Come Follow Me

To the Saints in Modesto:

We are so delighted that we can look back with you over the last 25 years and see some of the ways God has worked in your own lives as well as in and around Greater Modesto. We at International Renewal Ministries rejoice with you.

And we also look forward to the wonderful things God wants to do over the next 25 (plus!) years.

May this book be a resource and a blessing to you as you continue to "seek His face more than His hand!"

Dennis Fuqua
Executive Director,
International Renewal Ministries

Jody Mayhew
Women's Director
International Renewal Ministries

Come Follow Me

365 Days Walking in the Spirit

By
Jody Mayhew

two worlds press

www.twoworldsmedia.com

© 2016 By Jody Mayhew

Published by Two Worlds Press
A division of Two Worlds Media
Brush Prairie, WA

Scripture references are from the New American Standard Bible (NASB), 1973, 1995 edition, unless otherwise indicated.

ISBN-13: 978-1979146616
ISBN-10: 1979146616

SPECIAL LOCAL EDITION (Modesto, CA.)

Printed in the United States of America.

Dedication

I believe we are living at a time when the unity of the Body of Christ is of critical importance. Learning to live and operate in covenantal 'oneness' is necessary to bring about our maturity in Christ. I am privileged to walk with marvelous partners in the gospel and to share ministry opportunities with Abide Ministries. I dedicate this book to these faithful men and women who join me in service to our King.

Table of Contents

Acknowledgements

Without the contributions and encouragement of many friends, this book would not have been published. Since writing is not a favorite activity, editing and the effort it takes to prepare a book once it is written, would have certainly overwhelmed me.

I want to extend my heartfelt gratitude and thanksgiving to Sarah Cuny for all the work she did in line editing this book. Through hours of effort, she took on the grammar and punctuation corrections. I also want to thank my small army of readers who took a chapter or two and read, corrected, and made their helpful comments: Karen Williams, Laura Long, Heidi Sadler, Melissa Atkinson, Anna Lortz, Tammy Busby, and Mel Bombardier. The feedback has been encouraging and their work means you can hold this book in your hands today.

Thanks to my husband, who took my ideas for a cover design and made it come alive. His ability to navigate such a complicated formatting was a huge contribution as well.

For all who followed me as I first brought this material together as a YouTube podcast, thank you. I was encouraged by all of your feedback and comments.

Foreword

Yearlong commitments would frighten most of us. How will I ever follow through for 365 days? Yet Jody Mayhew has made a habit of such commitments. From drawing an image to capture one of the names of God for every day of the year or, as in the case of *Come Follow Me*, a daily video blog with two or three minute meditations on walking in the Spirit, she has joyfully taken on such commitments with relish and perseverance.

The book you hold in your hand is the printed version of those video presentations. It is a guide to a year of walking in the Spirit. Whether you begin in January or embark at some other time during the year, this Spirit-walk will challenge and inspire you thanks to Jody's insightful thoughts and penetrating questions. Let this book be your companion for a year of growing in Jesus as you accept His invitation to *"Come Follow Me."*

DNM

Part 1
Original Design

1. From the Dust

"Then the Lord God formed man of dust from the ground, and breathed into his nostrils the breath of life; and man became a living being." ~ Genesis 2:7

God created the world and its environs over the course of six days, declaring all good. Then, as the completion of the first week drew near, the Lord formed man from the dust of the ground, breathed His own breath into the still form lying before Him, and the dust trembled to life, the first Adam. We were designed to live and move in a body that expresses its needs and carries out our desires. It is the tent that our soul and spirit inhabit. We are a soul; with our mind, will, and emotions helping us interpret the natural realm. The soul houses our unique personality and gifts, and interprets the natural, visible realm for us. And, because God is Spirit, we were designed to walk in the Spirit and in continual fellowship with God.

At the time of creation, the Lord created beings that were uniquely suited to govern the realms they inhabited. Angels were created with the capacity to be responsive and minister. Humans were created for relationship and as a visible display of the image of the One who formed them.

We were designed to dwell on the earth, but to navigate the heavenlies. Angels were considered the heavenly host, but accessed the earth. God, who is both spirit and love, designed man to be a visible display of His invisible Presence, and to express His nature by love relationships.

Question: Since we are designed to operate with body, soul, and spirit — how aware are you of their distinct functions?

2. Inhabit the Earth

*"And He is the image of the invisible God, the
first-born of all creation. For by Him all things were
created, both in the heavens and on earth, visible
and invisible, whether thrones or dominions or
rulers or authorities—all things have been created
by Him and for Him." ~ Colossians 1:15-16*

For six days God created, and for six days God said it was
good. The Spirit moved over the surface of the waters and all
that had been without form became at His voice. He spoke
and there was light. Earth and waters were separated from
one another. The earth began to sprout and the trees brought
forth flower and fruit. Swarms of living creatures, birds in the
air and beasts after their kind, began to move at the impulse
of His voice. Creation was responding to the voice of Creator
God and all was good.

As we consider the days of creation, we are inclined to focus
on the visible realm—what we can see with our eyes or touch
with our hands. Yet, even in the realms of earth, the Lord was
creating that which was invisible. Our natural eye would
prove inadequate to discover all that the Lord was speaking
into existence. From the beginning, our vision and access to
the spiritual realm was going to require that we operate with
a spiritual navigation system.

*"Things which eye has not seen and ear has not heard, and which
have not entered the heart of man, all that God has prepared for those
who love Him"* (1 Corinthians 2:9).

Question: What invisible gifts from the Lord are you thankful for today?

3. It is Good

"And God saw all that He had made, and behold,
it was very good ..." ~ Genesis 1:31

In our economy of words, we are continually looking for superlatives, to describe something with greater value. Advertising attempts to draw our attention using word inflation to magnify and puff up. Magnificent is used to describe both sunsets and coffee. Awesome is used in worship and to describe a local sale at the mall.

By inflating the value of the common, we lose our capacity to understand and describe the holy.

As each day of creation drew to a close, the Lord looked at what had been formed and declared it was good. On our scale of word values, that would be "average". Perhaps we have failed to truly understand the power of words because of our misuse of them.

Wrapped up in the meaning of good is the idea of benevolent goodness. It is a sacrificial benevolence for the sake of the other. When God was creating, it was with us in mind. Each word lovingly formed that which was best for us. He was the Creator of good, and He wished to decide what was good for us. When Eve reached for a good, apart from God, she overvalued her own judgment, and undervalued the Giver of good.

God used the word good to describe Himself when Moses asked to see Him (Exodus 33:18). He is good and continues to have good in mind for His children. When we allow Him to choose a path for us, it will be for our good.

Question: Why and when is the goodness of God challenged in your life? Has the issue of His goodness been settled in your thinking?

4

4. Male and Female

"And God created man in His own image, in the image of God He created him; male and female He created them." ~ Genesis 1:27

Creator God desired to unfold a mystery in the natural realm. He desired to display a prophetic picture to His creation of the relationship He desired with them. God, who is Spirit, would make Himself known by relating to His creation in the role of Bridegroom. Humanity would be invited into the role of the Bride, one who would take her part opposite her Divine Counterpart. Mankind, by design, was created both male and female, that we might display the image of God. Marriage was to display, to a watching world, the very nature of His triune likeness. Marriage implies intimacy, a vital, holy communion between part and counterpart. So often we find couples living parallel lives rather than the merged oneness that God had in mind. It is that merged oneness that gives an accurate representation of Christ with His Church in the world. When the church fails to mature and is more familiar with herself than with her Divine Counterpart, she models an entirely different illustration in both the heavenly and earthly realms. Too often the church only knows how to be intimate with the church. When we can introduce people to church, but don't know how to encourage intimacy with the Beloved, we model an attraction to our own likeness. May all that we are as His Church display through our intimacy with Jesus the precious oneness that He had in mind.

Question: Where has the church forfeited the holy display of Himself that God had in mind?

5. Oneness — 1=2=1

*"There is one body and one Spirit, just as also you
were called in one hope of your calling; one Lord,
one faith, one baptism, one God and Father of all
who is overall and through all and in all.
~ Ephesians 4:4-6*

Knit into the very fabric of the creation is a revelation of the oneness of God. God is community that functions in unity, rather than uniformity. He made man to reflect in the natural what is true in the realm of the Spirit. He formed man from the dust of the ground and then breathed into his nostrils the breath of life; man became a living being, one. God's response to this creation was, *"It is not good for the man to be alone; I will make him a helper suitable for him"* (Genesis 2:18). As a deep sleep comes upon Adam, God removes one of his ribs and creates woman. One becomes two. As He brings this gift to Adam, to take as his wife, God declares that the two will become one (Genesis 3:24). This is a holy mystery, heavenly math. God chooses to represent His community in unity in human marriage. This imagery predates the fall of man, and is specific in what it communicates: Christ and His Bride— the Church.

Question: What strategy of the evil one most successfully interrupts the unity of the Body?

6. Oneness—In Rebellion

"...Holy Father, keep them in Thy name, the
name which Thou hast given Me, that they may be
one, even as we are." ~ John 17:11

There is power in unity—even in rebellion. *"And they said, 'Come, let us build for ourselves a city, and a tower whose top will reach into heaven, and let us make for ourselves a name; lest we be scattered abroad over the face of the whole earth.' And the Lord came down to see the city and the tower which the sons of men had built. And the Lord said, 'Behold, they are one people, and they all have the same language. And this is what they began to do, and now nothing which they purpose to do will be impossible for them'"* (Genesis 11:4-6). With such power available in union, mankind could perfect rebellion or be a perfect reflection of the image and likeness of God. God scattered their confederacy until that time when He would bring mankind together in a holy oneness in Christ. Caiaphas, the high priest during the last days of Jesus, unknowingly prophesied that *"... Jesus was going to die for the nation, and not for the nation only, but that He might also gather together into one the children of God who are scattered abroad"* (John 11:51-52). The new creation in Christ is to be displayed in a oneness that bears witness to the nature of God.

Question: Which of your relationships display a holy oneness?

7. God is Community

"Hear, O Israel! The LORD is our God, the
LORD is one!"~ Deuteronomy 6:4

The verse found at Deuteronomy 6:4 is called the *Shema*, "hear" in Hebrew, and is a central part of Jewish prayer. It declares the sovereignty of the one God. It is the initial thought taught to a Jewish child. It takes the message of Deuteronomy 6:4-9 and breathes it into one statement, "Hear, O Israel, the Lord our God is one Lord." In a world where there were multitudes of gods and idols worshipped and served, Israel stood apart, and worshipped the One whose name was too holy to even pronounce.

As Christians, we also believe that God is one. Yet, within the nature of the one true God, there are three distinct facets or personalities. The Bible clearly describes God the Father, God the Son, and God the Holy Spirit. We use the word trinity to describe this three-part (tri) oneness (unity).

Since we have been created to display God's image and likeness, walking in relational oneness bears witness to our profession of faith. Since God IS community, our means of displaying His image and likeness will require our participation in the Body of Christ. Jesus prayed for us, *"that they may all be one; even as You, Father, are in Me and I in You, that they also may be in Us, so that the world may believe that You sent Me"* (John 17:21). Walking by the Spirit is our means of preserving the gift of oneness and displaying the very Body of Jesus alive and powerful on the earth today.

Question: Are you willing to sacrifice unity with someone or sacrifice for it? Allow the Holy Spirit to show you if there are any breached relationships that He would like to repair.

---

8. Reorienting our Heart

"Teach me Your way, O Lord; I will walk in Your truth; unite my heart to fear Your name."
~ Psalm 86:11

As I was putting together a teaching on the topic of lust, I came across a verse that arrested my attention. James 1:13-14 states: *"Let no one say when he is tempted, 'I am being tempted by God'; for God cannot be tempted by evil, and He Himself does not tempt anyone. But each one is tempted when he is carried away and enticed by his own lust."*

As I considered the connection between temptation and lust, my thoughts were drawn to the original temptation and the condition of heart that took that first bait. How could this verse describe the condition of Eve's heart? Was she enticed by lust? How could this be true, if temptation precedes sin, and is not sin, in and of itself?

Our answer lies in a word translation. There

> *The one great petition which ought to be the chief thing every heart seeks for itself—that the life of God in the soul may have full sway, that Christ may be fully formed within, and that we may be filled to all the fullness of God. This is what God has promised.*
>
> *Andrew Murray*
> *Waiting on God*

is a Greek word that is used for two different English words. It is the word: *epithumeo*. It means "to have the affections directed toward anything; to long after." As long as the nature of our desire is toward that which is holy, righteous, and good, the word is interpreted "desire". When our desire is drawn astray, the word is interpreted "lust".

We were designed with a capacity to desire. This draws our heart and our affections outward from ourselves toward relational connectivity with another. As our heart is rightly oriented, our desires will be rightly expressed. If our heart is tempted to turn toward lesser loves, we often forfeit true intimacy.

Reading on in James 1:15-16, we are warned, *"Then when lust has conceived, it gives birth to sin; and when sin is accomplished, it brings forth death. Do not be deceived, my beloved brethren."*

Learning to walk in the Spirit teaches us to daily reorient our heart to the One who we claim to follow.

Question: When do you find yourself most vulnerable to enticement or temptation? How does this influence your level of spiritual desire?

9. Free will

"… choose for yourselves today whom you will serve … as for me and my house, we will serve the Lord." ~ Joshua 24:15

To bear the image and likeness of a holy God is a tall order. When the Lord created man to be a visible depiction of His invisible presence, it was a privilege as well as a responsibility. A few years ago, I set out to draw and paint one of the names of the Lord for each day of the year. There are well over 365 names to choose from and a majority of them reflect an aspect of His image and likeness. One such name is Sovereign Lord. The word sovereign means, "supreme ruler, possessing supreme or ultimate power." How would God go about creating man in His image and likeness in such a way that His sovereignty could be seen? He gave man free will.

Now I tend to think that this is a fairly dangerous quality when it gets into the wrong

I cannot give up my will—I must exercise it, putting it into action. I must will to obey, and I must will to receive God's Spirit. When God gives me a vision of truth, there is never a question of what He will do, but only of what I will do.

Oswald Chambers
My Utmost for His Highest

hands. And at the time of the fall, that is exactly what happened. It was in our hands.

We had been entrusted with one of God's most potent expressions of Himself, and we were to exercise such a gift in the context of relationship with our Heavenly Father. Learning to express free will was designed for hearts that walked in loving submission.

Jesus lived the expressed will of the Father as a Son. He demonstrated from His childhood onward what this pattern of living looks like. Philippians 2:5-7 captures it: *"Have this attitude in yourselves which was also in Christ Jesus, who, although He existed in the form of God, did not regard equality with God a thing to be grasped, but emptied Himself, taking the form of a bondservant and being made in the likeness of men. And being found in appearance as a man, He humbled Himself by becoming obedient to the point of death, even death on a cross."*

Our actions are an ongoing expression of the indwelling life of Christ. I have the privilege of presenting my body daily, as an expression of worship—not my will but His be done. I am always free to choose.

Question: Is it possible to know Jesus as Lord, yet refuse to obey Him?

---

10. Imprinting

"Therefore you are to be perfect, as your heavenly
Father is perfect." ~ Matthew 5:48

God spoke and His living, powerful words brought forth creation. By His word, *"By the word of the Lord the heavens were made, their starry host by the breath of his mouth"* (Psalm 33:6 NIV). Built into His design was the means for replicating this creation; not only to reproduce after its kind, but the means of understanding how to navigate their environment. These patterns for adapting were to pass on from one generation to the next through something called imprinting.

Imprinting refers to a critical period of time early in an animal's life when it forms attachments and develops a concept of its own identity. Birds and mammals are born with a pre-programmed drive to imprint onto their mother. Imprinting provides animals with information about who they are and who they will find attractive at adulthood.

Mankind, created to display the image and likeness of God, was to reflect this display of God's nature and character through relationship. The only way of reproducing His image and likeness is to reflect His inner presence.

At the fall of man in Genesis 3, we were separated from the One whose likeness we were to bear. Without submission we wandered, bent, never truly discovering our identity, and imprinting on every lesser thing.

Question: *Can you think of any lesser things that your heart and mind have imprinted on?*

11. Unity

"And the glory which You have given Me I have given to them, that they may be one, just as We are one; I in them, and You in Me, that they may be perfected in unity, so that the world may know that You did send Me, and loved them, even as You loved Me." ~ John 17:22-23

There are two great forces at work in our world. One is fission: the action of dividing or splitting something into two or more parts. When the nucleus of an atom is split, it releases large amounts of energy, such as the atom bomb. The other great force is fusion: the process or result of joining two or more things together to form a single entity. Through blending or melting, the separate things are formed into one. This is the theory behind the hydrogen bomb—which is more powerful than the atomic bomb.

God is a united whole, a display of the power of oneness. His identity is wrapped up in this oneness and He chooses to display His image and likeness through us. When Jesus

In a Christian community everything depends upon whether each individual is an indispensable link in a chain. Only when even the smallest link is securely interlocked is the chain unbreakable.

Dietrich Bonhoeffer
Life Together

prays for his disciples in His high priestly prayer from John 17, He prays that we will be one even as He and the Father are one.

Two significant places in scripture have been given to the people of God to display this kind of oneness. One is marriage. Jesus describes the union of marriage as the same kind of relationship that He has with His church. The second way we can experience oneness is in the body of Christ. Jesus is the Head of the church, and we are to live as members one of another. This unity is given as a gift. Instead of working hard to attain such unity, we are called to maintain it. We receive it as a gift at the beginning of the relationship, and through obedient maintaining, we mature in love. When Jesus prays, "that they may be perfected in unity", it was not a prayer for some time of future achievement. The Greek word for perfected means to be made mature or complete. When we maintain this unity, we mature in love and the world is a witness to the fact that the Father sent the Son because He deeply loved us.

Question: *When have you walked sacrificially in order to maintain love?*

12. Loving

"See how great a love the Father has bestowed
upon us, that we would be called children of God;
and such we are. For this reason the world does not
know us, because it did not know Him."
~ 1 John 3:1

When asked what the great commandment in the Law was, Jesus replied, *"'You shall love the Lord your God will all your heart, and with all your soul, and with all your mind. This is the great and foremost commandment.' The second is like it, 'You shall love your neighbor as yourself.' On these two commandments depend the whole Law and the Prophets"* (Matthew 22:37-40). Since God is love, the expression of love is the most viable expression of relationship with God.

The quality of love described in the commandment is *agape* love. This Greek word is often translated "love" in the New Testament. It is a faithful, sacrificial love that displays the same quality of love that God has for us. It is the kind of love described in I Corinthians 13:4-8a, *"Love is patient, love is kind and is not jealous; love does not brag and is not arrogant, does not act unbecomingly; it does not seek its own, is not provoked, does not take into account a wrong suffered, does not rejoice in unrighteousness, but rejoices with the truth; bears all things, believes all things, hopes all things, endures all things. Love never fails."*

This kind of love is the energy released in the fusion of oneness. This kind of love extends the power of belonging to each individual part. This kind of love allows His Kingdom to come and His will be done on earth as it is in heaven.

Question: *What has God used to increase your capacity to love?*

13. Living Loved

"We love, because He first loved us."
~ I John 4:19

After the fall of mankind and the introduction of sin, the Law was given. Yet Romans 3:20 states: *"... by the works of the Law no flesh will be justified in His sight; for through the Law comes the knowledge of sin."* We learn from the Law the nature of a Holy God and the requirement of holiness for restored fellowship. But scripture states that *"... all have sinned and fall short of the glory of God"* (Romans 3:23). Even the greatest commandment in the Law, to love the Lord with all your heart, soul, and mind, and your neighbor as yourself—is impossible to fulfill. It is Old Covenant. It is Law and we forever fall short of fulfilling it from our own strength.

Jesus initiates a New Covenant with us. He also introduces a new law. John 13:34-35 states, *"A new commandment I give to you, that*

> *You will know them by their fruit, he said. A good tree bears good fruit, a bad one bad fruit. If the people telling a story love each other and live together with depth and grace, then their story is true. If they don't, then their story is silliness—or worse.*
>
> John Alexander
> *The Secular Squeez*

you love one another, even as I have loved you, that you also love one another. By this all men will know that you are My disciples, if you have love for one another." Love is still the main thing, but flows from a different source. Under the Law, man is the source and must prove love with his own effort. With the New Covenant, the Lord is the source, and we are the recipients and then the delivery system for what we have received.

We should not be surprised then at how the evil one works to keep us from believing we are loved.

One of my favorite verses for ministry is I John 4:16-19:

"And we have come to know and have believed the love which God has for us. God is love, and the one who abides in love abides in God, and God abides in him. By this, love is perfected with us, that we may have confidence in the day of judgment; because as He is, so also are we in this world. There is no fear in love; but perfect love casts out fear, because fear involves punishment, and the one who fears is not perfected in love. We love, because He first loved us."

For the Lord to access His creation, He gains access through the giving and receiving of Love. This is the entry point—the divine strategy of recovery, the ransoming of hearts, the making of sons.

Question: Do you ever struggle with believing you are loved by God? Do you recognize the obstacle to believing?

---

14. *Breath and Dust*

"...unless one is born of water and the Spirit, he cannot enter into the Kingdom of God. That which is born of the flesh is flesh, and that which is born of the Spirit is Spirit." ~ John 3:5-6

On the day God formed man from the dust, He breathed into his nostrils the breath of life and man became a living being (Genesis 2:7). Dust for flesh and breath for spirit, Adam sat up. Without the breath, merely flesh. (Psalm 103:14). At the fall of man—merely flesh.

In Ezekiel 37, we witness a conversation between the Lord and the prophet. Set down in the middle of a valley of dry bones, the Lord questions Ezekiel, "Can these bones live?" The Lord then said, *"Prophecy to the dry bones, hear the word of the Lord. Thus says the Lord God to these bones, 'Behold, I will cause breath to enter you that you may come to life. I will put sinews on you,*

Breathe on me, Breath of God, fill me with life anew, that I may love what thou dost love, and do what thou wouldst do.

Breathe on me, Breath of God, till I am wholly thine, till all this earthly part of me glows with thy fire divine.

Breathe on me, Breath of God, so shall I never die, but live with thee the perfect life of thine eternity.

Edwin Hatch
From the Hymn

make flesh grow back on you, cover you with skin, and put breath in you that you may come alive; and you will know that I am the Lord.'" Ezekiel prophesied. The bones rattled together, becoming one, but they were without breath. At the command of the Lord, Ezekiel prophesies to the breath, *"and the breath came into them, and they came to life, and stood on their feet, an exceedingly great army"* (Ezekiel 37:1-10).

Centuries later, following the resurrection, Jesus enters a room where His disciples have gathered. He blows on them, saying, *"Receive the Holy Spirit"* (John 20:22). They rattled together into a body, and then waited in Jerusalem for the breath from heaven. On Pentecost, a mighty wind poured forth and the church stood up, a mighty army.

Question: How would you describe the state of the church—dry bones or a mighty army?

15. The Creator Inspires Response

*"O Lord. Our Lord, How majestic is Thy name in
all the earth, Who hast displayed Thy splendor
above the heavens!" ~ Psalm 8:1*

With each breath and each day, God said it was good, for
the sake of His goodness and His love. Because God is the
Creator, He is also the Owner; and because He owns all, He
gives. That leaves a creation in the position to make some
kind of response. Because of the vastness of the gift, the response often feels inadequate. We can mouth words of appre-
ciation, but experiencing exquisite beauty draws from a
deeper creative well. My heart is in a state of continual longing to tell the Lord with pen or brush or lens, that, yes, I see
what great gifts have been lovingly imagined by Him for a
joyful response on my part.

As Creator, He is the source of all life and built into His creation an ability to bear life as well. This heavenly community—Father, Son and Spirit—are brooding over the hearts of
His created ones and inspiring expressions of life and love.

Humanity is without excuse when it comes to thanksgiving.
*"For even though they knew God, they did not honor Him as God,
or give thanks"* (Romans 1:21).

*Question: What did God build into the creation to remind us that He is
the Creator?*

16. God Gave

*"... seeing that His divine power has granted to
us everything pertaining to life and godliness,
through the true knowledge of Him who called us by
His own glory and excellence. For by these He has
granted to us His precious and magnificent
promises, in order that by them you might become
partakers of the divine nature, having escaped the
corruption that is in the world by lust."*
~ *I Peter 1:2-4*

There are two kingdoms at work on the earth, the kingdom of the world and the kingdom of our God and King. In Greek, the prince of darkness who relies on worldly systems and slaves of sin to carry out his will is called *kosmo-krater (world-ruler)*. The other realm, ruled by God Almighty (Greek, *panto-krater* or ruler of all) is built on relationships—sons who have learned the nature of their true identity.

Each kingdom has its own economy. One operates on the basis of greed: buying and selling, relentless unsatisfactory consumption, debt and poverty, and slavery to ever increasing appetites. The other kingdom is governed by a good father who has chosen to freely give all good things to His children. He is the provider, and the foundation for this Kingdom is giving and receiving. In the Kingdom of God, there is an inheritance to draw on and a stewardship to carry out. We have all been entrusted with time, talents, territory, treasure, and a temple to care for. It is time to transfer our trust and future investments to the true King and His Kingdom.

*Question: What happens if we remain in submission to the ways of a
system that is not overseen by the Lord?*

17. The Word Put On Flesh

"Who told you that you were naked? Have you eaten from the tree of which I commanded you not to eat?" ~ Genesis 3:11

The Lord of Glory did not regard equality with the Father as something to be grasped, but willingly emptied Himself of privilege and location, and put on flesh. He came and dwelt among us in human disguise, clothing Himself with our nature and limitations so that we might, in turn, put on His fullness and be clothed once more in the Spirit. At the fall, we forfeited the royal apparel of His presence and glory, and were left with merely flesh. O, the devastating nakedness of it all! When Jesus came, robed only in skin, He demonstrated the way home to the Father's house, and the path of restoration to our original design. He disrobed, putting on flesh, and dwelt among us, so that we could relearn the way of putting on the Spirit and walking in Him. *"Beloved, now we are children of God, and it has not appeared as yet what we shall be. We know that, when He appears, we shall be like Him, because we shall see Him just as He is. And everyone who has this hope fixed on Him purifies himself, just as He is pure"* (1 John 3:2-3).

Today, the Lord desires to put on your flesh, continuing to be among His people, releasing the fullness of the Father's will on earth as it is in heaven. We can make the exchange if we dress the opposite way, putting on His Spirit.

Question: Is there any obstacle you face in putting aside your old identity and putting on Christ?

18. From Seed to Fruit

"Now He who supplies seed to the sower and bread for food, will supply and multiply your seed for sowing and increase the harvest of your righteousness; you will be enriched in everything for all liberality, which through us is producing thanksgiving to God." ~ 2 Corinthians 9:10-11

Within the nature of God's design for His creation was the ability to reproduce itself. *"Then God said, 'Behold, I have given you every plant yielding seed that is on the surface of all the earth, and every tree which has fruit yielding seed; it shall be food for you'"* (Genesis 1:29). All the potential for future fruit and harvest is locked up in the seed. The seed is always the way a plant or person begins, and upon reaching maturity, the way life is passed on through them. In Genesis 3, when God intervened at the corruption of mankind, He promised that a Seed would come who would restore His creation to its intended fruitfulness. If we fail to recognize God's work—when He approaches us in seed form—we can miss the future fruit that is borne through believing. When we pray, the Lord will often respond by enlivening

Every aspect of the time we spend together in the worshiping Christian community influences the kind of people we are becoming.

Marva Dawn
The Hilarity of Community.

His word in our heart, and delivering a promise that carries the hope of future fruit. We can miss the fact that He has answered our prayer when He gives a seed of promise to us. Thinking an answer looks like fruit, and not like seed, has us holding onto the seed in our clenched fist and raising that fist in the air, in prayer, instead of receiving the heaven-blessed response, and allowing it to grow in our hearts through faith.

When you hear someone teach, it is their fruit, but it is your seed. We tend to treat teaching as a meal, and eat the seed, becoming forgetful hearers instead of faithful doers of His word. As we become more familiar with His Kingdom, we realize He will continually nourish us. But we also use the seed He delivers to our heart, allowing it to grow and be released as fruit through us.

Question: *As you wait in faith for a promise from the Lord to bear fruit, what is the condition of the soil of your heart?*

---

19. Living a Merged Life

"Abide in Me, and I in you. As the branch cannot bear fruit of itself, unless it abides in the vine, so neither can you, unless you abide in Me."
~ John 15:4

We live in a country that has always placed a high value on independence. From the founding fathers to the generation currently growing to adulthood, we have valued the rugged individualism of the pioneer, the independent-minded, the self-made individual who is able to stand on their own two feet alone. This is a foreign way to the Kingdom of God.

When Jesus prayed for His disciples, in the high priestly prayer (John 17), He prayed that we would be one—even as He and the Father are one. He came to restore us to a merged life with the Father, the Son, the Holy Spirit, and the body of Christ.

To live a merged life is to live united, combined, and blended together so that the outcome is oneness.

In order to walk in this life of the Spirit, we will need to adopt the way of humility. Humility is a declaration of dependence, and allows the will of the Father, the way of the Son, the practices of the Holy Spirit, and the needs of the Body to be elevated above our own.

This laying down of the self-life, and the call to live, united in Him, restores us to the fullness of our original design—the way to walk in the Spirit.

Question: Is there a trial that you have gone through that exposed independence or self-sufficiency in your heart?

20. *Navigating the Realms of Creation*

*"Jesus answered and said to him, 'Because I said
to you that I saw you under the fig tree, do you
believe? You shall see greater things than these ...
Truly, truly, I say to you, you shall see the heavens
opened, and the angels of God ascending and
descending on the Son of Man.'" ~ John 1:50-51*

In the beginning, we had the capacity to walk with God in the cool of the day. We had the ability to hear His voice and respond. Man had access to the presence of God without fear of death. When sin entered, and corrupted creation, not only was access to the Tree of Life barred, but the habitation of the Garden of Eden was closed to us as well. When Jesus came to restore our relationship with the Father, we regained entry to the heavenly realms of creation. Paul prays in Ephesians 1:18-21, *"that the eyes of your heart may be enlightened, so that you may know what is the hope of His calling, what are the riches of the glory of His inheritance in the saints, and what is the surpassing greatness of His power toward us who believe. These are in accordance with the working of the strength of His might which He brought about in Christ, when He raised Him from the dead, and seated Him at His right hand in the heavenly places, far above all rule and authority and power and dominion, and every name that is named, not only in this age, but also in the one to come."*

When we are reborn, and the life of His Spirit indwells us, we recover the capacity to walk with God, and to navigate both the visible, and the invisible, heavenly realms of creation once more.

Question: Are you aware of your spiritual gifts and calling?

21. Order out of Chaos

*"The earth was formless and void, and darkness
was on the surface of the deep; and the Spirit of God
was moving over the surface of the waters."*
~ Genesis 1:12

I appreciate order in my world. I have not always been this way. In my first few years of marriage, I knew how to clean, but had little understanding of what it takes to manage a home. I would use every dish before choosing to wash one. If the counters grew too cluttered, I made use of the floor. When clothes were dirty, they could face mildew before I would get around to washing them. When a baby was introduced to the mix, it felt like my life was spinning out of control.

Meanwhile, as a new Christian, I was learning to love the word of God. I asked the Lord, in prayer, if I could teach His word someday. It is the only time I have heard the Lord laugh. Well, it was more like a chuckle, but His response grabbed my heart. "How can I let you care for My house, when you have not learned to care for your own?"

That moment of conviction led to a year's worth of repentance, bringing order from chaos in my realm of the Kingdom. I have been teaching His word now for 39 years.

"… let us also lay aside every encumbrance, and the sin which so easily entangles us, and let us run with endurance the race that is set before us, fixing our eyes on Jesus, the author and perfecter of faith, who for the joy set before Him endured the cross, despising the shame, and has sat down at the right hand of the throne of God." (Hebrews 12:1-2).

Question: Is there anything cluttering your life and keeping you from walking in your gifts and calling?

22. *Living Blessed*

"Behold, My servant whom I have chosen; My
beloved in whom My soul is well-pleased; I will put
My Spirit upon Him, and He shall
proclaim justice" ~ Matthew 12:18

In the Old Testament, at the end of a patriarch's life, they would extend a blessing to their children. Wrapped up in the words uttered was a promise of benefit, an inclusion in the inheritance, and proclamation of identity. It was a time when resources and role were transferred from one generation to another, and if you were the first-born, a double portion.

We read in these stories how sons manipulated in order to receive a better blessing, and how others received lesser benefit because of previous behavior. Blessing established future well-being and reward; sons lived in order to be blessed.

On the day Jesus was baptized, and His public ministry began, the Father gave voice from heaven and blessed the Son. *"And after being baptized, Jesus went up immediately from the water; and behold, the heavens were opened, and He saw the Spirit of God descending as a dove, and coming upon Him, and behold, a voice out of the heavens, saying, 'This is My beloved Son, in whom I am well-pleased'"* (Matthew 3:16-17).

Jesus lived from blessing rather than for it. The Father conferred His identity upon His Son, voiced His pleasure, and extended the Holy Spirit as a dove to rest upon Him. He lived from that blessing into the darkest days of history, into the hours when He experienced the Father's wrath against sin, right on into the resurrection and ascension.

Question: Do you consider it difficult to walk in a way that would be pleasing to the Lord?

23. Ministry of Reconciliation

*"Now all these things are from God, who
reconciled us to Himself through Christ, and gave
us the ministry of reconciliation"*
~ 2 Corinthians 5:18

When God created man in His image, we were designed to display His triune likeness in community. Is it any wonder then, that when the evil one attempts to steal, kill, and destroy, that he purposely targets relationships? The accuser of the brethren works to bring division through slander, deception, and offended hearts. The prince of darkness works to unite hearts in an evil opposition to the Lord (Genesis 11:6).

The Father's strategy to recover His creation was satisfied in His Son. *"For it was the Father's good pleasure for all the fullness to dwell in Him, and through Him to reconcile all things to Himself, having made peace through the blood of His cross; through Him, I say, whether things on earth or things in heaven. And although you were formerly alienated and hostile in mind, engaged in evil*

He drew a circle that shut me out—Heretic, rebel, a thing to flout. But love and I had the wit to win; we drew a circle that took him in.

Edwin Markham

deeds, yet He has now reconciled you in His fleshly body through death, in order to present you before Him holy and blameless and beyond reproach ..." (Colossians 1:19-22).

The great breech between God and man was reconciled at the cross of Christ. All are invited to come. The mercy seat is still open to all who will receive salvation. The message of such great news has now been entrusted to His Body. We have the capacity to be a living witness to this—not just a declarer of doctrine, but a demonstration of it. To be a living witness means we carry the presence of the Holy Spirit into every situation and His power conducts His will through us.

"Now all these things are from God, who reconciled us to Himself through Christ, and gave us the ministry of reconciliation, namely, that God was in Christ reconciling the world to Himself, not counting their trespasses against them, and He has committed to us the word of reconciliation. Therefore, we are ambassadors for Christ, as though God were entreating through us; we beg you on behalf of Christ, be reconciled to God" (2 Corinthians 5:18-20).

Question: *Do you have any unreconciled relationships? Ask the Holy Spirit for His strategy for restoration.*

24. Sonship

*"And He is the radiance of His glory and the
exact representation of His nature, and upholds all
things by the word of His power ..." ~ Hebrews 1:3*

When the Lord created man, we were formed in the image of God, according to His likeness. We were formed to be image bearers, sons, reflections of the nature and likeness of the Father on earth, as it is in heaven. As we stood in His presence, exposed to His counsel, relationally expressing His glory, we expressed the Father's design and desire. At the fall, separated by sin, naked without the reflection of His glory, we lost our relational connect. And instead of being formed in His likeness, we began to be a marred, deformed creation.

At the incarnation, Jesus comes to give fallen man an exact representation of the Father's image. John 14 shares that if you have seen Him, you have seen the Father. He also comes to purchase redemption for His fallen creation. Upon our purchase, we are restored to relationship once more. But we are unfamiliar with how this restored relationship is expressed.

Jesus modeled this restored relationship for us. As we observe His Sonship, we learn our own.

Question: *When it comes to your relationship with the heavenly Father, do you live more like a servant, an orphan, or a son?*

32

25. Rulership

"Thy throne, O God, is forever and ever."
~ Psalm 45:6

The word dominion means to have the rule or power over. God, who is sovereign, has complete power and authority over His creation and He has delegated that ability to rule to us. Psalm 8:6-8 states, *"You make him to rule over the works of Your hands; You have put all things under his feet, all sheep and oxen, and also the beasts of the field, the birds of the heavens, and the fish of the sea, whatever passes through the paths of the seas."*

Upon the creation of man, he was entrusted with the oversight, the place of command over the creation. The assignment was to subdue the earth, rule over this creation, and cause it to be fruitful and multiply.

Untethered at the fall, our own rebellion is often displayed in an unrighteous attempt to rule over others instead of being under His rule ourselves.

God desires to write a redemption story even when we have gone completely astray; when we have cut our moorings and are lost at sea. His redemption allows for our return to submission.

Bringing the creation into submission would be a reflection of our own submission to the Creator, and allow for the rule of His Kingdom to come to earth as it is in heaven.

Question: *Is there any area of your life where you tend to act on your own initiative, rather than a submissive response to His voice?*

26. Cooperation

"...and be subject to one another in the fear of Christ." ~ Ephesians 5:21

The definition of cooperation is the process of working together to the same end—Creator with creation, husband with wife, parent with child, Head with body. Learning to walk in this kind of harmony requires a mutual submission to the leading of the Holy Spirit. God's ways must be relearned by a creation that has lived a very self-oriented life.

God gives people gifts to equip the body for this kind of cooperative functioning. *"And He gave some as apostles, and some as prophets, and some as evangelists, and some as pastors and teachers, for the equipping of the saints for the work of service, to the building up of the body of Christ; until we all attain to the unity of the faith, and of the knowledge of the Son of God, to a mature man, to the measure of the stature which belongs to the fullness of Christ...speaking the truth in love, we are to grow up in all aspects into Him, who is the head, even Christ, from whom the whole body, being fitted and held together by that which every joint supplies, according to the proper working of each individual part, causes the growth of the body for the building up of itself in love"* (Ephesians 4:11-13, 15-16).

Where unity is lacking, we still live in a state of immaturity. To the degree that we walk in the power of the life of the Head, cooperating with His will and purpose, we gain intimacy with the Lord, and a growing love for one another.

Question: How have the people gifts mentioned in Ephesians 4:11 helped you to walk in unity (cooperation) with the body of Christ?

---

27. Be Fruitful and Multiply

"Be fruitful and multiply, and fill the earth…"
~ Genesis 1:28

The DNA of creation is to be fruitful and multiply. Built into the design of every plant is the ability to both flower and bear fruit. Carried within each seed is the complete replication of itself. Creator God built into the design of all life the ability to reproduce in its own likeness.

"And God created man in His own image, in the image of God He created him; male and female He created them. And God blessed them; and God said to them, 'Be fruitful and multiply, and fill the earth…'" (Genesis 1:27-28).

This command was given two times in the Old Testament. First, in the creation story, when God entrusted the stewardship of His creation to Adam and Eve. Then, God gave it a second time following the flood. (Genesis 9:1).

"Be fruitful and multiply" shows up in the New Testament as well. In the parable of the talent (Matthew 25:14-30), the Lord indicates that faithfulness in stewardship reaps an obedient harvest. In the parable of the soils (Matthew 13:3-23), we are shown the obstacles to fruitfulness and the way to multiplication. Then, the final words in the Gospel of Matthew: *"All authority has been given to Me in heaven and on earth. Go therefore and make disciples of all the nations, baptizing them in the name of the Father and the Son and the Holy Spirit, teaching them to observe all that I commanded you; and lo, I am with you always, even to the end of the age"* (Matthew 28:18-20).

Question: *What talents has the Lord entrusted to you to do business with until His return?*

28. Vision

*"Therefore, gird your minds for action, keep sober
in spirit, fix your hope completely on the grace to be
brought to you at the revelation of Jesus Christ."*
~ I Peter 1:13

Our original design was a fulfillment of God's vision. Both man and woman were formed to bear His image and likeness, walk in a holy, loving relationship, and bear witness to the Lord's vision. His vision—something He saw, before He spoke—became as He released His breath. Since we bear His likeness, vision operates in and through us as well. *"Where there is no vision, the people perish"* (Proverbs 29:18). Having vision for the purposes of God allows us to participate in those purposes. Seeing the unseen keeps us walking by the Spirit, relying on our inward navigation system. Vision fuels our hope. Speaking to all believers, I Peter 1:8-9 says, *"And though we do not see Him now, but believe in Him, you greatly rejoice with joy inexpressible and full of glory, obtaining as the outcome of your faith the salvation of your souls"* (1 Peter 1:8-9).

Question: *What is one way in which knowing the vision and purposes of God helps you make a daily decision?*

29. For Beauty and Food

*"The Lord God caused to grow every tree that is
pleasing to the sight and good for food." ~ Gen. 2:9*

Austere means severe or strict in manner, having no com-
forts, harsh or ascetic. Jesus used the word twice in the parable of the minas (Luke 19:21-22). It describes the false opinion
and misconception of one man of his master, and also of many
hearts toward God. Those who live in sinful disobedience can
never be fully relieved of a guilty conscience, so their conclusions about God are often distorted. Willful wrongdoing
tends to create a defensiveness that hides and obscures the
goodness of the Father toward His creation. Instead of experiencing the fullness of His love, fallen man experiences limitation and a marring of His intended design.

When God planted His garden, *"out of the ground the Lord
God caused to grow every tree that is pleasing to the sight and good
for food ..."* (Genesis 2:9). Built into His handiwork was the
idea of bringing pleasure, satisfying longing, and blessing.

It would serve us well to learn from the deception that undermined Eve. *"When the woman saw that the tree was good for
food, and that it was a delight to the eyes, and that the tree was de-
sirable to make one wise, she took from its fruit and ate; and she gave
also to her husband with her, and he ate"* (Genesis 3:6). Pay attention. He made all trees to be good for food. He had forbidden
one tree. We were never to pursue wisdom apart from God.
It is His desire to always bring that to us relationally. Left to
ourselves, deciding what is good and what is evil, will only
distance us from the beauty and food God longs to provide.

*Question: Is there any area of your life where you doubt God's goodness
toward you?*

30. Fellowship

"...for we cannot stop speaking what we have seen and heard." ~ Acts 4:20

When the Holy Spirit came upon the early church, they continually devoted themselves to the apostles teaching, fellowship, breaking of bread, and prayer. No one set in place a list of rules to keep, but the Spirit began to move within to bring about this pattern for life of hearing the word together, eating together, praying together, and fellowship. What is so important about fellowship? 1 John 1:1-3 gives insight: *"What was from the beginning, what we have heard, what we have held and our hands handled, concerning the Word of Life—and the life was manifested and we have seen and bear witness and proclaim to you the eternal life, which was with the Father and was manifested to us—what we have seen and heard we proclaim to you also, that you also may have fellowship with us; and indeed our fellowship is with the Father, and with His Son Jesus Christ."* Far more than a coffee date to chat about kids, or sports, or current events, fellowship is God's means of distribution in His Body. What He gives to one part of the church can be shared and multiplied to feed the other members. God builds and strengthens His Body by the proper working of each individual part, causing growth and maturity.

Question: *Do you have a good God story you can share with others this week?*

---

31. Exact Likeness

*"Phillip said to Him, 'Lord, show us the Father,
and it is enough for us.' Jesus said to him, 'Have I
been so long with you, and yet you have not come to
know Me, Phillip? He who has seen Me has seen the
Father; how do you say, 'Show us the Father'?"*
~ John 14:8-9

At the completion of seven days of creation, God saw that it was good; His word brought forth all that was in His heart. Everything displayed His will and purpose, on earth, as it was in heaven. However, when the fall of man took place in the Garden, sin and corruption began their assault. Over time, every good thing bore the likeness of death, rather than life. When God sent forth His Son, Hebrews 1:1-3, states: *"God, after He spoke long ago to the father's in the prophets in many portions and in many ways, in these last days has spoken to us in His Son, whom He appointed heir of all things, through whom also He made the world. And He is the radiance of His glory and the exact representation of His nature, and upholds all things by the word of His power ..."* God began again. His Word put on flesh and dwelt among us. A new Adam was sent to be an exact representation of the Father. Thy Kingdom came ... and it is good.

Question: *Consider three ways that the Lord has shown you His goodness this week.*

Part 2

Going Astray

32. Deceived

"Do not be deceived, my beloved brethren."
~ James 1:16

There are three significant strategies of the evil one that have impacted the people of God for multiple centuries. These strategies are so aligned with his wicked nature that his names correspond to each activity. Satan is the accuser, and we are usually aware when he is whispering a charge against us. He is also the tempter, actively pursuing us with bait in hand. We tend to recognize both of these attempts to war against us. But with the third strategy, we are consistently oblivious to the manner of infiltration that the deceiver has made in our lives. When you are accused, you know it. When you are tempted, you know it. When you are deceived, you don't see it, or it wouldn't be a deception. When we consider the topic of deception, we tend to focus on what comes out of our mouths, rather than what goes into our hearts. We focus on when we are lying rather than when we are being lied to.

If we acknowledge the potency of deception, we tend to regard it as an infection. Just like germs can introduce a virus into our systems, we believe lies only last for a season and we can easily escape their snare. The reality is that deception is much closer to something being imbedded, cancer-like, and built into our very framework. Deception is designed to lurk like a hidden IED (improvised explosive device), and explode with devastating consequences at an unforeseen moment.

Question: List three deceptions that are influencing the very foundation of our culture. These may not seem evil.

33. Lust of the Flesh

*"Do not love the world, nor the things in the
world. If anyone loves the world, the love of the
Father is not in him."*
~ I John 2:15

Satan laid a trap when he enticed Eve. The bait was the forbidden fruit, but the trap was a plot designed to reorient Eve's desires from God's blessing, and attract her off course. The initial deception relied on getting Eve to act on her own initiative, to operate with a level of independence, rather than being led. Filled with desire, she became aroused to the potential of a choice made from her own hunger rather than the Lord's command. With no forethought to an act of treason, she wandered toward rebellion by allowing the lust of the flesh, the lust of the eyes, and the boastful pride of life determine her course.

These patterns of desire operate when we live our lives by our own human strengths and weaknesses. As a Christian, though we have been given the life of the indwelling Holy Spirit, we often walk as mere men. We use the same means of navigating our lives as we used prior to our salvation. "See it, want it, get it" becomes our mode of operation. To be led by the Spirit means He is the author and the authority behind every action we take. Submission to His will needs to become our learned response.

Question: When are you most vulnerable to being misled by a fleshly desire?

34. Living for a Lesser Love

"Beloved, if God so loved us, we also ought to love one another." ~ 1 John 4:11

When my first-born was almost two she learned what the word "love" meant. As we would drive along in the car, she would sing out from the back seat, "I love Jesus, I love mommy, I love French fries." Love is often used to describe what we desire and to give us a glimpse into the state of our heart. Jesus was asked, "Teacher, which is the greatest commandment in the Law?" And Jesus answered, *"You shall love the Lord your God with all your heart, and with all your soul, and with all your mind. This is the great and foremost commandment. The second is like it, you shall love your neighbor as yourself"* (Matthew 22:37-39). Each heart has an ability to love and to express that desire—it's just a matter of what or who that desire is aimed toward. The evil one is not as concerned about what he tempts us with, but who he tempts us from.

Paul prays for us in Ephesians 3:14-19: *"For this reason, I bow my knees before the Father, from whom every family in heaven and on earth derives its name, that He would grant you, according to the riches of His glory, to be strengthened with power through His Spirit in the inner man; so that Christ may dwell in your hearts through faith; and that you, being rooted and grounded in love, may be able to comprehend with all the saints what is the breadth and length and height and depth, and to know the love of Christ which surpasses knowledge, that you may be filled up to all the fullness of God."*

Question: *What word best describes the state of your heart toward God?*

35. Going Astray

*"All of us like sheep have gone astray, each of us
has turned to his own way; but the Lord has caused
the iniquity of us all to fall on Him."*
~ Isaiah 53:6

Walking in the Spirit is not operating in our own strength of soul—our mind, will, and emotions. It is not the reformation of our natural man—restraining our appetites and taming our affections. It is inviting the Holy Spirit to indwell us fully, in our heart. I have been reading a book called *You Are What You Love: The Spiritual Power of Habit*, by James K. A. Smith. He describes how we live from what we love, more than from what we believe. Is it any wonder then, when asked, "What is the greatest commandment in the Law?", Jesus responds, *"You shall love the Lord your God with all your heart, and with all your soul, and with all your strength, and with all your mind; and your neighbor as yourself"* (Luke 10:27).

Walking with the Lord is a relationship, and we must learn living in oneness, being led, walking in the Spirit, from the heart. It requires fixing the eye of our heart on Him.

Yet, as God described His relationship with His people, He said, *"Therefore I was angry with this generation, and said, 'They always go astray in their heart; and they did not know my ways"* (Hebrews 3:10).

Idolatry is to have our heart aimed at lesser things, turning aside from our first love, and going astray.

Question: Have you ever gone astray in your spiritual journey? What lesser love captured your attention?

36. Did not Honor Him

"This people honors Me with their lips, but their heart is far away from Me. But in vain do they worship Me, teaching as doctrines the precepts of men."

~ Matthew 15:8-9

To honor someone is to display a level of respect appropriate to who they are or what they have done. It is to not think more highly of ourselves than we ought, but to emphasize the value of another above ourselves. Consider Paul's words to the Romans: *"For the wrath of God is revealed from heaven against all ungodliness and unrighteousness of men, who suppress the truth in unrighteousness, because that which is known about God is evident within them; for God made it evident to them. For since the creation of the world His invisible attributes, His eternal power and divine nature, have been clearly seen, being understood through what has been made, so that they are without excuse. For even though they knew God, they did not honor Him as God, or give thanks; but they became futile in their speculations, and their foolish heart was darkened"* (Romans 1:20-21).

Worship is the response of our heart toward who or what we value. In choosing to undervalue God, by neglecting to honor Him or give thanks, we become those who *"...exchange the truth of God for a lie, and worship and serve the creature rather than the Creator"* (Romans 1:25).

Question: Do you have any regular ways of giving honor to the Lord?

37. *Did not Give Thanks*

"Bless the Lord, O my soul; and all that is within
me, bless His holy name. Bless the Lord, O my soul,
and forget none of His benefits."
~ Psalm 103:1-2

Gratitude is our means of entering into God's presence. Psalm 100 is an exhortation for all men to display a heart of thankfulness to the Lord:

> *Shout joyfully to the Lord, all the earth.*
> *Serve the Lord with gladness;*
> *Come before Him with joyful singing.*
> *Know that the Lord Himself is God;*
> *It is He who has made us, and not we ourselves;*
> *We are His people and the sheep of His pasture.*
> *Enter His gates with thanksgiving,*
> *and His courts with praise.*
> *Give thanks to Him; bless His name.*
> *For the Lord is good;*
> *His loving kindness is everlasting,*
> *and His faithfulness to all generations.*

Giving thanks to the Lord is the only gift we can give in response to who He is and all that He has done on our behalf. To withhold our thanksgiving from the One to whom it is due, is to forfeit His presence.

Question: When are you inclined to forget to express gratitude to the Lord?

47

38. I Will Ascend

"And whoever exalts himself shall be humbled;
and whoever humbles himself shall be exalted."
~ Matthew 23:12

Jesus was an accurate display, in His sonship, of the image and likeness of His Father. *"Although He existed in the form of God, did not regard equality with God a thing to be grasped, but emptied Himself, taking the form of a bond-servant, and being made in the likeness of men"* (Philippians 2:6-7). Though He was God in flesh appearing, He modeled the appropriate behavior of a son toward the Heavenly Father. Humility marked His nature, His words, and His actions.

The evil one showed his contempt for Almighty God when he took an opposite position. In Isaiah 14:12-15, the king of Babylon is used as a type of Satan. *"How you have fallen from heaven, O star of the morning, son of the dawn! You have been cut down to the earth, you who have weakened the nations! But you said in your heart, 'I will ascend to heaven; I will raise my throne above the stars of God, and I will sit on the mount of assembly in the recesses of the north. I will ascend above the heights of the clouds; I will make myself like the Most High."*

The roots of the boastful pride of life come from the evil one and his pride. Those who exalt themselves have joined their hearts to the rebellion.

Question: *Are you ever tempted to think of yourself more highly than you ought?*

39. Has God Said?

"...Who is this that darkens counsel by words
without knowledge?" ~ Job 38:2

It is no coincidence that the first deception sown into the heart and mind of Eve was in the form of a question. Why do we stumble more from a question than we do from a statement? With a statement, we are able to judge it for truth or error without personal engagement. A question instantly engages us, and often requires a response before we have time to consider our reply. *"Has God said?"* (Genesis 3:1) purposefully introduced doubt into a holy and whole relationship. This was the first thought Eve had ever encountered from the realm of darkness. It called for her to make a decision apart from the known will of her Creator. The Father's instructions, given for her protection, are cast with a shadow, as the evil one tries to imply that God has been purposely withholding good from her.

Prior to the third chapter of Genesis, Adam and Eve regularly encountered God in the garden. They walked with God—Truth embodied—on a daily basis. Their communication with their God and with one another was free of all guile, manipulation, or accusation. Then the father of lies, with his question, sowed doubt and undermined that relationship.

Satan is assaulting God's authority by questioning His Law. The usurper is always at work to undermine the Truth, by sowing doubt. Since this same ploy is aimed at the sons of God today, *"Commit your way to the Lord, trust also in Him, and He will do it"* (Psalm 37:5).

Question: Is there any area of your life where you have struggled with doubt?

40. Did God Know

*"...for God is greater than our heart, and knows
all things." ~ I John 3:20*

When God asked, *"Where are you?"* in Genesis 3:9, He was not seeking Adam and Eve's physical location. He went on to ask, *"Who told you that you were naked?"*, *"Have you eaten from the tree of which I commanded you not to eat?"*, and *"What is this you have done?"* (Genesis 3:11, 13). Does God know? Why would an all-knowing God need to ask a question? God must not know.

Oh yes He does. Remember, when God asks a question in scripture, it is never because He needs information, rather, it is for our sake. There is something that we need to know. At the core of this challenge to our omniscient God is the opportunity for humans to learn submission. Since we were created in His image and likeness, our free-will is a reflection of His sovereignty. When we remain in communion with Him, our submission will always lead us to wisdom. When we linger too long at the wrong tree—the Tree of the Knowledge of Good and Evil—we will return over and over again to using human reasoning for our decisions.

What kind of fruit is borne of a heart that disregards, or even challenges, His omniscience? One that can be conned into thinking, "no one will ever know ..." No one will know if you watch porn on your computer. No one will know if you say something inappropriate to just a few others. No one will know if you cheat or steal. But does God know? Yes He does. The suggestion that He doesn't know is one of the oldest tricks in The Book.

Question: Has the Lord ever asked you a question? Do you know why?

41. Lord God

"Who do people say that the Son of Man is?"
~ Matthew 16:13

The first reference to God, in Genesis 1, uses the Hebrew word *Elohim*. In the traditional Jewish view, this is the name of God as Creator and Judge. Upon the creation of man, another name is introduced, *YHWH*, and it is translated "Lord God".

As the history of mankind begins to unfold, we go from "God said, God saw, and God made" in chapter one, to "the Lord God formed, the Lord God commanded, and the Lord said" in chapter two. The only name we see upon the creation of man is, Lord God. This is the way He made Himself known to His creation, as Lord. Little wonder, when Satan approaches Eve that he gets the name wrong (Genesis 3:1-3). We can understand the evil one's reluctance to honor God as Lord, but "Lord God" is the only name by which He has ever been known to Eve. There is a level of protection in using it to identify Him. Using His name accurately is important to God, and when a new name is introduced, in both the Old and New Testament, it is an invitation to know Him as such.

When Eve repeats the name "God" instead of "Lord God", she has lessened the relationship. Today we often hear the name "God" used. It can be easily uttered from the screen, in print, on Facebook, and in conversations with unbelievers. We can sneak in that name, but it is significant when the name Lord is uttered. Lord perks up the ear, and implies a bowed heart. No wonder it is a more difficult name to say.

Question: Is it possible to know Jesus as Lord, yet refuse to obey Him?

42. Led Astray to Idols

"You know that when you were pagans, you were
led astray to the dumb idols ..."
~ I Corinthians 12:2

You may think you have free will; your decisions seem to flow from your own thinking and desire. Yet, there is something at work, always leading us in a course away from the will of God. It is a sin nature, and we are born with it.

Paul describes how it works in Romans, *"For we know that the law is spiritual; but I am of flesh, sold into bondage to sin. For that which I am doing, I do not understand; for I am not practicing what I would like to do, but I am doing the very thing I hate. But if I do the very thing I do not wish to do, I agree with the Law, confessing that it is good. So now, no longer am I the one doing it, but sin which indwells me. For I know that nothing good dwells in me, that is, in my flesh; for the wishing is present in me, but the doing of the good is not. For the good that I wish, I do not do; but I practice the very evil that I do not wish"* (Romans 7:14-19).

While we profess great freedoms, our behaviors betray us. There is another power at work, determining our steps. When Christ comes into our lives, we experience what liberty tastes like. Jesus said, *"If you abide in My word, then you are truly disciples of Mine; and you shall know the truth, and the truth shall make you free"* (John 8:31-32).

True freedom comes through submission. And sin comes from being led into bondage.

Question: Have you experienced any cycles of sin? What has helped you break free and walk in the Spirit?

43. Independence

"He who separates himself seeks his own desire, he
quarrels against all sound wisdom."
~ Proverbs 18:1

Day after day of creation, God saw *"that it was good"* until He made man. And then He said that it was *"not good for the man to be alone"*, so He made him a suitable helper. For mankind to reflect the image and likeness of their God, they would have to be a "we". This holy unity was an extension of the love relationship that God had displayed toward man, and would be a source of comfort, companionship, partnership, and protection. Ecclesiastes 4:9-12 says, *"Two are better than one because they have a good return for their labor. For if either of them falls, the one will lift up his companion. But woe to the one who falls when there is not another to lift him up. Furthermore, if two lie down together they keep warm, but how can one be warm alone? And if one can overpower him who is alone, two can resist him. A cord of three strands is not quickly torn apart."*

It is a subtle rebellion that initiates independence. In thinking highly of oneself and trusting oneself to be adequate for all of life's contingencies, a separation occurs that breeches the ways of God, opening the door for a powerless isolation. We are often tempted to stand alone—to withdraw in conflict, rather than repair the union. The way of the world is to be self-protective, self-made, and self-oriented—forfeiting holy communion.

Question: What commands of God require that you carry them out in the context of community?

44. Two Ways

*"Every man's way is right in his own eyes, but
the Lord weighs the hearts." ~ Proverbs 21:2*

As New Testament believers, we do not live under the burden of Old Testament Law. Yet, while attempting to live in
that freedom, there is often a tendency toward license, rather
than liberty. Living in and from grace means that we are set
free from our old sin nature, and able to discover the ways of
the Lord. Ever since the garden, the Lord has set before us two
ways of living, choosing, and walking. We always have a
choice to make—free-will to exercise. There were two trees in
the garden—one would bring life and one would bring death.
There were two offerings from the first sons—one was received and one required correction. There were two kinds of
sons in Proverbs—the wise and the foolish. There were true
prophets and false prophets, good kings and wicked kings,
the obedient and the disobedient. Jesus said, *"Enter by the narrow gate; for the gate is wide, and the way is broad that leads to
destruction, and many are those who enter by it. For the gate is
small, and the way is narrow that leads to life, and few are those who
find it"* (Matthew 7:13-14). Jesus always extends a way linked
with life and truth, but you can't always discern this with
your natural senses. It takes walking with and being led by
the Holy Spirit to discern the blessed way.

*Question: Why do we tend to disconnect consequences from daily oppor-
tunities and choices?*

45. High Places for Lesser Loves

*"You shall have no other gods before Me. You
shall not make for yourself an idol, or any likeness
of what is in heaven above or on the earth beneath or
in the water under the earth. You shall not worship
them or serve them; for I, the Lord your God, am a
jealous God" ~ Exodus 20:3-5a*

Throughout Israel's history in God, they continued to return to the high places, to install gods they had made with their own hands to a pedestal of worship. Rivals for their heart, residue from their days in Egypt, these idols were exalted in the face of a holy God. Idolatry can only be described as spiritual adultery.

It began on the plains of Shinar—when the ideas of men carried in rebellious hearts, joined together to build a tower that would access heaven. *"And the Lord said, 'Behold, they are one people, and they all have the same language. And this is what they began to do, and now nothing which they purpose to do will be impossible for them. Come, let Us go down and there confuse*

> **If it is I who determine where God is to be found, then I shall always find a God who corresponds to me in some way, *who is obliging, who is connected with my own nature. But if God determines where he is to be found, then it will be in a place which is not immediately pleasing ... This place is the Cross of Christ.***
>
> *Dietrich Bonhoeffer*

55

their language, that they may not understand one another's speech.'
So the Lord scattered them abroad from there over the face of the
whole earth; and they stopped building the city" (Genesis 11:6-8).

To walk in any kind of idolatry turns us from being led by
the Spirit to taking directions from idols. Consider how the
prophet Ezekiel rebuked the spiritual leadership of his day:

"Son of man, these men have set up their idols in their hearts, and
have put right before their faces the stumbling block of their iniquity.
Should I be consulted by them at all? Therefore speak to them and
tell them, 'Thus says the Lord God, "Any man of the house of Israel
who sets up his idols in his heart, puts right before his face the stum-
bling block of his iniquity, and then comes to the prophet, I the Lord
will be brought to give him an answer in the matter in view of the
multitude of his idols, in order to lay hold of the hearts of the house
of Israel who are estranged from Me through all their idols."'"

Question: How can you recognize the lesser things that you have ele-
vated in your heart — to the point that they now rival your relationship
with the Lord?

---

46. Compass of the Heart

*"When Thou didst say, 'Seek My face,' my heart
said to Thee, 'Thy face, O Lord, I shall seek.'"*
~ Psalm 27:8

A compass is a small instrument that uses the magnetism within the earth to orient us in a specific direction and help us navigate our journey. Because it is built to consistently point north, it helps us to make accurate travel choices.

One might think that our spiritual compass would be the mind. With accurate doctrine, foundational teaching laid down in each member, the church is sure to maintain her course in an expedient and precise manner. The problem is—we don't. *"For that which I am doing, I do not understand; for I am not practicing what I would like to do, but I am doing the very thing I hate"* (Romans 7:15). I might want to pursue a certain course—and know in my mind that a certain path is the wisest, healthiest, most productive, etc.—but my ultimate direction is always cued by my heart.

Inviting the Holy Spirit to abide within, and then positioning ourselves to follow His leadership, is the reorienting of the heart and the way to walk in the Spirit.

Question: What are some indicators to you that your heart has gone off course?

47. The Rest of God

*"Therefore, let us fear lest, while a promise
remains of entering His rest, any one of you should
seem to have come short of it." ~ Hebrews 4:1*

Man was created on the sixth day. *"And God saw all that He had made, and behold, it was very good"* (Genesis 1:31). If you review the first chapter of Genesis, you realize that the continual description of the passing of time is rehearsed with, *"there was evening and there was morning, one day."* It is counted from sundown on one day through the morning of the following day. So, somewhere, late on the sixth day, the man and the woman were brought forth. The very first day they will ever experience is about to begin, and it is called the Sabbath.

After six days of creation, *"the heavens and the earth were completed ... And by the seventh day God completed His work which He had done; and He rested on the seventh day from all His work which He had done. Then God blessed the seventh day and sanctified it, because in it He rested from all His work which God had created and made"* (Genesis 2:1-3). God worked, then rested. Adam rested, then worked.

Instead of working for rest, we must learn to work from rest. Listen to the words of Jesus, *"Come to Me, all who are weary and heavy-laden, and I will give you rest. Take My yoke upon you, and learn from Me, for I am gentle and humble in heart; and you shall find rest for your souls. For My yoke is easy, and My load is light"* (Matthew 11:28-30).

Question: What kind of resting produces the greatest refreshment in your life?

48. Live Like an Orphan

*"… I ascend to My Father and your Father, and
My God and your God." ~ John 20:17*

If I only had one portion of scripture to use in ministry for the rest of my life, it would be I John 4:16-19: *"And we have come to know and have believed the love which God has for us. God is love, and the one who abides in love abides in God, and God abides in him. By this, love is perfected with us, that we may have confidence in the day of judgment; because as He is, so also are we in this world. There is no fear in love; but perfect love casts out fear, because fear involves punishment, and the one who fears is not perfected in love. We love, because He first loved us."* Knowing and believing that you are loved is key for the transformation of the heart, and restores the ability to believe that you belong to Father God. The evil one is quick to interfere in this process; accusing us and filling our soul with thoughts of fear, guilt, and shame.

Orphans look at their world through the lens of lack rather than from the perspective of love bestowed from the Beloved to His creation. The call for us is to reconnect to our original design: sons of God.

Question: *Are there ways you fail to live into the adoption as sons described in Ephesians 1:5?*

49. Live Like a Slave

"You were called to freedom, brethren; only do not
turn your freedom into an opportunity for the flesh,
but through love serve one another. ~ Gal. 5:13

Jesus declared, *"If you abide in My word, then you are truly disciples of Mine; and you shall know the truth, and the truth shall make you free"* (John 8:31-32). The Apostle Paul found himself ministering to those who had heard, but were caught in two traps leading to bondage again. The first is sin. Those who continue to sin, after being set free, return to bondage. *"This I say therefore, and affirm together with the Lord, that you walk no longer just as the Gentiles also walk, in the futility of their mind, being darkened in their understanding, excluded from the life of God, because of the ignorance that is in them, because of the hardness of their heart; and they ... have given themselves over to sensuality, for the practice of every kind of impurity with greediness. But you did not learn Christ in this way ..."* (Ephesians 4:17-20).

The second trap is the Law. *"This is the only thing I want to find out from you: did you receive the Spirit by the works of the Law, or by hearing with faith? Are you so foolish? Having begun by the Spirit, are you now being perfected by the flesh?"* (Galatians 3:2).

Truth is a Person more than a set of doctrines, and true freedom comes when we learn to be led by the Holy Spirit. *"...Walk by the Spirit, and you will not carry out the desire of the flesh. For the flesh sets its desire against the Spirit, and the Spirit against the flesh; for these are in opposition to one another, so that you may not do the things that you please. But if you are led by the Spirit, you are not under the Law"* (Galatians 5:17-18).

Question: *In the natural realm, freedom has been something that is fought for. Is it something to be fought for in the spiritual realm?*

50. Nature of our Opponent

*"And they overcame him because of the blood of
the Lamb and because of the word of their
testimony, and they did not love their life even to
death." ~ Revelation 12:11*

A good story has a number of common characteristics. There is the initial hook—the way the author gets the attention of the reader. An element of desire is included—someone within the story who has a goal to achieve. The third element is conflict—some opposition arises that interferes with the characters' ability to achieve their goal. Within the framework of the story, a number of challenges and obstacles are faced, followed by a climax and resolution. God did not set out to just write a good story. He is the story (the living Word) and we are inserted into the greatest story that has ever been told. And it is true. The face of conflict in His-Story is a being known as Satan, the deceiver, the accuser of the brethren, Lucifer, the evil one. We are a part of God's plan to destroy his works (1 John 3:8). All human stories of good against evil find their source material in this large work that we are participating in. The final chapter declares the winner. Let us live like we believe His story.

Question: How are you able to recognize spiritual conflict? What is your best defensive tactic?

51. Doing what is right in our own eyes

*"In those days there was no king in Israel; every
man did what was right in his own eyes."*
~ Judges 17:6

Untethered from the living God after the fall, man wandered far from the Father's heart and will. Without God's Spirit, man was left to navigate each day of his life by his own mind, will, and emotions. Instead of reflecting the image and likeness of the Creator, we were distorted by every misled decision. It is difficult to govern a people who only look to themselves for authority and take little regard for the ways of the Lord. The book of Judges was characterized by such a rebellious people, for whom God Himself raised up leaders to rescue them from their apostasy, and their frequent idolatry and falling away.

It is insightful to look up the definition of anarchy. It is "the absence of government and absolute freedom of the individual, regarded as a political ideal." This is how Israel lived for approximately 350 years—without God as King, or man in subjection. It is not too far afield of how humanity is navigating today. On the brink of anarchy, with all seeming restrain removed, we are vulnerable to all that would overwhelm, overpower, and overtake us. Submission is our only way back to God's heart.

Question: Where or with whom do you practice submission?

52. Division

*"Let all bitterness and wrath and anger and
clamor and slander be put away from you, along
with all malice." ~ Ephesians 4:31*

God's intention at creation was to have oneness with Him. After the fall, it was to restore us to union. From the creation plan to Christ's triumphant return, the evil one works to bring destruction through division. It is an ancient strategy of war to divide and conquer. Intrusive thoughts undermine, careless words divide, and arrogant attitudes separate. We experience weakness when we are divided, and great strength when we are joined. In John's Gospel, Caiaphas, the high priest, prophesied that Jesus was going to die for the nation that He might also gather together the children of God who are scattered abroad (scattered since Genesis 11). It is Jesus, who was ...*"before all things, and in Him all things hold together"* (Colossians 1:17).

The church has been entrusted with God's divine antidote to the poisonous works of division. *"Love is patient, love is kind, and is not jealous; does not brag and is not arrogant, does not act unbecomingly; it does not seek its own, is not provoked, does not take into account a wrong suffered, does not rejoice in unrighteousness, but rejoices with the truth; bears all things, believes all things, hopes all things, endures all things. Love never fails"* (1 Corinthians 13:4-8a).

Let us consider and walk in these familiar vows: "What God has joined together, let no man put asunder (separate)."

Question: Do you have any severed relationships? Have the wounds healed? Is there any hope of reconciliation?

53. Distraction

*"... let us also lay aside every encumbrance, and
the sin which so easily entangles us, and let us run
with endurance the race that is set before us, fixing
our eyes on Jesus ..." ~ Hebrews 12:1-2*

As the church, we are engaged in an ancient spiritual conflict with the prince of darkness. He continually attempts to steal, kill, and destroy—to blind us from seeing and walking in the abundant life of the Spirit. It is critical that we understand the nature of our enemy and uncover his strategies. His attack usually begins with a thought/a fiery dart. If he can get us to meditate on his idea, fear and anxiety begin to set in. Those ideas, once rehearsed, become familiar, then owned as our own. We begin to act on what we are hearing, so we keep it (James 1:22-25). Then, out of the abundance of our heart— we speak (Luke 6:45). Sin has been conceived and it is designed to bring forth death (James 1:15).

Nehemiah was a man used of God to rebuild the wall surrounding Jerusalem. He faced cunning opposition, and was able to identify each of their strategies and come up with the right response. *"But we prayed to our God, and because of them we set up a guard against them day and night"* (Nehemiah 4:9).

The church must discover what we are falling for—where we are yielding—and resist the distractions.

Question: Have you ever lost anything by being distracted?

54. Distortion

"For wisdom will enter your heart, and knowledge will be pleasant to your soul; discretion will guard you, understanding will watch over you, to deliver you from the way of evil, from the man who speaks perverse things ..." ~ Proverbs 2:10-12

Distortion means to give a misleading account or impression, to twist something out of its true meaning. When this strategy is used by the evil one, it is usually aimed at distorting God's nature and character, particularly His goodness. It is also used to keep us from understanding our true identity.

Any time that God's nature can be distorted or marred, our ability to trust is at stake. Without trust, faith evaporates, and the enemy triumphs. The Apostle Paul continually prays that we would have eyes to see and apprehend what is true for us in the heavenly realm (Ephesians 1:17-19, 3:16-19, Colossians 1:9-12).

Since we were designed to be a reflection of the image and likeness of the Father, we must understand the great love extended to us, so we might be restored to relational intimacy. The only way to take a stand against such a great gift is for the enemy of our souls to keep us believing that our sin, guilt, and shame define us.

Question: *How does distortion become an effective tactic of the evil one?*

55. Fear

"For you have not received a spirit of slavery
leading to fear again ..." ~ Romans 8:15a

There is a unique acronym that helps us understand the strategy behind fear: False Evidence Appearing Real. As long as Satan can keep us believing lies, distortions, and threats, he can keep us from possessing the abundant life God intends for us. Ever since the garden, fear has taken advantage of God's people. When Adam and Eve chose to hide rather than confess, it was because they were afraid. When sin is crouching at the door, we are tempted to fear rather than learning to master it. When we are weary from suffering, fear can set in—causing us to give in to despair rather than finding nourishment from hope.

Anxiety and fear are causing God's people to shrink back with doubt, rather than move into possession of His Kingdom. When we yield to this kind of thinking over a period of time, a spiritual stronghold is established. A stronghold happens when we believe that something contrary to God's will is unchangeable. Fear exaggerates an outcome of the enemy's design and minimizes the power of the living God.

George Mueller said, "The beginning of anxiety is the end of faith, and the beginning of true faith is the end of anxiety."

Question: What is your most effective weapon when dealing with fear or anxiety? How does this protect and defend you?

56. Blame

"And the man said, 'The woman whom Thou
gavest to be with me, she gave me from
the tree, and I ate.'" ~ Genesis 3:12

Blame is when we take the responsibility for a sin or fault and place it on the shoulders of another. It is a way to avoid the gift of conviction and become deceived into believing that another should bear the responsibility for our sin. It is a strategy of avoidance that partners with the accuser of the brethren. Whenever sin is involved, the accuser can multiply its effect by deploying this false defense.

"And He, when He comes, will convict the world concerning sin, and righteousness, and judgment" (John 16:8). It is a gift of the Holy Spirit to bring an offense into the light, so that it can be confessed and forgiven. It is a false means offered by the evil one to blame another instead of receiving our own discipline, cleansing, and redemption.

The Lord knew that the burden of sin was too great to bear, but never intended for it to be shifted to any other but Himself.

Question: Have you ever found yourself blaming another for the state of your heart?

57. Shame

*"... and He Himself bore our sins in His body on
the cross, that we might die to sin and live to
righteousness; for by His wounds you were healed."*
~ 1 Peter 2:24

We experience shame when we continue to live under the judgment on fallen man, even though it was paid for by Jesus on the cross. It is often based on perfectionism, a standard we set for ourselves that can never be achieved and which leads to a false sense of failure and feelings of shame. It is the unachievable bench-mark that is put in place when I am the one who is in control. It is the result of believing my holiness hinges on my perfect behavior. The way to experience my creation design—bearing the image and likeness of the Father—is from proximity, rather than performance.

Due to walking in the strength of our soul instead of by the Holy Spirit, there is a tendency to evaluate the condition of our spirituality through our senses. Often, our feelings are not an accurate reflection of the truth. If we allow our sin or our feelings or our circumstances to define us, we will struggle to maintain the well-being (*shalom*) of God.

He died for our sin, that we might be made perfect by His righteousness.

Question: What circumstance is most able to distort your sense of identity and leave you with a burden of shame?

58. World Systems

*"For though we walk in the flesh, we do not war
according to the flesh, for the weapons of our
warfare are not of the flesh, but divinely powerful
for the destruction of fortresses."*
~ 2 Corinthians 10:3-4

During the wilderness temptation, Satan took Jesus to a high mountain, *"and showed Him all the kingdoms of the world, and their glory; and he said to Him, 'All these things will I give You if You fall down and worship me'"* (Matthew 4:8-9). Satan was offering Jesus an opportunity to rule the earth through exalting him as the ruler of this world (*Kosmokrater*). Jesus was not the last person to be offered this kind of rulership. Men daily trade their souls for a moment of fame, yielding themselves to wickedness.

The kingdom of the world is made up of systems, what some have called cultural mountains. These include business, government, arts and entertainment, education, family, and religion. To the degree Satan accomplishes his will and purpose through these systems is the basis of his earthly rule.

When Jesus triumphed over the devil by His crucifixion, resurrection, and ascension, He set in place the Kingdom of God. It is based on relationships. These relationships, operating in harmony with our King, have the power and authority to destroy all the works of the devil.

Question: What did Jesus mean when He said that we are in the world, but not of it (John 17:16)?

59. Reproduction

*"Indeed, the Lord will give what is good; and our
land will yield its produce." ~ Psalm 85:12*

Within every seed is the potential to bear mature fruit. It was a part of creation's design to reproduce according to its likeness. *"Then God said, 'Let the earth sprout vegetation, plants yielding seed, and fruit trees bearing fruit after their kind, with seed in them, on the earth'; and it was so"* (Genesis 1:11). Plants, animals, and people had the capacity to be fruitful and multiply, to fill the earth with all that God said was good. When the devil invaded time and space in the Garden, he came as the father of lies, to reproduce after his kind. He came to sow doubt and deception, and to corrupt the creation for his will and purposes. Like tares sown among wheat, and with lies sown next to truth, the intruder came to steal, kill, and destroy. Jesus came that we might have abundant life, yielding 30, 60, and 100 fold increase for His word, sown in our hearts.

Question: Does God's word find good soil in your heart? Are you seeing fruit from His seed sown?

Part 3
Soul and Spirit

60. Soul vs. Spirit

"That which is born of the flesh is flesh, and that which is born of the Spirit is spirit." ~ John 3:6

"Thus the heavens and the earth were completed, and all their hosts" (Genesis 2:1). Certain beings (angels) were formed to dwell in heavenly places, while others (mankind) were to steward an earthly domain.

At the time of creation, because man would dwell in the realm of time and space, he was given a body which would serve as a tent to dwell in. Since he would be able to interact with his environment, he also had a soul. The soul is made up of mind (I think), will (I want), and emotions (I feel). But because man was made to bear the image and likeness of God, he was spirit. Though designed to flourish in earthly realms, mankind was uniquely created to access the heavenly realm as well. As beings made in God's image and likeness, we were given the authority and responsibility to govern the earth until the fall. Once sin was introduced, separation occurred. God from man … man from woman … soul from Spirit.

Question: Do you tend to walk more as a natural man/woman or one who is spiritually alive?

61. Soul vs. Spirit (2)

"... it is sown a natural body, it is raised a
spiritual body. If there is a natural body, there is
also a spiritual body."
~ I Corinthians 15:44

At the fall, when mankind was disconnected spiritually, we began to compensate by operating from our body and soul together (flesh). The soul became enlarged, and took on a role it was never designed to accomplish, that of taking the lead, and directing our path. The indwelling life of the Holy Spirit was forfeited, and we were given to wander. Left to the leadership of the soul, our decisions were based on "I think it" (mind), "I want it" (will), or "I feel it" (emotions). Without the governing work of the Spirit, we were earth creatures who could no longer perceive the spiritual realm. When mankind turned away from submission to God, we were left with only strength of soul.

Question: Where are you relying on your soul for what only the Holy Spirit can accomplish?

73

62. Conversion

"... always carrying about in the body the dying of Jesus, that the life of Jesus also may be manifested in our body." ~ 2 Corinthians 4:10

At the cross, payment was made for sin, and at the resurrection, provision was made for newness of life. As we receive His punishment on our behalf, our sins are paid for. As we identify with His risen life, we also are raised in the likeness of His resurrection, with the new life of His indwelling Spirit. Having walked by strength of soul, man must relearn the ways of the Spirit and the submission of the flesh. The process of conversion becomes our daily experience as we put off the flesh and put on the Spirit. *"... For if you are living according to the flesh, you must die; but if by the Spirit you are putting to death the deeds of the body, you will live"* (Romans 8:13).

Question: How can you recognize an opportunity to die to the ways of your flesh?

63. Strength vs. Weakness

*"My grace is sufficient for you, for power is
perfected in weakness." ~ 2 Corinthians 12:9*

One might be tempted to believe that the way to mature in
Christ is the perfecting of our soul's strengths. If we train our
mind, focus our will, and restrain our emotions we might become more Christ-like. *"There is a way which seems right to a
man, but it's end is the way of death"* (Proverbs 14:12). The ways
of the Kingdom of God are opposite to the ways of the world,
and involve how we face our weaknesses. *"Because the foolish-
ness of God is wiser than men, and the weakness of God is stronger
than men ... God has chosen the foolish things of the world to shame
the wise, and God has chosen the weak things of the world to shame
the things which are strong, and the base things of the world and the
despised, God has chosen, the things that are not, that He might
nullify the things that are, that no man should boast before God"*
(1 Corinthians 1:25, 27-29).

Question: *What area of your life could benefit from exchanging your
weakness for His strength?*

64. Huios

"For the anxious longing of the creation waits
eagerly for the revealing of the sons [huios] of God."
~ *Romans 8:19*

We were designed to live with our body and soul in submission to the leadership of the Holy Spirit. After the fall, man lived apart from the life of the Spirit functioning from fallen flesh (body-soul-Spirit). Without His indwelling presence, mankind was unable to reflect the true image and likeness of our holy God. When Jesus came to reconcile us to the Father, He not only made peace for us, He made us family. He lived among us as a visible model of Sonship—submission of body and soul to the life of the Spirit. In the Greek language, four different words can be interpreted "son"; two of them are *tekna* and *huios*. When Jesus is described as the Son of God, *huios* is combined with, *Theou*, the Greek word for God (*Huios Theou*). *Tekna* refers to those who were born of God, and *huios* refers to those who show maturity by acting as sons and displaying the image and likeness of God and His character. Romans 8:14 declares, *"For all who are being led by the Spirit of God, these are sons [huios] of God."* As we learn to be led by the Holy Spirit rather than operating in the strength of our soul, we bear the image and likeness of our Father.

Question: Do you recognize the difference between your soul and the Spirit, and how they function?

65. Strength of Mind

"For the Lord gives wisdom; from His mouth
come knowledge and understanding."
~ Proverbs 2:6

Ever since the Garden and the choice made to partake of the wrong tree, man has fixed his desire on the Tree of the Knowledge of Good and Evil. No matter how well trained your mind has become, how many titles gained, or doctorates awarded, a mind in pursuit of knowledge apart from the Spirit is a mind given to the flesh. Curiosity allied with pride can quickly take a mind off course and toward a vain outcome. For our mind to accurately assess any situation, it must be directed by and under the authority of the Holy Spirit. When properly submitted, wisdom is found.

Question: How have you learned to gain wisdom about something, and not just knowledge?

66. Stimulated Emotions

"And the peace of God, which surpasses all comprehension, shall guard your hearts and your minds in Christ Jesus."
~ Philippians 4:7

Emotions tend to reflect the conditions of our environment, both internally and externally. They happen in response to stimuli we experience or rehearse, and their accuracy concerning the true nature of our condition can be suspect. There tend to be eight basic emotions: fear, anger, sadness, joy, disgust, trust, anticipation, and surprise. The emotions we dislike, we work to avoid or suppress. The feelings we enjoy, we look forward to or attempt to prolong.

Because emotions give us clues concerning the state of our environment, they tend to rely on the natural realm for their source. People can confuse an emotional response with a true spiritual encounter. Learning to recognize emotional sensitivity from true spiritual perception is an indication of maturity in the believer.

Question: *How do you recognize the difference between an emotional and a spiritual response?*

67. Strength of Will

*"...Father, if Thou art willing, remove this cup
from Me; yet not My will, but Thine be done."*
~ Luke 22:42

Will power gives the ability to say no to chocolate cake. It also gets an athlete out of bed and into the gym before dawn. It has kept a prisoner alive in a concentration camp, a patient alive until a relative arrives, and a toddler awake instead of napping. The unsubmitted will, though admirable at times, is still the power of flesh. Stubbornness—which is to be fixed or set in purpose or opinion—can become a fleshly way that ultimately is resistant to the leading of the Holy Spirit.

When our will is rightly submitted to the Holy Spirit, it no longer functions by stubborn persistence, but is the means to faithfulness, sustaining the will of God in our lives.

Question: *Where has the Lord asked you to follow Him that was against your will?*

68. Body + Soul = Flesh

*"But now we have been released from the Law,
having died to that by which we were bound, so that
we serve in newness of the Spirit and not in oldness
of the letter." ~Romans 7:6*

Man was never designed to live apart from the One whose image and likeness we are to bear. Both body and soul were created to live in submission to the Spirit and not move by their own impulse. When they operate on their own, apart from God, it is described as flesh in scripture. Flesh cannot be subdued by the Law, in fact, it is aroused by it (Romans 7:5). This alliance is in opposition to the Spirit, and the Spirit is in opposition to the flesh, and this conflict never goes away (Galatians 5:17).

Rather than trying to restrain our old nature, we are called to daily recognize the ways the Holy Spirit is leading, and follow Him.

Question: When is your flesh most likely to oppose the work of the Holy Spirit?

69. Religious Flesh

*"Woe to you, scribes and Pharisees, hypocrites!
For you clean the outside of the cup and of the dish,
but inside they are full of robbery and self-
indulgence." ~ Matthew 23:25*

There are very religious people who have doctrinally sound knowledge about God, but are far from having a relationship with Him. The Apostle Paul described himself in Philippians 3: *"... although I myself might have confidence even in the flesh. If anyone else has a mind to put confidence in the flesh, I far more: circumcised the eighth day, of the nation of Israel, of the tribe of Benjamin, a Hebrew of Hebrews; as to the Law, a Pharisee; as to zeal, a persecutor of the church; as to the righteousness which is in the Law, found blameless. But whatever things were gain to me, those things I have counted as loss for the sake of Christ...I count all things to be loss in view of the surpassing value of knowing Christ Jesus my Lord ..."* (Philippians 3:4-8).

The Holy Spirit and God's word work together. If the word is only received as knowledge, the heart remains unchanged. When the Spirit ministers the word, it is *"living and active and sharper than any two-edged sword, and piercing as far as the division of soul and spirit, of both joints and marrow, and able to judge the thoughts and intentions of the heart"* (Hebrews 4:12).

Question: Have you ever believed the truth about the scriptures in your head, but failed to believe it with your heart?

70. Search Engine

"... which things we also speak, not in words
taught by human wisdom, but in those taught by
the Spirit, combining spiritual thoughts with
spiritual words." ~ I Corinthians 2:13

The human mind is like a search engine—accessing and bringing to mind all manner of intelligence that has been stored over the years. It draws on a range of collected experiences, learned facts, and memorable data. It is information driven, and can rehearse and rearrange the thoughts that are stored in a variety of ways. Without a filter, these thoughts can emerge to incite our speech and behavior on a regular basis. When we come to Christ, we are able to yield to the Spirit as a filter for our thoughts. As we learn to submit this wonderful gift of the mind to the leadership of the Holy Spirit, we learn to discern the voice of the Lord. Revelation—as opposed to information—is the way the Holy Spirit inserts His direction into our thinking to influence our immediate situation. Information is the accumulation of facts, revelation is when God discloses himself and His will relative to our circumstances.

Question: *How readily can you distinguish the voice of the Lord from stored information in your mind?*

71. *Human or Divine*

"And the Word became flesh, and dwelt among
us, and we beheld His glory, glory as of the only
begotten from the Father, full of grace and truth."
~ John 1:14

Over 2,000 years ago, Jesus put on flesh and dwelt among us. Leaving His throne of glory to be made manifest as the Son of Man, He laid aside privilege to restore His creation. Spirit stepped into time and space and put on flesh, so that a redeemed creation could get dressed the reversed way—putting off flesh, and putting on Spirit. Jesus, through the Body of Christ, is still God in flesh appearing.

When the Father poured out the Holy Spirit upon His people, we were once more filled with divine life—the third person of the Triune God, the Holy Spirit, indwelling man. He is the source of our new life, our transformation, our power, and authority. He determines our gifting, our calling, our identity, and our destiny. If the Lord has chosen to indwell us, it is critical that we learn how to discern His will, His ways, His desires, His word, so that we might cooperate with all that He desires to do in us and through us.

Question: *How has the Lord desired to express Himself through your life this week?*

83

72. *How we speak*

"Death and life are in the power of the tongue,
and those who love it will eat its fruit."
~ Proverbs 18:21

Words have great power. When the Lord uttered His voice, creation came forth. As His Word was released, His will was made known, His goodness seen, and His ways were established. Life and blessing were the fruit of His speaking.

When the evil one spoke in Genesis 3, his purpose was to steal, kill, and destroy. He was a liar, and the father of lies, looking for a heart to conceive his seed. His words robbed and ransacked creation.

Jesus came to be the exact representation of His Father. *"For I did not speak on My own initiative, but the Father Himself who sent Me has given Me commandment, what to say and what to speak"* (John 12:49). Life came forth from all that He said.

The tongue is a very small part of our body, but scripture says, *"... no one can tame the tongue; it is a restless evil and full of deadly poison. With it we bless our Lord and Father; and with it we curse men, who have been made in the likeness of God; from the same mouth come both blessing and cursing. My brethren, these things ought not to be this way."* As followers of Jesus, we must learn His ways, and only say what we hear the Father saying.

Question: Who have you blessed this week?

73. Do What I See Him Doing

*"Truly, truly, I say to you, the Son can do
nothing of Himself, unless it is something He sees
the Father doing; for whatever the Father does, these
things the Son also does in like manner."*
~ John 5:19

"God, after He spoke long ago to the father's in the prophets in many portions and in many ways, in these last days has spoken to us in His Son...and He is the radiance of His glory and the exact representation of His nature, and upholds all things by the word of His power" (Hebrews 1:1-3). God created man to display His nature and likeness. After the fall, mankind became a reflection of every lesser thing. The Father sent the Son to bear witness in the physical realm to His true image and likeness. Jesus, through His purposeful submission to the Father, displayed what mature sons are supposed to look like. *"I do nothing on My own initiative ... He who sent Me is with Me; He has not left Me alone, for I always do the things that are pleasing to Him"* (John 8:28-29). *"Truly, truly, I say to you, the Son can do nothing of Himself, unless it is something He sees the Father doing; for whatever the Father does, these things the Son also does in like manner. For the Father loves the Son, and shows Him all things that He Himself is doing; and greater works than these will He show Him, that you may marvel"* (John 5:19-20).

Question: How have your actions been transformed by the indwelling life of the Holy Spirit?

74. *Not On Your Own Initiative*

*"And He who sent Me is with Me; He has not left
Me alone, for I always do the things that are
pleasing to Him." ~ John 8:29*

The person who is best suited for leadership is the one who knows how to follow, and does so.

In order to have great authority, one must understand the power found in submission. These statements stand in contradiction to the ways of the world, but are the path that was demonstrated to us in the life of the Son of God.

Though never less than God, Jesus humbled Himself, living as the Son of Man. He limited His behavior to the ways available to all of us. He took all that He thought, felt, and wanted, and brought them as an offering to His Father. He exchanged who He was, and what He had, for the will of His Father and what the Father wanted done on earth as it is in heaven. Of all that was accomplished in and through the life of Christ, it was not based on His own initiative, but on what the Father was directing and inspiring (John 8:28).

Question: How difficult is it for you to live in submission to the will of another?

75. *Discerning the Source*

"Turn to my reproof, Behold, I will pour out my
spirit on you; I will make my words known to you."
~ Proverbs 1:23

Not all thoughts come from the same source. When we begin to interrogate our thinking for the source of our ideas, we uncover numerous avenues or entry points. Humans have the capacity to store experiences and think about them later. By remembering, we can reconsider an event and take away further ideas. Reasoning and logic are ways we consider a thought and then decide how to act upon it.

Thoughts also enter the mind from two other sources. The evil one has the ability to aim a fiery dart at us, which is an intrusive thought, ultimately designed to steal, kill, and destroy. Paying attention to what response a thought elicits can help discover its author.

The other source is the Holy Spirit speaking to our spirit, introducing thoughts that come from the heart of God. Learning to trust these leadings help us to mature, and to think with the mind of Christ.

Question: How have you learned to test a thought or way of thinking?

76. Learning from the Heart

*"… If you confess with your mouth Jesus as
Lord, and believe in your heart that God raised Him
from the dead, you shall be saved; for with the heart
man believes, resulting in righteousness, and with
the mouth he confesses, resulting in salvation."*
~ Romans 10:9-10

We might be persuaded to believe that right doctrine leads
to a response of faith. Yet, thinking accurately doesn't always
transform our heart. Information in our head is no rival to the
whispering of the Holy Spirit within. Most learning in the
West is aimed at collecting and rehearsing the right facts and
figures, without regard for the state of our heart or values.
Rather than mastering material, Christians are to reflect the
presence of indwelling Wisdom.

If learning is aimed at the heart, instead of the head, each
one might bear a different result from the presence
of the Teacher.

Question: What heart question has the Lord recently posed to you?

77. *Word Written on the Heart*

"But their minds were hardened; for until this very day at the reading of the old covenant the same veil remains unlifted, because it is removed in Christ." ~ 2 Corinthians 3:14

God chose to make a New Covenant with His people. Instead of being written on stone, and doing little to transform hard hearts, He declared, *"I will put My law within them, and on their heart I will write it; and I will be their God, and they shall be My people."* (Jeremiah 31:33).

When a woman caught in adultery was thrown to the ground in front of Jesus, He was asked what the Law required. He stooped down, and with His finger, wrote on the dust. What was He writing? Perhaps the better question might be, what was He demonstrating. The Law written on stone kills, but the Spirit gives life (2 Corinthians 3:6). What is man made of? Dust. Jesus came to fulfill writing His New Covenant on human hearts—writing in the dust. When that takes place, we can go, and sin no more.

Question: Do you recognize the difference between condemnation and the convicting work of the Holy Spirit?

78. *Natural Mind*

*"Let this mind be in you, which was also in Christ
Jesus …" ~ Philippians 2:5 KJV*

Though the human brain is exquisitely complex, it does not have the capacity to access the thoughts of God. Left to our own thinking, we find ourselves inadequate to discern the ways of the Lord. *"Things which eye has not seen and ear has not heard, and which have not entered the heart of man, all that God has prepared for those who love Him"* (1 Corinthians 2:9). *"But, these things are spiritually discerned; God revealing them to us by His Spirit"* (1 Corinthians 2:10). Since God speaks, *"… not in words taught by human wisdom, but in those taught by the Spirit, combining spiritual thoughts with spiritual words"* (1 Corinthians 2:13), it is critical for us to discern the power and intent of His words, and to know the mind of Christ.

To walk and speak, to pray and discern, we must yield our natural capacity and abilities, and not trust in what our fleshly human nature can access or produce. We must learn how to appraise all things spiritually, and then walk in submission to the Holy One, given to guide us.

Question: How do you confirm that you are thinking like God would think about a matter?

79. Viewpoint

"For from Him and through Him and to Him are
all things …" ~ Romans 11:36

Under the Old Covenant Law, a priesthood was allowed to approach the Lord through sacrifice and offerings. The statutes kept them mindful of what was required to please God— performing His will through their words and ways. Tabernacled within the Holy of Holies, God was set apart, unapproachable by most, and all preparations were for Him. Now, Christ has come to dwell, by His Holy Spirit, in the hearts of His people. As He makes His residence within us, we are transformed into His likeness (2 Corinthians 3:17-18). We are a living tabernacle, pitched in the midst of the world, bearing the likeness of the living God. Now, as His royal priesthood, we can respond from Him, actively carrying His presence forth and establishing His Kingdom purposes.

Question: Knowing that you are chosen to carry the Lord's presence—
how does this influence your behavior?

80. *The Wounded Soul*

*"The Lord is my shepherd, I shall not want. He
makes me lie down in green pastures; He leads me
beside quiet waters. He restores my soul."*
~ Psalm 23:1-3

The soul is designed to be an incredible interface between
our natural environment and our spirit. Divinely designed to
be in submission to the Holy Spirit, we are able to navigate
our lives with His wisdom and counsel. Our soul is also subject to a level of buffeting as we move through our daily journey. We can become wounded in our thinking, our feelings,
and our desires. Once wounded, our perception becomes bent
and deformed until that injury is addressed. Some of the
deepest wounds we experience, such as betrayal, rejection,
and abandonment, can have a life-altering influence until
they are addressed.

When the Holy Spirit comes to indwell the believer, we have
the opportunity for this conversion to impact every aspect of
our being. Our soul, in the presence of the Comforter, can
begin to lay hold of what we were created for.

---

*Question: When you hear the words betrayal, rejection, and abandon-
ment, does any person or situation come to mind? Ask the Holy Spirit
about the state of your heart.*

81. Healing the Wounded Soul

*"I would have despaired unless I had believed that
I would see the goodness of the Lord in the land of
the living. Wait for the Lord; be strong, and let your
heart take courage; yes, wait for the Lord."*
~ Psalm 27:13-14

Soul wounds often go untended for a period of time without being healed. We come up with a variety of ways to live with our wounds and their symptoms. With the passage of time it is no longer just a wound that needs tending, but the onset of infection and walking with a limp. If a wound remains open, the evil one can infect the wound with deception—creating a larger need for healing and deliverance. If we continue too long with significant pain, we limp due to the pain or to escape the suffering. When the Holy Spirit is involved, the God of all comfort, He will always move us toward His shalom—well-being. The healing process will take us through the steps of confession, forgiveness, re-orienting our thoughts and beliefs, and relearning how to walk by the Spirit, rather than from our pain.

Question: Do you have someone you trust to go to when you have suffered a heart wound? If not, why not?

82. *Leaning on Your Own Understanding*

*"... for if you cry for discernment, lift your voice
for understanding; if you seek her as silver, and
search for her as for hidden treasures; then you will
discern the fear of the Lord, and discover the
knowledge of God." ~ Proverbs 2:2-5*

Knowledge addresses the facts about a situation. To understand, means we perceive the meaning of something. Wisdom is the outcome of walking with correct understanding. When man sinned, and became separated from God, he was limited to information that came from his body and soul, his flesh. He could draw conclusions from knowledge—human thinking, feelings, and desires—and he was often led astray. Walking by the Spirit means we choose to not *"lean on our own understanding, but in all [our] ways acknowledge Him, and He will direct [our] steps"* (Proverbs 3:6).

Though Jesus was God in flesh appearing, He chose to not "lean on His own understanding", but modeled a dependency on the Father for how to approach every situation in which He found Himself. He has invited us into the same counsel. We can walk with Wisdom, and display God.

Question: Is it more difficult to depend on the Lord's leading for your thoughts, your feelings, or your desires?

83. *What Would Jesus Do?*

"For the Father loves the Son, and shows Him all
things that He Himself is doing; and greater works
than these will He show Him, that you may
marvel." ~ John 5:20

Charles Sheldon, in his book *In His Steps*, posed the question through his characters, "What would Jesus do?" and answered that a Christian should then go and do likewise. For over a century, this novel has challenged believers to bring their lives in conformity to the life of Christ in all matters.

But what if we have been asking ourselves the wrong question? In imitating Jesus, we can miss one of His most vital lessons. He only said what He heard the Father saying. We are not to copy Jesus' words, but the way He received them. Jesus only did what He saw the Father doing. We don't copy His behaviors, but the way He learned how He was to behave. He never acted on His own initiative. Once our own will is in a place of submission, the release of the Father's ways begin to flow through us as well. Our own faith comes through our own privileged hearing as we access His presence.

Question: *How is God's will most often confirmed in your life?*

84. Navigation

*"The wind blows where it wishes and you hear the
sound of it, but do not know where it comes from
and where it is going; so is everyone who is born of
the Spirit." ~ John 3:8*

There are three different approaches people take on their
spiritual journey with the Lord. Some treat it as though it
were a train ride. At the point of salvation, you receive your
ticket to your final destination, heaven. You merely board the
train, enjoying the ride, because all has been paid for. You are
merely a passenger and observer.

Others approach the journey as a passenger in a car. You
have a vehicle and a map. Just follow the script and keep the
rules, and you should find your way there.

But our journey is more like a ship driven by the wind of His
Spirit and charting our way by fixing our eyes on the heavens.
The Spirit leads us daily and supplies the power for any for-
ward movement.

Question: *Have you ever taken a journey without knowing where you
were headed?*

85. *Church Government*

"And he had a son whose name was Saul, a choice
and handsome man, and there was not a more
handsome person than he among the sons of Israel;
from his shoulders and up he was taller than any of
the people." ~ I Samuel 9:2

There was a time in the history of Israel when they requested a king. *"Now appoint a king for us to judge us like all the nations"* (1 Samuel 8:5). Though this was displeasing to the prophet Samuel, the Lord's response was, *"Listen to the voice of the people in regard to all that they say to you, for they have not rejected you, but they have rejected Me from being king over them"* (1 Samuel 8:7). Throughout history, humans have sought to elevate man to a position that can only rightfully be satisfied by God. Mankind's willingness to disregard the leadership of God has often brought him into servitude instead of freedom. Today, the church can find itself in subjection to human authority, rather than divine authority. Our willingness to forfeit God's ways for the will of man can still only produce a "Saul".

Question: What kind of government did the Lord institute in His church?

86. Fullness of Deity

"... until we all attain to the unity of the faith,
and of the knowledge of the Son of God, to a mature
man, to the measure of the stature which belongs to
the fullness of Christ." ~ Ephesians 4:13

"For in Him all the fullness of Deity dwells in bodily form" (Colossians 2:9). Though Christ was God in flesh appearing (1 Timothy 3:16), He did not regard equality with God as a thing to be grasped (Philippians 2:6), but lived in humble dependence upon the Father. Jesus bore witness to all that sons were supposed to display of the image and likeness of God. Every possible aspect of His Father's divinity was displayed through His humanity. Christ is now the head of the body, His church, and when we live into this corporately, we experience His fullness once more in bodily form. *"For of His fullness we have all received, and grace upon grace"* (John 1:16). *"And He put all things in subjection under His feet, and gave Him as head over all things to the church, which is His body, the fullness of Him who fills all in all"* (Ephesians 2:22-23). As we live and move together in the life of His Spirit, we experience Christ in His fullness in our midst.

Question: When have you experienced the fullness of Christ in a corporate setting?

87. *Human Divisions*

"Be of the same mind toward one another; do not
be haughty in mind, but associate with the lowly.
Do not be wise in your own estimation."
~ Romans 12:16

The world has divided itself on the basis of race, gender, status, occupation, preferences, and income. Instead of diversity being a gift, it now leads to hate language. National boundaries are fiercely guarded, while moral boundaries are coming under a relentless demand for sameness. Within God's economy, differences contribute to the betterment of the whole. In the kingdom of the world, they are used to subjugate one group to another. Racism exists because of our tendency to elevate one part of society, while demeaning another. Sexism, the stereotyping and discrimination of women, has existed throughout history, and is often fueled by the stance of the church toward the feminine gender. Classism, the prejudice of one social class over another, separates the rich from the poor—the haves, from the have-nots. Human efforts can not remove these offenses, but Christ can. *"For you are all sons of God through faith in Christ Jesus. For all of you who were baptized into Christ have clothed yourselves with Christ. There is neither Jew nor Greek, there is neither slave nor free man, there is neither male nor female; for you are all one in Christ Jesus"* (Galatians 3:26-28). All previous distinctions that separated can now become gift as we abide in Christ.

Questions: Is there any evidence of human divisions in your church?

88. *Traditions of Men*

"Neglecting the commandment of God, you hold to the tradition of men... You nicely set aside the commandment of God in order to keep your tradition." ~ Mark: 7:8-9

The traditions of men often interrupt the ways of God. Religious practices that are rooted in performance and perfection of self fail to display the will or the word of the Father. Jesus found Himself in more conflict with the scribes and Pharisees than with the sinners among the people. He charged them with shutting off the kingdom of heaven from men—not entering themselves, or allowing others to enter (Matthew 23:13). Without the indwelling Spirit, the best human effort can only produce religious flesh. Apart from His presence, living His life, in us and through us, we forfeit what we have been given in Christ. As the church, we are to be a living display of Christ in our midst. If we attempt to serve Him from our own strength, the image is marred.

Question: Do you recognize any religious traditions that are not scriptural?

89. Creation is Longing

"The heavens are telling of the glory of God; and
their expanse is declaring the work of His hands.
Day to day pours forth speech, and night to night
reveals knowledge."
~ Psalm 19:1-2

"For the anxious longing of the creation waits eagerly for the revealing of the sons of God. For the creation was subjected to futility, not of its own will, but because of Him who subjected it, in hope that the creation itself also will be set free from its slavery to corruption into the freedom of the glory of the children of God" (Romans 8:19-21). When we fell prey to sin in the Garden, all of God's will and purpose in the design of His creation was also disrupted. The stewardship of this planet, entrusted to Adam and Eve, has yet to be recovered and released. "We are His workmanship, created in Christ Jesus for good works, which God prepared beforehand, that we should walk in them" (Ephesians 2:10). As God's children learn to walk in the Spirit they mature into the likeness of the Father. They become what they were intended to be, mature sons (*huios*) and the creation is longing for that original design to be brought to fruition (Romans 8:14).

Question: How would maturity as sons of God make a difference in the stewardship of our planet?

90. Soulishness

"For those who are according to the flesh set their
minds on the things of the flesh, but those who are
according to the Spirit, the things of the Spirit."
~ *Romans 5:5*

Many attempt to act on the Lord's behalf without receiving instruction from Him. Our mind, will, and emotions can be trained to perform for God—a pattern more representative of the Old Covenant, than the New. Religious performance has the appearance of godliness, but denies its power (2 Timothy 3:5). Once we are filled with the Holy Spirit, we must learn to walk in submission to His will, His word, and His ways. Our soul will always attempt to rival the indwelling work of the Holy Spirit. *"For the flesh sets its desire against the Spirit, and the Spirit against the flesh; for these are in opposition to one another, so that you may not do the things that you please"* (Galatians 5:17). We mature in Christ as we live in submission to the Head of the Church, in all things. Learning to hear His voice, both personally and corporately, is how we are led by Him. Then, we can carry the presence of the Holy Spirit into every situation and His power conducts His will through us.

Question: How does this description of the work of the Holy Spirit rede-fine ministry?

Part 4

Egypt and the Promised Land

91. The Wilderness Journey

"Thou art the God who workest wonders; Thou
hast made known Thy strength among the peoples.
Thou hast by Thy power redeemed Thy people, the
sons of Jacob and Joseph." ~ Psalm 77:13-15

The wilderness was a time of testing and trial for Israel. Born into slavery in Egypt, they were unaccustomed to the ways of the Lord. The Father needed to reorient His people to Himself.

The stories of Israel's forty year sojourn have numerous lessons for us today. *"For I don't want you to be unaware, brethren, that our fathers were all under the cloud, and all passed through the sea; and all were baptized into Moses in the cloud and in the sea; and all ate the same spiritual food; and all drank the same spiritual drink, for they were drinking from a spiritual rock which followed them; and the rock was Christ. Nevertheless, with most of them God was not well-pleased; for they were laid low in the wilderness. Now these things happened as examples for us; that we should not crave evil things, as they also craved ..."* (1 Corinthians 10:1-6).

Hidden within the story of deliverance from Egypt and the journey to the Promised Land, is our own redemption story. There is a saying that goes: The Old Testament is the New Testament concealed, and the New Testament is the Old Testament revealed. When we read them, it is similar to the way we put a large puzzle together, by continually looking for places that match. The wilderness story is when God begins to retrain His people to be led.

Question: How has the Lord taught you to trust Him in the midst of a trial?

92. Putting God to the Test

*"Today if you hear His voice, do not harden your
hearts as when they provoked Me, as in the day of
trial in the wilderness, where your fathers tried Me
by testing Me, and saw My works for forty years."*
~ Hebrews 3:7-9

In the day of trial in the wilderness, instead of being tested themselves, Israel put God to the test. Exodus 17:7 states, *"And he named the place Massah and Meribah because of the quarrel of the sons of Israel, and because they tested the Lord, saying, 'Is the Lord among us, or not?'"*

In the day of our trial, this can be worded in so many different ways. God: Are you really Provider—or not? Are you really Protector—or not? Are you really good? Are you with us—or not? In our trials, we have been assured that He is with us; that we can cry for help and ask for wisdom. Though we might fail the wilderness test, the Lord never fails to fulfill His names, His nature, and His character. He is Provider—He will provide. He is Protector—our security is certain. He is—God with us—Immanuel. *"Consider it all joy, my brethren, when you encounter various trials, knowing that the testing of your faith produces endurance. And let endurance have its perfect result, that you may be perfect and complete, lacking in nothing"* (James 1:2-4). Trials bring strength and maturity. They should never be cause to require God to prove Himself.

Question: Is there any area of your walk with God where you are putting Him to the test?

93. Water From the Rock

*"Jesus said to her, 'If you knew the gift of God,
and who it is who says to you, "Give Me a drink,"
you would have asked Him, and He would have
given you living water.'"*
~ John 4:10

When God brings a people to Himself by means of a desert, He is creating a scenario that should lead to trust. As the need for water arises, the Lord tells Moses, *"Pass before the people and take with you some of the elders of Israel; and take in your hand your staff with which you struck the Nile, and go. Behold, I will stand before you there on the rock at Horeb; and you shall strike the rock, and water will come out of it, that the people may drink."* The passage concludes with, *"And Moses did so in the sight of the elders of Israel"* (Exodus 17:5-6).

Picture the scene: a large rock in the midst of the people that Moses is commanded to strike—using the staff that had accomplished all the previous displays of

> *[T]he prayers offered in the state of dryness are those which please Him best ... Do not be deceived, Wormwood. Our cause is never more in danger than when a human, no longer desiring, but still intending, to do [God's] will, looks round upon a universe from which every trace of Him seems to have vanished, and asks why he has been forsaken, and still obeys.*
>
> C.S. Lewis
> The Screwtape Letters

power—and—God will be standing on that rock. At the striking of the rock, a mighty flow of water is released, and the nation is satisfied. Later, in Numbers 20:2-12, when the people thirst, God instructs Moses to speak to the rock—to release a river. In a moment of anger, Moses strikes it again, forfeiting entrance to the Promised Land for his disobedience. God is displaying the future prophetically in this event.

At the cross, when Jesus is struck once—salvation is poured forth. *"For it was fitting that we should have such a high priest, holy, innocent, undefiled, separated from sinners and exalted above the heavens; who does not need daily, like those high priests, to offer up sacrifices, first for His own sins, and then for the sins of the people, because this He did once for all when He offered up Himself"* (Hebrews 7:26-27). Struck once and Living Water is released. When Moses struck the rock a second time, he ruined the imagery.

Question: *Have you ever disregarded a command of the Lord because you thought you knew what to do?*

---

94. Dependence

*"I can do nothing on My own initiative. As I
hear, I judge; and My judgment is just, because I do
not seek My own will, but the will of Him
who sent Me." ~ John 5:30*

Within the nature of the One God, there are three Persons—
the Father, the Son, and the Holy Spirit. Equally God, with
separate roles, they demonstrate among themselves the
power of unity. When man was created, though he had free
will, he was invited to participate in this community of One.
Bearing the Father's image and likeness on earth would require that we operate from a position of dependence, since
that was how the Trinity operated with one another.

There is a remarkable glimpse we get of the Father and Son
speaking to one another just prior to the Incarnation. *"Therefore, when He comes into the world, He says, 'Sacrifice and offering
Thou hast not desired, but a body Thou hast prepared for Me; in
whole burnt offerings and sacrifices for sin Thou hast taken no pleasure.' Then I said, 'Behold, I have come (in the roll of the book it is
written of Me) to do Thy will, O God'"* (Hebrews 10:5-7). True
humility is exhibited by the Son here in taking all of His life,
and making a declaration of dependence.

*Question: Are you more likely to live in complete dependence upon the
Lord–His will and His ways—when you feel strong or when you feel
weak?*

95. Two Crossings

*"They did not keep the covenant of God, and
refused to walk in His law; and they forgot His
deeds, and His miracles that He had shown them.
He wrought wonders before their fathers, in the
land of Egypt, in the field of Zoan. He divided the
sea, and caused them to pass through; and He made
the waters stand up like a heap." ~ Psalm 78:10-13*

Crossing water on dry ground stands out as a significant miracle in the Old Testament. It happens twice on Israel's wilderness journey—once leaving Egypt, and the second upon entering the Promised Land. Two bodies of water divided the territory. Egypt was divided from the wilderness by the Red Sea, and the wilderness was divided from the Promised Land by the River Jordan. These bodies of water had the ability to restrict movement for the nation, but the Lord intervened. Egypt, the wilderness, and the Promised Land represent three stages in our ongoing walk with the Lord.

Egypt is a type of the kingdom of darkness—with Pharaoh symboliz-

*Deep River, My home is
over Jordan.*

*Deep River, Lord. I want
to cross over into
campground.*

*Oh, don't you want to go,
To the Gospel feast;
That Promised Land,
Where all is peace?*

Negro Spritual

ing Satan. Prior to salvation, we were dead in our sins, participating in the kingdom of the world, excluded from the life of God. At salvation, we are released from the kingdom of darkness (as blood has been applied to our hearts), and begin our initial journey of following the Lord. This initial response usually brings us to the waters of baptism, which is symbolic of a life laid down, and then raised to newness of Life. Crossing the Red Sea is a picture of our deliverance from the kingdom of darkness into a relationship with God as Father.

Multiple pieces of music treat crossing the Jordan as man's transition upon death from earth to heaven. This crossing does mark a transition, but it is to be experienced this side of eternity.

While the first cross-ing represents Christ's cross that purchased our salvation, this second cross-ing is our opportunity to die to self and live into our Kingdom calling.

Question: What do you think the wilderness represents in our own journey with the Lord?

---

96. Repentance

*"Therefore bring forth fruit in keeping with
repentance." ~ Matthew 3:8*

While Israel is being led through the desert by the pillar of
fire, which is a type of the Holy Spirit, they are still immature,
and are being tutored by the Law. This season of their journey
helps us to learn about repentance. Repentance has two parts.
We must learn to repent FROM—from our old life, old ways,
patterns, and thoughts. We also must learn to repent TO.
Without learning to repent TO, we stay wandering in a continual state of sin management.

Grace removes us from our former manner of life—a life
dominated by fear, guilt, and sin. Faith brings us into the fullness of all God desires to restore to His people in the Kingdom. Israel failed to believe God, and as a result, were *"laid
low in the wilderness"* (1 Corinthians 10:5). Though an entire
nation was delivered FROM Egypt, only two went in TO the
Promised Land. Joshua and Caleb believed God fully, and
thus, possessed the land.

*Question: Do you ever turn back in your thinking to your old life? Have
you discovered anything that precipitates this?*

97. Kept Through

> *"Consider it all joy, my brethren, when you encounter various trials, knowing that the testing of your faith produces endurance. And let endurance have its perfect result, that you may be perfect and complete, lacking in nothing." ~ James 1:2-4*

Israel was led TO the wilderness by God, and THROUGH the wilderness by God. The wilderness redefines what is important, narrowing our focus to the basics. Sometimes we believe God's promises will keep us FROM trials, when He intends to keep us THROUGH them.

Consider this wisdom, from the writer of Hebrews: *"For since He Himself was tempted in that which He has suffered, He is able to come to the aid of those who are tempted,"* and, *"Although He was a Son, He learned obedience from the things which He suffered. And having been made perfect, He became to all those who obey Him the source of eternal salvation"* (Hebrews 2:18, 5:8-9).

So often we think that temptation comes as an appeal to our senses and appetites. What if we are continually being tempted in our sufferings—and yielding—because we don't recognize it as a temptation? In a trial, I am tempted to say my own thoughts, take my own actions, and choose my own path—to escape pain, conflict, and pressure.

There is a narrow way that leads to life, and the Son is willing to instruct us in His ways, lest we wander forty years in the wilderness, too.

Question: What are some of the old ways you are tempted to think, act, or speak in the midst of a trial?

---

98. *Possessing the Land*

"And so we see that they were not able to enter because of unbelief." ~ Hebrews 3:19

There are words to an old praise chorus that deliver a powerful charge to us. "He did not bring us out this far, to bring us back again; He brought us out, to bring us in, to the Promised Land ..."

While Israel's time in the desert was their opportunity to learn how to follow the leading of the Holy Spirit, God's purpose was deliverance from one domain and possession of another. The generation that left Egypt failed to obey, never possessing the land. Due to unbelief, they died in the wilderness; they received the Law, but failed to believe the Lord. It was their children that possessed the land.

That next generation did not enter under the leadership of Moses, who represents the covenant of Law. They were led by Joshua, who is a type of Jesus. Circumcision of an entire generation took place at Gilgal, just prior to their assault on Jericho (Joshua 5:2-9). This indicated that flesh and blood cannot inherit the Kingdom of God (1 Corinthians 15:50); it must be by the power of the Holy Spirit.

Question: Is there an area of your life where "flesh" is interrupting your ability to walk in the Spirit? Thoughts? Attitudes? Actions?

99. Food for the Journey

*"For this reason I say to you, do not be anxious
for your life, as to what you shall eat, or what you
shall drink; nor for your body, as to what you shall
put on. Is not life more than food, and the body than
clothing?"* ~ Matthew 6:25

In the beginning, God demonstrated His goodness by His willingness to be our provider. Eve's independent response took her from holy food to a meal of her own liking. As the children of Israel left Egypt and began to follow the presence of the Lord to His promised possession, He demonstrated His willingness to be their provider. *"And the sons of Israel said to them, 'Would that we had died by the Lord's hand in the land of Egypt, when we sat by the pots of meat, when we ate bread to the full; for you have brought us out into this wilderness to kill this whole assembly with hunger.' Then the Lord said to Moses, 'Behold, I will rain bread from heaven for you; and the people shall go out and gather a day's portion every day, that I may test them, whether or not they will walk in My instruction'"* (Exodus 16:3-4). The Lord continually promises His provision, but wandering hearts are turned away by their own appetites.

Question: When have you been led astray by an appetite?

100. Possession by Request

"Ask, and it shall be given to you; seek, and you
shall find; knock, and it shall be opened to you."
~ Matthew 7:7

As we consider Israel's possession of the Promised Land, it is similar to our possession of the Kingdom of God. It cannot be possessed by works of the flesh, but only at the direction of the Holy Spirit. It is also possessed by faith and request, as we see in the life of Caleb, son of Jephunneh. Joshua and Caleb had been among those sent to spy out the land for the children of Israel. They were the only two who brought back a report that agreed with God. Nevertheless, they were required to wander with the disobedient until that entire generation died in the wilderness (Joshua 14:6-13, Numbers 13:30). Caleb had heard the command, responded with faith, and then suffered the corporate faithlessness of Israel.

After forty years, Caleb was no longer a warrior in the prime of his life and strength, but he was a tested servant who trusted the Captain of the Host (Joshua 5:13-15). Now in the land, he had believed a promise for 45 years. He asked for the land—a place that was inhabited and would require further warfare. He made his request. In response to his request, he is granted the hill country of Hebron, which means the place of communion.

Question: *Has the Lord promised you something? Have you asked for it to be released to you? Is it time to possess it?*

101. Possession: Requesting as Sons

*"You lust and do not have; so you commit
murder. And you are envious and cannot obtain; so
you fight and quarrel. You do not have because you
do not ask." ~ James 4:2*

Jesus modeled Sonship for a creation that had lived their entire lives as orphans or slaves. He demonstrated how to live with the Father and how to learn dependence through making requests. *"If you abide in Me, and My words abide in you, ask whatever you wish, and it shall be done for you. By this is My Father glorified, that you bear much fruit, and so prove to be My disciples"* (John 15:7-8).

Asking unites His word (the seed) with our faith. Asking moves us from what we can obtain by our own will and efforts, to the realm of the supernatural. It reorients our hearts toward our intended design—sons.

Question: *What interrupts your confidence in voicing your requests to the Father?*

102. Possession by Capacity

*"His master said to him, 'Well done, good and
faithful slave; you were faithful with a few things, I
will put you in charge of many things; enter into
the joy of your master.'" ~ Matthew 25:23*

Israel possessed the land when they had the capacity to sustain what they had been given. When they entered Canaan, it was possessed by nations that were greater than themselves. They were charged to enter and to *"not be afraid of them; you shall well remember what the Lord your God did to Pharaoh and to all Egypt: the great trials which your eyes saw and the signs and the wonders and the mighty hand and the outstretched arm by which the Lord your God brought you out. So shall the Lord your God do to all the peoples of whom you are afraid ... You shall not dread them, for the Lord your God is in your midst, a great and awesome God ... And the Lord your God will clear away these nations before you little by little; you will not be able to put an end to them quickly, lest the wild beasts grow too numerous for you"* (Deuteronomy 7:18-22).

Possession was based on Israel's ability to apprehend and appropriate. We see the same lesson in the New Testament when the master entrusts His kingdom to His servants in the parable of the talents (Matthew 25:14-30). They each received a portion to steward based on their ability, and by obedience, increased their fruitfulness. Receiving ... Believing ... Obedience ... Waiting ... Reward.

Question: Whenever you hear the Lord speak (through a scripture or a teacher or in prayer)—what do you do to activate what you heard? Do you understand how to enlarge your capacity?

---

103. Secret to Possession

*"So that you may walk in a manner worthy of the
Lord, to please Him in all respects, bearing fruit in
every good work and increasing in the knowledge of
God; strengthened with all power, according to His
glorious might, for the attaining of all steadfastness
and patience ..." ~ Colossians 1:10-11*

The secret to possessing the Promised Land was not in
Israel's great military prowess. It was based on who they were
partnered with. The land would only be possessed little by
little, so Israel needed to increase their capacity to receive. The
definition of capacity is: the maximum amount something can
contain; the ability or power to do, experience, or understand
something; and the ability to receive, hold or absorb
something.

As Christians, we must also be stretched in our capacity to
receive all that the Lord would entrust to us, until *"I can do all
things through Him who strengthens me"* (Philippians 4:13).

*Question: What is something you have been praying and believing for?
As you wait, what has increased your capacity to believe?*

104. Possession by Remembering

*"Our fathers in Egypt did not understand Thy
wonders; they did not remember Thine abundant
kindnesses, but rebelled by the sea…they quickly
forgot His works; they did not wait for His counsel,
but craved intensely in the wilderness, and tempted
God in the desert … They forgot God their Savior,
who had done great things …"*
~ Psalm 106:7,13-14, 21

We tend to treat life as though it were linear, as a series of events, coming and going on a daily basis. What if all that has come into your life is cumulative in nature, and instead of passing through, it was designed to bring increase?

(For reference and further thought, the definition of cumulative: is to increase in quantity, degree, and force by successive additions).

Psalm 103 exhorts a people to remember all they have been given: *"Bless the Lord, O my soul; and all that is within me, bless His holy name. Bless the Lord, O my soul, and forget none of His benefits; Who pardons all your iniquities; Who heals all your diseases; Who redeems your life from the pit; Who crowns you with loving kindness and compassion; Who satisfies your years with good things, so that your youth is renewed like the eagle."*

The trouble with Israel was just how often they forgot and did not remember. When we fail to remember His goodness, we test Him in the day of trial. When we take the time to remember all His benefits, our heart is re-formed to thanksgiving.

Question: What is your first memory of encountering the Lord?

105. Altars and Wells

*"And when He had given thanks, He broke it, and
said, 'This is My body, which is for you; do this in
remembrance of Me.' In the same way He took the
cup also, after supper, saying, 'This cup is the new
covenant in My blood; do this, as often as you drink
it, in remembrance of Me.'"*
~ *I Corinthians 11:24-25*

God has ways of reminding His people of who He is and
what He has done. Often an encounter with the Lord was
marked by the building and naming of an altar. When God
chose to display Himself in significant provision, a well was
often named to reflect this. The Lord also chose to remind Israel of who He was through the yearly feasts. Part of each of
these celebrations was the rehearsing of their common story.

Psalm 78 urges one generation to speak to the next their God
stories. Pass on to the next generation the praises of the Lord;
tell of His strengths and His wondrous works. Fathers are
commanded to pass along to their children both the statutes
and the stories. Yet, Israel failed to remember. *"They did not
keep the covenant of God, and refused to walk in His law; and they
forgot His deeds, and His miracles that He had shown them"*
(Psalm 78:10-11).

Remembering is our way of cultivating faith for the next
generation. When we only pass on the statutes, we are forgetting the very heart of our message.

*Question: Which God-story in your own life stirs up faith in
remembering it?*

106. Possession by Faith

*"But My righteous one shall live by faith; and if
he shrinks back, My soul has no pleasure in him."*
~ Hebrews 10:38

While faith must be exercised in order to dispossess enemies from the Promised Land, it must also be expressed in order to enter in. Possession by faith is to have confidence in and reliance upon God. The entire chapter of Hebrews 11 celebrates those who listened, learned, and obeyed the Word of God. Those mentioned laid hold of the unseen because it was promised, not because it was visible yet. While Hebrews 11 celebrates those who learned to walk by faith, I Corinthians 10:5 tells us, *"Nevertheless, with most of them God was not well-pleased, for they were laid low in the wilderness."*

We often treat possession by faith as something we lay hold of as individuals. There is significant personal application, but much of Israel's story is aimed at a people. We must pay attention to the kind of remark made by Jesus: *"O unbelieving and perverted generation, how long shall I be with you? How long shall I put up with you?"* (Matthew 17:17).

Question: *Within the church, what are the symptoms of an unbelieving generation?*

107. Possession by Providence

*"What is the outcome then, brethren? When you
assemble, each one has a psalm, has a teaching, has a
revelation, has a tongue, has an interpretation. Let
all things be done for edification."*
~ I Corinthians 14:26

Possession of the Promised Land also came through providence, through the care and oversight of God. The Lord distributed a portion to each tribe through allotment; He chose, and divided their inheritance to them. Though Joshua was advanced in years, and much of the land remained to be possessed, he made the apportionments known to each tribe. By making their territory personal, there could be a renewed commitment to contend.

What application does that have for us? *"Now there are varieties of gifts, but the same Spirit. And there are varieties of ministries, and the same Lord. And there are varieties of effects, but the same God who works all things in all persons. But to each one is given the manifestation of the Spirit for the common good ... one and the same Spirit works all these things, distributing to each one individually just as He will. For even as the body is one and yet has many members, and all the members of the body, though they are many, are one body, so also is Christ"* (1 Corinthians 12:4-7, 11-12). Each one of us is uniquely designed to carry out the word, will, and work of the Holy Spirit. The advancement of the Kingdom of God requires the whole Body of Christ to complete the purpose of God.

Question: Have you learned to recognize your spiritual gifts?

108. Dispossessing the Land

"Submit therefore to God. Resist the devil and he will flee from you." ~ James 4:7

When Israel entered the Promised Land, they already had neighbors, living in the very territory given to them by God. God required that they participate in the removal of any foreigners from the land, so Israel had to engage in battle in order to possess Canaan. Their enemies were only dislocated as Israel was able to enter and possess.

The Kingdom of Heaven is being established where the kingdom of darkness is already doing business. In our own spiritual journey, we need to subdue forces of wickedness, and yield territory in our own lives to the Lord. The world always attempts to gain the allegiance of our flesh. The flesh is continually opposed to the Spirit and attempts to control our choices through impulse and appetite. The evil one searches for access and authority to oppose the Christian. We must be vigilant in hearing the voice of the Father, and respond to His strategies with His authority and power.

Question: Do you have any compromised territory in your heart? mind? will?

109. Keeping the Seed

"And the one on whom seed was sown on the good soil, this is the man who hears the word and understands it; who indeed bears fruit, and brings forth, some a hundred-fold, some sixty, and some thirty." ~ Matthew 13:23

If possession is through remembering, and Israel always for-got—what do we need to learn? *"Therefore putting aside all filthiness and all that remains of wickedness, in humility receive the word implanted, which is able to save your souls. But prove your-selves doers of the word, and not merely hearers who delude them-selves. For if anyone is a hearer of the word and not a doer, he is like a man who looks at his natural face in a mirror; for once he has looked at himself and gone away, he has immediately forgotten what kind of person he was"* (James 1:21-24).

When the Lord speaks by a gift of the Holy Spirit through the Word, in prayer, or through a teaching, it is seed. Our ten-dency is to eat the seed. What if—instead—it is to be acti-vated. The appropriate response to hearing is doing. Activat-ing seed is the guarantee of a future harvest rather than satis-fying ourselves in the moment with a meal.

Question: Where is the Word alive to you right now? Is it a scripture you've just read or remembered? Was it from a lesson or a sermon? Ask the Lord for a way to activate that seed. Ask: What do I do with this?

110. Pharaoh—Type of Satan

"Now these things happened to them as an
example, and they were written for our instruction,
upon whom the ends of the ages have come."
~ I Corinthians 10:11

St. Augustine said this about the New and Old Testament,
"The new is in the old contained; the old is in the new
explained." Rather than just a series of stories about ancient
characters and history, the Old Testament paints a living
picture of New Testament truths. I Corinthians 10 rehearses
the fact that the journey of Israel from bondage to the
Promised Land was written for our instruction. As believers,
we are also on a journey from bondage, through redemption,
to inheritance.

The conflict Moses faced with Pharaoh gives immeasurable
insight into our own deliverance from the kingdom of
darkness and its prince. We may be familiar with spiritual
conflict, but this story of the exodus allows us to see the stages
of deliverance, the power and authority that are exercised,
and the calculated responses of the prince of darkness. Rather
than yielding to despondency when the trial seems
relentless—remember—the same God who led the children of
Israel out of Egypt is the God who is leading you.

*Question: Take some time to re-read the exodus account in Exodus 3-14.
What strategies of the evil one can you identify?*

111. Pillar of Fire

"And the Lord was going before them in a pillar of
cloud by day to lead them on the way, and in a
pillar of fire by night to give them light ..."
~ Exodus 13:21

When God gave the pillar of fire to lead His people from Egypt, through the desert, to the Promised Land, He was giving them His very presence. As a continual presence to guard and guide, the Lord tutored Israel on what it meant to be led. The imagery is this: *"The Lord your God who goes before you will Himself fight on your behalf, just as He did for you in Egypt before your eyes, and in the wilderness where you saw how the Lord your God carried you, just as a man carries his son, in all the way which you have walked, until you came to this place. But for all this, you did not trust the Lord your God, who goes before you on your way, to seek out a place for you to encamp, in fire by night and cloud by day, to show you the way in which you should go"* (Deuteronomy 1:30-33).

When the pillar moved, the people moved. When the pillar remained in one place, the people stayed encamped. Though Israel was led by their natural eye seeing the miraculous presence of God, they continued to go astray.

Then, on the day of Pentecost, the birthday of the Church, God sent His promised Holy Spirit. As a mighty wind came forth from heaven, the pillar was distributed now as tongues of fire upon each member of this new Body of Christ, and brought the presence of God to once more guide His people.

Question: How are you learning to discern the movement of the Holy Spirit in your own life?

112. *Tutored by the Law*

"But when the fullness of the time came, God sent
forth His Son, born of a woman, born under the
Law, in order that He might redeem those who were
under the Law, that we might receive the
adoption as sons." ~ Galatians 4:4-5

The Law was given to tutor a people in the ways and will of God. It did not have the ability to redeem, restore, or make perfect. *"Before faith came, we were kept in custody under the law, being shut up to the faith which was later to be revealed. Therefore, the law has become our tutor to lead us to Christ, that we may be justified by faith"* (Galatians 3:23-24).

Before Moses received the Law, Abraham believed in the Lord, and it was reckoned to him as righteousness. The Law underscored the great need for redemption, for a blood sacrifice that would satisfy the guilty verdict hanging over the entire world. When the burden of the Law was rolled onto one perfect Lamb ... it was finished.

Question: Where do you see legalism still at work in the church?

113. Plunder the Egyptians

"And God said to Abram, 'Know for certain that your descendants will be strangers in a land that is not theirs, where they will be enslaved and oppressed four hundred years. But I will also judge the nation whom they will serve; and afterward they will come out with many possessions.'"
~ Genesis 15:13-14

As Israel left Egypt after 400 years of slavery, they were instructed to request from their neighbors *"articles of silver and articles of gold, and clothing; … the Lord had given the people favor in the sight of the Egyptians, so that they let them have their request. Thus they plundered the Egyptians"* (Exodus 12:35-36). This certainly is a demonstration of the proverb that states *"the wealth of the wicked is stored up for the righteous"* (Proverbs 13:22). While the ways of the evil one are to steal, kill, and destroy (John 10:10), the ways of the Lord repaid the laborers for 400 years of back wages.

Question: Where do you see God transfer wealth in the scriptures?

114. Timing is Everything

"But of that day and hour no one knows, not even
the angels of heaven, nor the Son, but the Father
alone." ~ Matthew 24:36

The Lord is all about timing. Creation was not accomplished randomly but sequentially. There are rhythms and seasons to be observed. It is important that things are accomplished *"properly and in an orderly manner"* (1 Corinthians 14:40).

When Moses was approaching the age of forty, *"it entered his mind to visit his brethren, the sons of Israel"* (Acts 7:23). This is the first time Moses hears and responds to the Holy Spirit. What came into his mind was to visit—the action he took was to liberate. *"And he supposed that his brethren understood that God was granting them deliverance through him; but they did not understand"* (Acts 7:25). Hearing is one thing; supposing what action should be taken is another.

Jesus, on the other hand, was very precise in his obedience. *"… I do nothing on My own initiative, but I speak these things as the Father taught Me"* (John 8:28). He lived and moved in the prescribed rhythm of His Father. *"When the fullness of the time came, God sent forth His Son …"* (Galatians 4:4). God will fulfill all things at the right time.

Question: Have you ever heard right—but got the timing wrong?

115. Priesthood of Believers

"... but like the Holy One who called you, be holy
yourselves also in all your behavior."
~ 1 Peter 1:15

God created man for a love relationship and to live in Holy Communion and fellowship among the Father, the Son, and the Holy Spirit. Our response to that love is what worship is all about. It is the perfect expression of that love, and an ongoing feast and fuel for the relationship between God and His creation. Worship is also the corporate expression of our love relationship with the Living God and the reorienting of our desires toward Him. Before limiting Himself to one tribe of Israel with the Levites, the Lord had called for all of His people to worship and to draw near as holy to Him, as a priesthood of believers.

When the perfect Lamb was slain for the redemption of the world, the Lord once more called for *"a chosen race, a royal priesthood, a holy nation, a people for God's own possession, that you may proclaim the excellencies of Him who has called you out of darkness into His marvelous light; for you once were not a people, but now you are the people of God"* (1 Peter 2:9-10).

Question: What does ministry to the Lord look like in your life?

116. Learning Dependence

*"Trust in the Lord with all your heart, and do not
lean on your own understanding. In all your ways
acknowledge Him, and He will make your paths
straight." ~ Proverbs 3:5-6*

If the Son of God purposed to only say what He heard the
Father saying, do what He saw the Father doing, and not act
on His own initiative, then the hearts of God's rebellious creation can relearn the path of submission as well. As the Lord
extracts a people for Himself from the corruption of this
world, He intends to re-form them into the likeness of His
Son. Rather than maturity being marked by independence, it
is displayed in complete humility—a declaration of dependence upon the Father. A life lived for self must be exchanged
for the utter humility of living for Him, from Him,
and to Him.

Question: *When do you have the greatest difficulty asking for help?*

117. Nature of the Conflict

"… The Lord had also executed judgments on
their gods." ~ Numbers 33:4

Behind every war in the natural realm, a conflict exists in the hidden, invisible realm. *"For our struggle is not against flesh and blood, but against the rulers, against the powers, against the world forces of this darkness, against the spiritual forces of wickedness in the heavenly places"* (Ephesians 6:12). In the Old Testament story of the exodus of Israel from Egypt, the conflict appears to be with Pharaoh. Yet, God is at war in the invisible realm, against the gods of Egypt. *"For I will go through the land of Egypt on that night, and will strike down all the first-born in the land of Egypt, both man and beast; and against all the gods of Egypt I will execute judgments—I am the Lord"* (Exodus 12:12). By his own strength, Moses had only been able to free one of his brothers from the power of his oppressor. God had plans to deliver an entire nation of His people from the cruel bondage of Pharaoh. In order to secure a complete deliverance, the powers at work in the spiritual realm had to be defeated.

Question: What helps you perceive the true nature of your conflicts?

118. Overcoming

*"And they overcame him because of the blood of
the Lamb and because of the word of their
testimony, and they did not love their life even to
death." ~ Revelation 12:11*

The exhortation to the churches listed in the book of Revelation is to overcome. Overcoming is to succeed in dealing with a problem or difficulty, and, to defeat and prevail over an enemy. Both of these qualities of overcoming are featured in the wilderness journey of the children of God. The covenant that God made with Israel did not have the power to transform Israel. Rather it could only make the ways and word of God known, and illustrated their inability to fulfill the Law. The Exodus story exposed what happens when we attempt to follow the Lord in our own strength, our flesh. Overcoming is learning to have our flesh be in submission to the Holy Spirit, so that we might have power over sin. Israel also had to defeat and prevail over an enemy in order to be delivered from Egypt, and again, to access the Promised Land. Though the stages of warfare were being engaged in the natural realm, the triumph was taking place in the invisible, spiritual realm, as God triumphed over all the gods of Egypt.

Question: *How do you recognize the true nature of the conflict when you are being assaulted, threatened, or undermined?*

119. Remembering Feasts

"Now this day will be a memorial to you, and you shall celebrate it as a feast to the Lord; throughout your generations you are to celebrate it as a permanent ordinance." ~ Exodus 12:14

One of the regular patterns for Israel, as they celebrated their feasts, was to rehearse their history together. Whether it was through repetitive sacrifices being offered, or verbally remembering—one generation was called to pass on to the next the great stories of their faith. Passover was instituted by God as a way of remembering His great deliverance of His people from the power of Pharaoh's cruel bondage. The yearly reenactment of God's triumph over evil is foundational for continuing to press on toward the land of promise. While Passover celebrates deliverance from bondage and captivity (our old life prior to Christ), Pentecost celebrates laying hold of what we have been called toward. When Jesus came to establish the Kingdom of God, once more on earth, He instructed His disciples to wait until they had received power from on high. That power was poured out on Pentecost, filling and establishing the church as His new Temple—a place for God to tabernacle in the midst of His people.

Question: How do you celebrate your spiritual birth?

120. True Rest

*"For the one who has entered His rest has himself
also rested from his works, as God did from His."*
~ Hebrews 4:10

On the day Joshua led the children of Israel into the Promised Land, their spiritual journey was not ending, but merely realizing it's true purpose. An entire generation had to die in the wilderness, due to their unbelief, before the next generation could enter in. All of the good promises given by God were forfeited by a generation who believed their circumstances more than His word. As believers, we should *"... fear lest, while a promise remains of entering His rest, any one of you should seem to have come short of it. ... For if Joshua had given them rest, He would not have spoken of another day after that. There remains therefore a Sabbath rest for the people of God"* (Hebrews 4:1, 8-9). The way of Jesus is the way of His indwelling Holy Spirit. His way is to live from the new life of the Holy Spirit, rather than the power of our old life, through the strength of soul. Our soul does not lay hold of the promises of God, but attempts to please God with what our flesh can accomplish in His name. This old way is our own form of unbelief.

Question: Where do you see the current generation of the church laying hold of the promises of God?

Part 5

Stages of Maturity

121. Stages of Maturity

*"And after you have suffered for a little while, the
God of all grace, who called you to His eternal glory
in Christ, will Himself perfect, confirm, strengthen,
and establish you." ~ I Peter 5:10*

Advancing through different stages of maturity is an ongoing theme in the scriptures. The aged Apostle John, toward the end of his life and ministry, spoke to three distinct categories of believers: little children, young men, and fathers (1 John 2:12-14). Little children need to know and grow in the love of the Father. Their focus needs to rest on all that was accomplished for them at salvation. Young men are in need of endurance, and must focus on overcoming the evil one. They grow in all aspects to be like Him, by the power of the Word of God abiding in them. For fathers it's about knowing and being known by God. Intimacy is the result of living and walking from the life of the indwelling Spirit.

God's intention is to grow us through each of these stages as sons. When He invites us into relationship, He desires to train us as sons. He is also a God of the process, and takes up residence within—bearing His fruit through us.

Question: *Do you see evidence of these three stages of believers around you? Why is having all three around a sign of a spiritually healthy church?*

122. The Feasts—Passover

"Clean out the old leaven, that you may be a new lump, just as you are in fact unleavened. For Christ our Passover also has been sacrificed."
~ I Corinthians 5:7

God painted pictures of Himself in each of the Jewish holy days (holidays). These days not only gave the observer an image of the nature and character of God; they were to awaken within each one an invitation to follow Him and mature into His likeness. The first of these feasts for Israel is the first description of our spiritual journey as well. Passover rehearses the day when blood was applied to the door posts of each home, when God was bringing deliverance to Israel from their cruel bondage in Egypt. Applying the blood of a sacrificed lamb would mark the home of each one who God was saving from the angel of death. While the first-born perished in every Egyptian home, those who were "under the blood" were saved. As we begin our own life as a believer in Jesus, we receive His shed blood as our deliverance from death. This becomes our Passover celebration.

Question: *Do you remember the day the blood of the Lamb was applied to your own heart?*

123. The Feasts—Pentecost

"And it will come about after this that I will pour
out My Spirit on all mankind; and your sons and
daughters will prophesy, your old men will dream
dreams, your young men will see visions. And even
on the male and female servants I will pour out My
Spirit in those days." ~ Joel 2:28-29

Pentecost celebrated God's gift of the Law, written on stone, and given to Moses on Mount Sinai. It came 50 days after the Feast of First Fruits (when the Christian celebrates Jesus' resurrection), and was known to the Jews as the Feast of Weeks. It celebrated the early days of the wheat harvest, what emerged after a *"grain of wheat falls into the earth and dies...it bears much fruit"* (John 12:24).

Following the ascension of Jesus, the early disciples were told to wait in Jerusalem until they received power from on high—the outpouring of the promised Holy Spirit. Once the Spirit came, the disciples would be quickened to the same indwelling life that the Son lived with the Father—the Word writing the Father's will upon our hearts.

Question: Have you submitted your life to His life and power? Do you recognize the difference between His power and your own?

124. Tabernacles

*"And they were all filled with the Holy Spirit and
began to speak with other tongues, as the Spirit was
giving them utterance." ~ Acts 2:4*

A prophetic picture took place on the day of Pentecost, a visual illustration of God's plan for His people. *"And suddenly there came from heaven a noise like a violent, rushing wind, and it filled the whole house where they were sitting. And there appeared to them tongues as of fire distributing themselves, and they rested on each one of them"* (Acts 2:2-3). From the beginning, God had a people in His heart, and we see His story of mankind written in Genesis 1-11. In Genesis 12, the story narrows to one man, and his seed—until His Seed is brought forth as the Son of God. Then the story enlarges again to the whole of mankind. All are invited to be His people. The story takes us from one nation being delivered from another nation, then following the presence of God as a pillar of fire, that would abide over the tabernacle in the wilderness. When Israel came into the Promised Land, a permanent residence was established, and the Temple became the focus of worship. One place ... one nation ... until one Pentecost. In the fullness of time, God sent His Spirit to rest on His intended residence: mankind. With the Spirit now resting on each, and moving through each, a holy nation and a royal priesthood bring us into the fullness of God's design.

Question: How have you learned to trust the guidance of the Holy Spirit?

125. How the Seed Grows

"The soil produces crops by itself; first the blade,
then the head, then the mature grain in the head."
~ Mark 4:28

There are distinct stages of maturity that the seed grows through as it is sown in the heart. It enters as a small time capsule of God's will and word. The process to bring forth life is designed to take that small investment and bring it into the fullness of God's design. Once it is sown in a place that was prepared to receive, it can germinate. Seeds wait to germinate until three components are in place: water, correct temperature, and the right position in the soil. In the first days, the seed relies on its indwelling food supply. Then, when it is large enough to form leaves, it transforms light into food. It first takes root downward before it begins to bear fruit upward (Isaiah 37:31). Then the blade is visible—evidence of things that had been hoped for, though not yet mature. Following that the head of the seed begins to crown, promising a harvest of fruit. In the fullness of His time His fruit is brought forth.

Question: Can our own fruitfulness be effected by our exposure to light?
What would that look like?

126. Tale of Two Sons

"But we had to be merry and rejoice, for this
brother of yours was dead and has begun to live,
and was lost and has been found."
~ Luke 15:32

There is a story of two sons in the New Testament; one a law keeper and one a law breaker. The younger asks for his share of the estate, though his father has not passed, and squanders it all in his rebellion. At the end of himself—homeless and hungry—he returns in humility to his father's house, asking to work as a servant. The law breaker, now broken, receives the lavish grace extended by his father. The older son is offended with the father, having lived his whole life to perform and please. Living as a law keeper, he believed that works bring reward, and he does not understand what produces relationship. Since he labored to receive, he has no forgiveness for the slacker brother. Both sons missed the Fathers' heart. One found it.

Question: *When you read the story of the prodigal son (Luke 15:11-32), which of the three characters do you most identify with?*

127. Fullness of Deity

"... so we, who are many, are one body in Christ,
and individually members one of another."
~ Romans 12:5

The scriptures describe Jesus: *"For in Him all the fullness of deity dwells in bodily form, and in Him you have been made complete ..."* (Colossians 2:9). What Jesus accomplished as the Son of Man walking on Earth, now requires the Body of Christ in order to carry out the Father's purposes. We each have the capacity to be filled with His Holy Spirit, but must walk in this corporately to carry the fullness of deity.

Jesus prayed for His disciples in John 17:21 that they would be *"one, even as Thou Father, art in Me, and I in Thee, that they also may be in Us ..."* God is community. Father, Son, and Holy Spirit continually love one another and express that relationship—to us, and through us.

Man, created to be a visible expression of the image and likeness of God, can only accomplish this by living a merged life with the Body. The completion of what God has in mind for His creation takes place when all has been restored to oneness with Him and with one another.

Question: Where or when do you experience a vital expression of the corporate Body of Christ?

128. Crucifixion, Resurrection, Ascension

*"For if we have become united with Him in the
likeness of His death, certainly we shall be also in
the likeness of His resurrection."*
~ Romans 6:5

There are three historical events in the life of Jesus that are reflected as stages in our spiritual journey: crucifixion, resurrection, and ascension. All three took place at the culmination of His earthly life, but are offered to us from the beginning of our walk with Him.

As we learn to walk by His Spirit, we are invited to live in Him. *"I have been crucified with Christ; and it is no longer I who live, but Christ lives in me; and the life which I now live in the flesh I live by faith in the Son of God, who loved me, and delivered Himself up for me"* (Galatians 2:20). Dying daily is not something I can prescribe, but an opportunity I receive as the Lord desires to live His life through me. Recognizing the cross in my daily walk is the first key to living an exchanged life.

Question: *Was your will cross-ed this week? How did you deal with it?*

129. Resurrection

*"... that I may know Him, and the power of His
resurrection and the fellowship of His sufferings,
being conformed to His death; in order that I may
attain to the resurrection from the dead."*
~ Philippians 3:10-11

Jesus' crucifixion made the final payment for our debt of sin. His resurrection is what offers us newness of life. One wipes the old away, while the other makes all things new. *"For the death that He died, He died to sin, once for all; but the life that He lives, He lives to God. Even so consider yourselves to be dead to sin, but alive to God in Christ Jesus"* (Romans 6:10-11). When we are born again, His new life restores us to our original design as sons. We no longer live enslaved to sin and the desires of the flesh, but by the life of His indwelling Spirit. *"But if the Spirit of Him who raised Jesus from the dead dwells in you, He who raised Christ Jesus from the dead will also give life to your mortal bodies through His Spirit who indwells you"* (Romans 8:11). As we walk by His Spirit, rather than our own strength of soul, His resurrection power is released to accomplish His purposes through us.

Question: *Where has the Holy Spirit offered you a choice to walk His way this week?*

130. Ascension

*"Blessed be the God and Father of our Lord Jesus
Christ, who has blessed us with every spiritual
blessing in the heavenly places in Christ ..."*
~ Ephesians 1:3

The ascension of Jesus was more than the Lord's exit
strategy. Jesus modeled sonship during the days of His
earthly ministry, but at the time of His ascension He took on
His identity as the Great High Priest of our faith. The book of
Hebrews bears witness to both roles being fulfilled in Him
and the access that is now afforded to us. The book of
Ephesians can only truly be understood from the perspective
of His ascension: *"Blessed be the God and Father of our Lord Jesus
Christ, who has blessed us with every spiritual blessing in the
heavenly places in Christ,"* and, *"made us alive together with
Christ ... and raised us up with Him, and seated us with Him in the
heavenly places in Christ Jesus..."* (Ephesians 1:3, 2:5-6). It is
from this eternal position and perspective that we begin to
operate in His overcoming life. His position is now ours, in
Him. This is not a call for us to be some kind of ascended
masters, but to abide in the ascended One.

Question: *Do you find yourself living under your circumstances, or,
above the fray?*

131. Entrusted with a Stewardship

"... Well done, good and faithful slave; you were
faithful with a few things, I will put you in charge
of many things, enter into the joy of your master."
~ Matthew 25:21

In Christ, we are all *"sons of God through faith in Christ Jesus"* (Galatians 3:26). As sons, we are recipients of an inheritance, *"every spiritual blessing in the heavenly places in Christ"* (Ephesians 1:3). Thus, the Apostle Paul prays, *"that the eyes of your heart may be enlightened, that you may know what is the hope of His calling, what are the riches of the glory of His inheritance in the saints"* (Ephesians 1:18). As members of Christ and citizens of the Kingdom of God, our inheritance is a gift, preserved and kept for us. We are in His will.

Each one of us is also entrusted with a stewardship. We will give an account concerning how we have taken the gifts given to us, and over the course of our life invested them for the sake of our Master. In the parable of the talents (Matthew 25:14-30), each one receives according to their ability, and then, due to faithfulness sees their stewardship multiplied. We need to consider all that we have been entrusted with: time, talents, territory, treasure, temple, and our testimony.

Question: *Have you taken account of all you have been entrusted with for the sake of the Kingdom of God?*

---

132. Time

"There is an appointed time for everything. And
there is a time for every event under heaven ..."
~ Ecclesiastes 3:1

Tick ... tock ... minutes pass into hours, then hours pass into days.

As redeemed ones, we now live into an eternal future, but have a limited time to express that as earth-bound sons. Each one of us has an unknown quantity of time to accomplish *"... the good works which God prepared beforehand, that we should walk in them"* (Ephesians 2:10). Whatever these works happen to be, the Lord has designed them for the advancement of His Kingdom. Under His authority, and filled with His power, we are called to destroy the works of the evil one. The devil uses his own strategy to defend his realm and to get us to waste, squander, and be negligent with time. Abiding in Him means we will seize every opportunity for the Father to do His works through us.

Question: *When it comes to time, do you see yourself as casual, careless, or careful with it?*

133. Talents

"But one and the same Spirit works all these
things, distributing to each one individually just as
He wills." ~ I Corinthians 12:11

Every member of the Body of Christ has been gifted to display the Lord's image and likeness, and to carry His presence into every situation, allowing Him to accomplish His works through us. The more we become familiar with the movement of His indwelling Spirit, the more readily we cooperate with Him, releasing His life in and through us to perform His will. We have each been uniquely created to express His gifts through our lives, according to our ability (Matthew 25:15). As we are faithful to each opportunity, our ability increases, as well as fruit for the Kingdom. These talents are not given for the sake of our identity, but for the display of His love. As we are faithful to steward these talents and gifts, the ministry of Jesus continues upon the earth.

Question: What gifts or talents have you received from the Holy Spirit? What has He accomplished through you recently?

134. Stewardship—Treasure

*"But seek first His kingdom and His
righteousness, and all these things will be added to
you." ~ Matthew 6:33*

The Kingdom of God has a different value system than the kingdom of the world, and encourages a redefining of treasure. What the world elevates, the Lord brings low. Being reoriented to His ways, we become aware of how the Lord is the sustainer and provider for His creation, and intends to use us as His distribution system. Once He is acknowledged and received as Creator and Provider, we are free to respond as stewards rather than owners.

Through the use of money, we learn a faithful response in our stewardship, so the Lord can entrust the true riches to us. As children of God, we can cooperate with all the supernatural ways the Father uses to sustain His people.

Question: Make a list of all the treasure that the Lord has entrusted to you to steward.

135. Stewardship—Territory

*"For where two or three have gathered together in
My name, there I am in their midst."*
~ Matthew 18:20

When we consider the stewardship of a territory, it is less about land, and more about the spheres of influence we have with the people in our lives. The Lord uses us to be the visible image of Himself, as we walk in the Spirit. As the gifts of His Spirit are released through us, it impacts the well-being of the territory we inhabit. If believers make themselves available to be used by Him, the health and maturity of the entire Body of Christ is impacted. When we are careful to preserve unity in the bond of peace, Jesus is free to build up, strengthen, and edify others through us.

Each time a circle of relationship is established, it becomes a village that Jesus can access by His Spirit through His Body. If these circles include Him, churches of the heart are established.

Question: Who had the biggest influence on your spiritual journey? Do they know?

136. Temple

"For you have been bought with a price: therefore glorify God in your body." ~ I Corinthians 6:20

"Thus says the Lord, 'Heaven is My throne and the earth is My footstool. Where then is a house you could build for Me? And where is a place that I may rest?'" (Isaiah 66:1). God, creator of heaven and earth, cannot be contained in any man-made structure. Israel's tabernacle hosted His presence, but did not have the capacity to contain His whole. When Jesus walked upon the earth, *"all the fullness of deity [dwelt] in bodily form"* (Colossians 2:9). The Father illustrated in the life of His Son, His chosen dwelling place—in the heart of sons. Then, in Paul's letter to the Corinthians, *"Do you not know that you are a temple of God, and that the Spirit of God dwells in you? ... And that you are not your own?"* (1 Corinthians 3:16, 6:19). As individuals, we learn to host His abiding presence as we walk in the Spirit. Stewarding His presence together, we become the temple of the living God.

Question: *What qualities of Jesus do we display when we regard our lives as His temple?*

137. Testimony

"Return to your house and describe what great things God has done for you." ~ Luke 8:39

Everyone loves a good story, and when the central character is the Lord, it is a testimony. We have been called to steward the continuing narration of God's work in the midst of the world—the very word being written on our hearts and in our lives. Psalm 78 states the importance of one generation rehearsing God's statutes and stories to the next generation. The ways of God are passed on through remembering His statutes, and faith is enlarged as we tell of His amazing works in us or through us. Each day, God is writing new adventures in the lives of His saints, and displaying new mercies every morning. The Lord is able to evangelize those we love, as they see His-story being written on our lives.

Question: *Whose testimony has had the most effect on your life?*

138. Babes—Still Fleshly

"And I, brethren, could not speak to you as to
spiritual men, but as to men of flesh,
as to babes in Christ."
~ I Corinthians 3:1

Created to be an accurate representation of God's image and likeness, we were originally formed as body, soul, and spirit. At the fall, we forfeited the life of the Spirit. That left us with a body and soul to navigate our lives, and when they operate together without the leadership of the Spirit, that is the biblical description of flesh. Mankind, leaning on its own understanding, its feelings, and will, operated by strength of soul. At the time of new birth, through the cleansing work of the blood of Christ, we once more are inhabited by the Holy Spirit. His presence allows us to be transformed into His likeness, and thus into maturity as sons.

Galatians 5:17 states that the Spirit is opposed to the flesh, and the flesh is opposed to the Spirit, and that we are never free from this conflict. Spiritual growth takes place as we learn to bring our body and soul's desires into submission to the indwelling Holy Spirit.

Question: Where do you face the most opposition from your flesh?

139. Press On

"I press on toward the goal for the prize of the
upward call of God in Christ Jesus."
~ Philippians 3:14

Spiritual growth can take place when there is pressure—the continuous force exerted on or against an object. When we come under some form of pressure, it is called a trial and the fruit of the Spirit's work in us bears His fruit. Though we seldom appreciate suffering at the time, trials cause us to repent of our independence and turn to Him for sustenance. Trials also expose our personal coping or survival strategies, those things we learned prior to the Holy Spirit indwelling our life. Without His discipline, we tend to turn to our old ways, rather than the narrow way that leads to life.

There is another way pressure produces maturity. Paul describes it in his own life in Philippians 3:12-14: *"Not that I have already obtained it, or have already become perfect, but I press on in order that I may lay hold of that for which also I was laid hold of by Christ Jesus. Brethren, I do not regard myself as having laid hold of it yet; but one thing I do: forgetting what lies behind and reaching forward to what lies ahead, I press on toward the goal for the prize of the upward call of God in Christ Jesus."*

Question: Is there something you need to leave behind (forget), so that you might press on in your walk with the Lord?

140. Age and Stage

*"As you therefore have received Christ Jesus the
Lord, so walk in Him, having been firmly rooted
and now being built up in Him and established in
your faith, just as you were instructed, and
overflowing with gratitude."*
~ *Colossians 2:6-7*

There is a difference between a person's age and their level
of spiritual maturity. While age can be measured in days,
months, and years, maturity comes about when someone
reaches their full stage of development. When people are
walking responsibly with the capacity they have been given,
they tend to mature. From infancy to elder, there are lessons
to learn and grow from. An infant needs to learn they are
loved and how to receive comfort, while an elder learns the
wisdom of caring for an entire community. If we are walking
with the Holy Spirit, He has the ability to lead us through
trials in such a way that we can produce His fruit. When we
refuse to trust His wisdom and counsel, turning to our own
thoughts or emotions for guidance, we make little or no
progress.

Question: *Are you — or is someone that you know — stuck at a stage of
maturity?*

141. Mature Likeness

"... By this we know that we are in Him: the one
who says he abides in Him ought himself to walk in
the same manner as He walked."
~ 1 John 2:5-6

When we are born-again, and the Lord brings us into His family, there are two distinct stages in our spiritual journey. Two Greek words help us understand the stages of our sonship: *tekna* and *huios*. *Tekna* indicates that we have become children of God. Through new birth, we have been transferred from the kingdom of darkness into the kingdom of His Son. *Tekna* describes the nature of the relationship that has been conferred upon us through adoption. As new believers and babes in Christ, our first stage of sonship is referred to as *tekna*.

Huios is used to describe those sons who show maturity, who are bearing the image and likeness of the Father. Jesus was always called *huios*, and Romans 8:14 tells us, *"... all who are being led by the Spirit of God, these are sons [huios] of God."* Sonship is our means of maturing in Christ, as we daily learn to display His image and likeness.

Question: What stage of sonship do you find yourself in?

142. Lessons for the Carnal

"For whoever wishes to save his life shall lose it;
but whoever loses his life for My sake shall find it."
~ Matthew 16:25

When our behavior is ruled by our passions and appetites, rather than the Spirit of God, we are considered carnal. As sons, we are called to mature into His image and likeness, so our carnality must be addressed. One lesson that addresses carnal behavior is found in I Corinthians 7. Paul, who has chosen an unmarried life, declares the potential in such a sacrifice: freedom to pursue pleasing the Lord with undistracted devotion. He sacrifices an earthly intimacy for the sake of Christ. His instruction to those who struggle with their passions and appetites: get married. It almost sounds as though lust is best tucked into a marriage relationship. Wrong. As you read the instructions given to those who are called to marry rather than burn with passion, it calls for sacrifice as well. Husbands are to sacrifice for the sake of their wives, and wives for the sake of their husbands. Their body is no longer their own. In both cases, sacrificial love is the lesson.

Question: How is the Lord currently teaching you sacrificial love?

143. Zeal vs. Intimacy

"You were running well; who hindered you
from obeying the truth?"
~ Galatians 5:7

Zeal is described as great energy or enthusiasm in pursuit of a cause or an objective. When we are born again, our lives are ignited with a measure of zeal, given to start off our spiritual journey. Similar to a rocket leaving the launch pad, our lives need a surge of spiritual thrust to separate us from the gravitational pull of the world. Most of the fuel on-board a rocket is used in the first few minutes, as it presses toward escape velocity—the speed that guarantees clearing the gravitational forces working against it. As each stage is emptied of its fuel, it falls away, giving more freedom as the rocket heads toward its target. Our initial zeal supports our journey toward intimacy with Him. We have received enough fuel to break free from the world's pull on our lives, and deliver us to an ongoing walk of intimacy with the Lord. Intimacy is a new force of life and energy that is long-term and sustains our ongoing maturity.

Question: What can interrupt the success of zeal at the initial stages of our life in Christ?

144. *Doers of the Word*

"But prove yourselves doers of the word, and not
merely hearers who delude themselves."
~ James 1:22

The Word became flesh when Mary conceived the Seed by the power of the Holy Spirit. Her submission to the will of God brought forth the fulfillment of God's promise. God continues to work in His people today by conceiving His word in our hearts. When God speaks, His *"word is living and active and sharper than any two-edged sword, and piercing as far as the division of soul and spirit, of both joints and marrow, and able to judge the thoughts and intentions of the heart"* (Hebrews 4:12). When it is united with faith, in the womb of our hearts, it brings forth His desired fruit. Our part is to activate—to live into—all that He is speaking. Faith without the works that express it, is lifeless. When we cooperate with the Living Word moving in and through our lives, His will takes on the tangible expression that He desires.

Question: *Has the Lord made a promise to you from His word that needs to be activated (acted on) by you?*

145. *Parable of Soils*

"... unless a grain of wheat falls into the earth
and dies, it remains by itself alone; but if it dies, it
bears much fruit."
~ John 12:24

When God speaks a promise, the fulfillment of it is present there within the seed.

When the sower goes forth sowing his seed, there are four different responses to his effort. The parable of the soils, in Matthew and Luke, indicate that the responses differ because of the condition of the soil. When the seed is sown, it must be activated in an environment conducive to fruit bearing. The parable indicates that the sower sows, and the recipient hears, but only 1 in 4 brought forth fruit, some 30, some 60, some 100-fold. Learning to move in faith, past the obstacles that are resistant to that seed reaching maturity, is how we grow spiritually. As we remember and rehearse all that God sent His word to accomplish in our hearts, we see multiplication.

Question: *Do you have a promise from God that remains unfulfilled? Ask the Lord if there are any obstacles in the way.*

146. Milk Drinkers

*"Surely I have composed and quieted my soul; like
a weaned child rests against his mother, my soul is
like a weaned child within me."*
~ Psalm 131:2

Babies drink only milk because their bodies aren't ready to receive solid food. Teeth for solid food haven't been formed yet, so they are reliant on the nourishment they receive through the life of another. The Apostle Paul uses milk to describe the initial spiritual food that we receive following our new birth. It is food that has been pre-digested through the life of another believer, and transferred to our hungry spirits on a regular basis. Seasoned believers, realizing that they are not just eating for themselves, are careful to take in what will be most nourishing for the new infant. This transfer of life from one believer to another, allows the initial love bonds in the Body of Christ to form. Receiving nourishment in this way, and in this form, is not for the long-term. A healthy infant will grow quickly, adapt to solid food, and learn to feed themselves. Too many in the spiritual realm adapt to their initial means of feeding and are never weaned. They fail to thrive.

Question: Are you currently nourishing any spiritual children?

147. Meat Eaters

*"For everyone who partakes only of milk is not
accustomed to the word of righteousness, for he is a
babe. But solid food is for the mature, who because
of practice have their senses trained
to discern good and evil."*
~ Hebrews 5:13-14

In the scriptures food has always been an indication of our obedience and maturity. With all the food provided in the Garden of Eden, Eve still hungered for what she didn't have. When Moses led Israel into the wilderness on their journey to the Promised Land, God provided their food supernaturally. Manna, a bread that daily fell from heaven, tasted like wafers with honey. Yet, Israel grumbled, *"Would that we had died by the Lord's hand in the land of Egypt, when we sat by the pots of meat, when we ate bread to the full; for you have brought us out into this wilderness to kill this whole assembly with hunger"* (Exodus 16:3). God granted them meat in the wilderness, but their hearts, never satisfied, continued to crave. *"For this reason I say to you, do not be anxious for your life, as to what you shall eat, or what you shall drink ... for all these things the Gentiles eagerly seek; for your Heavenly Father knows that you need all these things"* (Matthew 6:25a,32). Jesus instructs us to *"... seek first His Kingdom and His righteousness; and all these things shall be added to you"* (Matthew 6:33). Perhaps, seeking His Kingdom is the best preparation for developing a capacity to eat meat.

Question: Are you ready to receive all that the Lord has prepared to nourish you in this season of your life?

148. Aspects of our Maturity

"For by these He has granted to us His precious
and magnificent promises, in order that by them
you might become partakers of the divine nature,
having escaped the corruption
that is in the world by lust."
~ 2 Peter 1:4

We are not just a physical body. We have multiple facets to our being, and mature in a variety of ways. Our physical body is designed to steadily grow until we reach full stature, and then begin to reproduce life. We are emotional beings, and grow through developmental stages as well. When conditions are harmful to our well-being, we can fail to thrive and remain emotionally as infant or child adults. Our emotions can heal and mature within the context of new life and a spiritual family that responds on God's behalf. When we are born-again, we have a spiritual life that can grow and thrive. Our inner life is overseen by Father God, and *"His divine power has granted to us everything pertaining to life and godliness, through the true knowledge of Him who called us by His own glory and excellence"* (2 Peter 1:3). Within the environment of the family of God, He desires to supply all that we need in order to reach our maturity in Christ.

Question: Are you mature for your age? In every aspect?

149. Slave of Sin

"But thanks be to God that though you were
slaves of sin, you became obedient from the heart to
that form of teaching to which you were committed,
and having been freed from sin,
you became slaves of righteousness."
~ Romans 6:17-18

When the Lord takes up residence in our hearts, it is the beginning of our conflict with sin, rather than its final day. Until we have the indwelling life of the Holy Spirit, we are held captive to the will of sin. Even as the children of Israel were held captive to Pharaoh in Egypt, we are held under the power of iniquity and corruption. *"... Everyone who commits sin is the slave of sin. And the slave does not remain in the house forever; the son does remain forever"* (John 8:34-35). The path to our freedom includes a daily choice to walk from His life, rather than our own. *"Even so consider yourselves to be dead to sin, but alive to God in Christ Jesus. Therefore do not let sin reign in your mortal body that you should obey its lusts, and do not go on presenting the members of your body to sin as instruments of unrighteousness; but present yourselves to God as those alive from the dead, and your members as instruments of righteousness to God. For sin shall not be master over you, for you are not under law, but under grace"* (Romans 6:11-14). The slave of sin does not remain forever; but you must learn to walk in freedom.

Question: Where do you face your greatest struggles with sin? How has the Lord empowered you to walk in freedom?

150. Reproduction

"Allow both to grow together
until the harvest ..."
~ Matthew 13:30

A hybrid plant is produced by crossing two chosen parent plants. The problem with hybrids though, is that their seed is sterile and does not reproduce true to its parent plant. Though this type of seed was developed to increase agricultural output and variety, it cannot reproduce. Heirloom seed has come down to us from generations of reproduction. It is open pollinated, which means by the wind, instead of through human intervention. I am not just addressing gardening here. I am addressing the gospel. *"The kingdom of heaven may be compared to a man who sowed good seed in his field. But while men were sleeping, his enemy came and sowed tares also among the wheat, and went away. But when the wheat sprang up and bore grain, then the tares became evident also. And the slaves of the landowner came and said to him, 'Sir, did you not sow good seed in your field? How then does it have tares?' And He said to them, 'An enemy has done this!' ..."* (Matthew 13:24-28). What seed have you received? Mixing the gospel with any other thing (even if it seems to be more readily received), makes a hybrid. It will not reproduce true.

Question: *Do you recognize any ways that the culture is being mixed with the gospel?*

151. Elders

*"Therefore I exhort the elders among you …
shepherd the flock of God among you, exercising
oversight not under compulsion, but voluntarily,
according to the will of God … proving to be
examples to the flock."*
~ I Peter 5:1,3

An elder is someone who has the maturity to oversee an entire community. Their wisdom and counsel is a gift to the young, while their authority is the fruit of their own life of submission to Him. The Apostle John wrote this to the church: *"I am writing to you fathers, because you know Him who has been from the beginning…"* (1 John 2:13). The Greek word for "know" is *ginosko,* and it describes a knowing that is not based on knowledge about, but a knowing that is intimate, transformative, and progressive. Those among us who have come to know the Lord in this way are those who can help the church discover the fullness of Christ. We live in times of unparalleled access to knowledge, but find a diminishing number who have discovered the path of knowing Him. *"So let us know, let us press on to know the Lord. His going forth is as certain as the dawn; and He will come to us like the rain, like the spring rain watering the earth"* (Hosea 6:3).

Question: Do you have any elders in your life that oversee your spiritual journey?

Part 6

Sonship

152. Temptation

*"For since He Himself was tempted in that which
He has suffered, He is able to come to the aid of
those who are tempted." ~ Hebrews 2:18*

Just as the pillar of fire led the children of Israel through their time of testing in the wilderness, the Holy Spirit, following Jesus' baptism, led Him to the wilderness to be tested. Israel continually failed, putting God to the test, rather than being tested themselves. I Corinthians 10:1-13 urges us to learn from their mistakes. Jesus faced the tempter and triumphed over all the works of the devil that we might learn from His victories. Forty days of fasting preceded the temptation. That might seem to be the worst part to us. But we learn a great truth from the perspective of the Son. When the devil challenged Him to make bread for Himself, Jesus responds by saying, *"It is written, man shall not live on bread alone, but on every word that proceeds out of the mouth of God"* (Matthew 4:4). For forty days, Jesus had been living on every word that came forth from the mouth of His Father. He had been feasting. The lifestyle of Jesus was to only do what He saw the Father doing, and to only say what He heard the Father speak (John 5:19,12:49). So, the moment the devil began to speak, Jesus knew it was not the voice of His Father. The temptation was not about bread alone, but who will give us directions.

Question: What has the Lord used in your life to prepare you to face a trial?

153. Fasting

*"But this kind does not go out except by prayer
and fasting." ~ Matthew 17:21*

In the story of His temptation (Matthew 4, Luke 4), Jesus feasts on His Father's word while fasting. As He hears His Father's will, He also discerns what is blocking that will from being done on earth as it is in heaven. Then, when Jesus encounters the enemy, He defeats him with His Father's strategies. We see in the Gospel of Luke that Jesus regularly returns to the wilderness or the mountains to spend time alone with His Father. Perhaps Luke 4 is the extended picture of what happens every time He withdraws to prayer. He submits to God, resists the evil one, and the enemy must flee (James 4:7). He removes the obstacles to God's work being done. After overcoming the forces of wickedness, He releases the power of His Father in healings and deliverances.

Question: What spiritual practices have prepared you for ministry opportunities this week?

154. He Knew Who He Was

*"And behold, a voice out of the heavens, saying,
'This is My beloved Son, in whom I am well-
pleased.'" ~ Matthew 3:17*

At the time of the Last Supper, *"Jesus, knowing that the Father had given all things into His hands, and that He had come forth from God, and was going back to God, rose from supper, and laid aside His garments; and taking a towel, He girded Himself about"* (John 13:3-4). Jesus knew who He was, so He did what He did. He had been blessed by His Father at the time of His baptism, and he lived from that blessing, rather than for it. He walked in oneness abiding in His Father, and His Father abiding in Him. He knew His inheritance; as He came forth from God, He used all that He had received. Jesus also knew His destiny, that He was going back to God. This Son lived His life as a full reflection of the image and likeness of His Father. With that hope and confidence, He was able to take the last hours of His life and model humility to His disciples. This display of dependence is our pattern for maturing in Christ.

Question: Do you live from the Father's blessing, or for it?

155. Rule and Dominion

"Humble yourselves, therefore, under the mighty hand of God, that He may exalt you at the proper time ..." ~ 1 Peter 5:6

Following the fifth day of creation, God designed a reflection of Himself for the natural, visible realm, by forming man to display His image and likeness. Formed to display this holy identity, we were also entrusted with a purpose: to steward the creation by ruling and establishing the Lord's dominion. In order to have a capacity to rule, mankind needed to learn to live under rule—to live led. In living under the governance of the Spirit, man would be an accurate reflection of God's authority. At the fall, we forfeited our position, and lived subject to the kingdom of darkness until the day of our redemption. Now in Christ, we have come under the authority of God once more, and have been restored to our stewardship. Our allegiance to God's rule is pledged every time we pray, *"Thy kingdom come, Thy will be done, on earth as it is in heaven"* (Matthew 6:10).

Question: How have you learned to bring your life in submission to the will of the Holy Spirit? What results have you noticed?

156. Filled with Power

"And for this purpose also I labor, striving
according to His power, which mightily works
within me." ~ Colossians 1:29

Jesus, following His resurrection, found His disciples and breathed on them, saying, *"Receive the Holy Spirit"* (John 20:22). He made them one body, as their sins were forgiven. They were commissioned to release this message to others as well. Then, in order to be witnesses to the risen Christ, the early disciples were told to wait in Jerusalem until they had received power (Acts 1:8). To be Christ's Body on earth, we are to carry the Holy Spirit's power into every situation, so that He can accomplish His will and work through us. In order to overcome the powers at work in the world (sin and Satan), we must be empowered from on high. In order to understand what we have been entrusted with, Paul prays for us in Ephesians 1:18-21: *"I pray that the eyes of your heart may be enlightened, so that you may know what is the hope of His calling, what are the riches of the glory of His inheritance in the Saints, and what is the surpassing greatness of His power toward us who believe. These are in accordance with the working of the strength of His might which He brought about in Christ, when He raised Him from the dead, and seated Him at His right hand in the heavenly places, far above all rule and authority and power and dominion, and every name that is named, not only in this age, but also in the one to come."*

Question: *Where have you seen the Lord demonstrate His power in and through your life?*

157. Belonging

"... that they may all be one; even as Thou,
Father, art in Me, and I in Thee, that they also may
be in Us; that the world may believe that Thou didst
send Me." ~ John 17:21

Orphans see the world through a different lens than do sons. Orphans live with an underlying sense of abandonment, forfeiting the sense of well-being that comes from a secure home life.

Rather than a deep-seated ability to trust others and believe for good, an orphan views life from the position of being his own provider and protector. Jesus came into the world a Seed, the promised Son for the line of David. He lived among us as One who was well acquainted with abandonment, betrayal, and rejection, but endured, knowing who He belonged to. Having put on flesh, He lived with His Father in the same manner on earth that He has invited us to experience. His oneness with the Father was sustained as He lived from the One He belonged to.

Question: *Is there any condition or situation in your past that has robbed you of a sense of belonging?*

158. Learning Submission

"… equip you in every good thing to do His will,
working in us that which is pleasing
in His sight …" ~ Hebrews 13:21

To a world that had completely gone astray, Jesus came as a living demonstration of submission. A conversation between the Father and the Lord Jesus takes place just prior to the Incarnation. *"Therefore when He comes into the world, He says, 'Sacrifice and offering Thou hast not desired, but a body Thou hast prepared for Me; in whole burnt offerings and sacrifices for sin Thou hast taken no pleasure.' Then I said, 'Behold, I have come (in the roll of the book it is written of Me) to do Thy will O God'"* (Hebrews 10:5-7). In the Kingdom of God, submission is the basis for all power and authority and so potent that the Son of God came to model it for us. To repent from following our own will and ways bears witness to our profession of faith.

Question: *When you hear the word submission—what is your initial response?*

159. Put on Spirit

"But put on the Lord Jesus Christ, and make no provision for the flesh in regard to its lusts."
~ Romans 13:14

In order to inhabit time and space, God put on flesh and dwelt among us. God, who is Spirit, took all that He was and confined Himself in Jesus, to all He created man to be. He came and took up where Adam had left off, so humanity could be restored to our original design—flesh fully inhabited and animated by the Holy Spirit of God. In the divine dressing room of the Incarnation, God, dressed as a man, came to model all that man was intended for. He invites us to this divine dressing room as well, to get dressed in the opposite direction and to put on Spirit. These are our new instructions: *"... that, in reference to your former manner of life, you lay aside the old self, which is being corrupted in accordance with the lusts of deceit, and that you be renewed in the spirit of your mind, and put on the new self, which in the likeness of God has been created in righteousness and holiness of the truth"* (Ephesians 4:22-24). Putting off flesh and putting on Spirit is a daily choice we make in order to walk in the Spirit.

Question: Where have you made a choice today, or this week, to put on Spirit?

160. Regaining Lost Capacities

*"Things which eye has not seen and ear has not
heard, and which have not entered the heart of man,
all that God has prepared for those who love Him."*
~ I Corinthians 2:9

God created in two realms—the visible, and the invisible (Colossians 1:15-16). In the beginning we were designed for and given the capacity to function in both realms. With our soul we interfaced with the natural realm, taking in and interpreting all of the information we absorbed. With our Spirit, we were able to access heavenly places, and commune with the Living God. At the fall, when we were disconnected spiritually from the Father, we lost our spiritual sight and hearing, and did not regain them again until Christ brought about salvation. When the Holy Spirit was reintroduced to His creation at Pentecost, He came that we might constantly conduct ourselves in the sphere of the Spirit. That we might determine every thought, word, and deed by the leading of the Spirit through His Word, and think every thought, speak every word, and do every deed in an attitude of entire dependence upon the Holy Spirit's empowering energy.

Question: How have you learned to be sensitive and aware of the spiritual realm?

161. Leaving to Follow

"Follow Me, and I will make you fishers of men."
~ Matthew 4:19

The pattern for leaving to follow shows up repeatedly in scripture. We first see it in the description of a marriage: *"For this cause a man shall leave his father and his mother, and shall cleave to his wife ..."* (Genesis 2:24). We see it again as God speaks to Abraham: *"Go forth from your country, and from your relatives and from your father's house, to the land which I will show you ..."* (Genesis 12:1). These two examples rehearse a spiritual principle of laying aside the old, and putting on the new. When Jesus approached each of the twelve disciples, He beckoned them to come and follow. This requires leaving an old lifestyle behind, and as an act of your will reordering the rest of your life to be led by the Holy Spirit. The Lord stirred up my walk with Him with the invitation: "If you will give up what you are satisfied with, I will give you what you are hungry for." Leaving, to follow, is the path that Jesus calls each disciple to travel in order to live into His life, instead of our own.

Question: Is there something that you are hungry for spiritually?

162. The Seed

"Therefore take care how you listen; for whoever has, to him shall more be given; and whoever does not have, even what he thinks he has shall be taken away from him." ~ Luke 8:18

When all seemed lost, at the corruption of mankind, God proclaimed His judgment upon the usurper, the devil, by the promise of a future seed. For generations, prophets and priests anticipated the One who would come to fulfill all that was promised. Then, at the center point of history, the Word became flesh by becoming that Seed. Sown as a promise to the fallen, and a threat to Satan, the full measure of the gift would wait until the good soil of Mary's womb. She heard the word, believed, and then in humility said, *"Behold, the bondslave of the Lord; be it done to me according to your word"* (Luke 1:38).

The way the Lord continues to bring forth His kingdom is through the sowing of seed. Seeds are sown into dark places when the conditions are conducive to growth. When soil is prepared, there can be a harvest of 30, 60, or 100-fold. When hearts are prepared, the Lord conceives His will by His living word, and our hearts become pregnant with promise. We are stretched, as the promise is enlarged through faith, and then bring forth fruit at the fullness of time.

Question: *What promise has the Lord conceived in your heart?*

163. Disciples and Multitude

"Peter began to say to Him, 'Behold, we have left everything and followed you.'" ~ Mark 10:28

Jesus attracted three different audiences: the disciples, the multitude, and enemies. They all came to observe Him for different reasons. Those who stood in opposition to His message were often those who had originally been entrusted with the word of God. Religious leaders flocked to His gatherings in order to mock and criticize, and eventually, to kill the Messenger.

The multitudes pressed around Jesus in order to hear the words this new teacher uttered. They came to be fed, and healed, and delivered from demonic possession. They surrounded Him, asking for signs and wonders, and then leaving Him to go their own ways. Multitudes came to gain — receiving a benefit without taking any responsibility.

Disciples were each called away to leave everything in order to follow Jesus. Sacrifice marks the path of a disciple. *"If anyone wishes to come after Me, let him deny himself, and take up his cross, and follow Me"* (Matthew 16:24). Relationship is offered to each one, as they reorient their lives to His Kingdom.

Question: How are churches setting themselves up to be attractive to multitudes or conducive to making disciples?

---

164. Great Commission

"Go therefore and make disciples of all nations,
baptizing them in the name of the Father and of the
Son and of the Holy Spirit, teaching them to observe
all that I have commanded you. And behold, I am
with you always, to the end of the age."

~ *Matthew 28:19-20*

The baton was passed to the disciples when Jesus gave them the Great Commission. *"All authority has been given Me in heaven and on earth. Go therefore and make disciples of all the nations, baptizing them in the name of the Father and the Son and the Holy Spirit, teaching them to observe all that I commanded you; and lo, I am with you always, even to the end of the age"* (Matthew 38:18-20). The first instruction each disciple had received was "Come, learn from Me." Now, after walking with the Lord and receiving the gift of the Holy Spirit, the instruction is to go into the whole world with their message. Jesus gave a command to go. This is not just a suggestion for a few, but for all who would be His disciples. This assignment stretches the boundaries of the Kingdom as each new life is added.

Perhaps when we are sent into the world, "teaching them to observe all that I commanded" has more to do with demonstrating the gospel relationally than with keeping the statutes. Jesus came to live among His people as an observable model of Sonship. He lived as a demonstration of walking in the Spirit, so we could learn to follow. Perhaps in an information driven world, disciple-making requires some re-modeling.

Question: Have you been discipled? Have you discipled others?

165. Fellowship

*"... but if we walk in the light as He Himself is in
the light, we have fellowship with one another, and
the blood of Jesus His Son cleanses us from all sin."*
~ 1 John 1:7

Following the Day of Pentecost, the church was *"continually
devoting themselves to the apostles teaching and to fellowship, to the
breaking of bread and to prayer"* (Acts 2:42). Fellowship was a
critical part of the maturity of the church.

We have used the word fellowship to describe the church
location where coffee is shared after the service. We meet over
a meal, or a game, or a party, and if other believers are there
together, it is considered fellowship.

If we fail to understand this element of church life, we forfeit
the profound impact it has for our gatherings. I John 1:1-3
gives us our best scriptural definition: *"What was from the beginning, what we have heard, what we have seen with our eyes, what
we beheld and our hands handled, concerning the Word of Life —
and the life was manifested, and we have seen and bear witness and
proclaim to you the eternal life, which was with the Father and was
manifested to us — what we have seen and heard we proclaim to you
also, that you also may have fellowship with us; and indeed our fellowship is with the Father, and with His Son Jesus Christ."* Fellowship happens when we each share with the other what we are
hearing the Lord say, and seeing the Lord do. It is a form of
bearing witness to one another, and an opportunity to build
one another up in our most holy faith.

*Question: Do you have a regular practice of rehearsing your God stories
with someone?*

166. A True Witness

*"For I gave you an example that you also should
do as I did to you." ~ John 13:15*

A true witness is not just a declarer of doctrine—but a demonstration of it. To be a living witness means we carry the presence of the Holy Spirit into every situation and His power conducts His will through us. Jesus, who was God in flesh appearing, demonstrated the word and the Spirit in and through His life, leaving us an example for living by the Spirit. Jesus modeled the way of walking as restored sons of God to a creation that had totally gone astray.

Just as you learn a language by hearing and speaking, you learn a lifestyle by observation and imitation. The gospel came to us through the life of the Son. He put on flesh and lived as an observable model of sonship. What we have received, we must now give away. This life is designed to be transferred to others relationally as well.

Question: How does this redefine the nature of witnessing for you?

167. *Wisdom From Above*

*"Now as they observed the confidence of Peter and
John, and understood that they were uneducated
and untrained men, they were marveling, and
began to recognize them as having been with Jesus."*
~ Acts 4:13

When Jesus was teaching in the temple, the Jews began to question, *"How has this man become learned, having never been educated?"* (John 7:15). As those who value education, we might have had a similar response. Yet Jesus taught from an indwelling wisdom received from His Father. *"My teaching is not Mine, but His who sent Me. If any man is willing to do His will, he shall know of the teaching, whether it is of God, or whether I speak from Myself. He who speaks from himself seeks his own glory; but He who is seeking the glory of the One who sent Him, He is true, and there is no unrighteousness in Him"* (John 7:16-18). He urges us repeatedly to ask for such wisdom from Him. *"...If any of you lacks wisdom, let him ask of God, who gives to all men generously and without reproach and it will be given to him"* (James 1:5). How do we recognize wisdom from God? The *"wisdom from above is first pure, then peaceable, gentle, reasonable, full of mercy and good fruits, unwavering, without hypocrisy"* (James 3:17).

Question: How do you recognize the difference between what you have been educated to believe, and that which has been given to you as wisdom from God?

168. Humility

"Humble yourselves, therefore, under the mighty hand of God, that He may exalt you at the proper time." ~ 1 Peter 5:6

The common definition of humility is a modest or low view of one's own importance. Humility is not just an assessment, or personal view of our lives, but our means of accessing the presence of the Lord. Neither is it the acknowledgment of sinfulness—but it is to acknowledge absolute dependence—having nothing, but receiving all things from God. When we make a declaration of dependence, we are making all that we have fully dependent on all that He is. When Jesus humbled Himself as it says in Philippians 2, He displayed, incarnate in human flesh, what it is to fully depend upon the Father. He emptied Himself of presence, privilege, and glory, that He might demonstrate the position we are to take. Jesus modeled humility by not saying His own words (He only said what He heard the Father say), by not taking His own actions (He only did what He saw the Father doing), and He never acted on His own will (He did nothing from His own initiative). This humility took Him all the way to the cross, with the words, *"not My will, but Yours be done"* (Matthew 26:39).

Question: What has God used to reveal pride in your life?

169. Learned Obedience in Suffering

"Therefore, since Christ has suffered in the flesh,
arm yourselves also with the same purpose, because
he who has suffered in the flesh has ceased from sin,
so as to live the rest of the time in the flesh no
longer for the lusts of men, but for the will of God."
~ 1 Peter 4:1-2

Suffering comes into our lives as we undergo pain, distress, injury or loss. Ever since the fall, it is an element we face in our lives that has great potential for transforming us. In the midst of crisis, suffering, and pain, we can mature or defect. Jesus demonstrated the way of the Father. *"Although He was a Son, He learned obedience from the things which He suffered. And having been made perfect, He became to all those who obey Him the source of eternal salvation"* (Hebrews 5:8-9). Although He was sinless, until He suffered He was untested. Testing is a gift that puts all that we are and have under pressure, and results in bringing us near to the Lord, or turning away in rebellion.

We must realize that we are tempted as much in our sufferings as we are by our appetites. *"For since He Himself was tempted in that which He has suffered, He is able to come to the aid of those who are tempted"* (Hebrews 2:18). In the midst of a trial we have the opportunity to reorient our lives toward the Comforter, rather than the ways we have practiced comforting ourselves. This is a form of repentance.

Question: *Do you recognize any way that you comfort yourself in the middle of a trial?*

170. The Lord's Prayer

"Thy kingdom come. Thy will be done, on earth as it is in heaven." ~ Matthew 6:10

Within the context of the Lord's Prayer, Jesus gives us insight into the relationship we now have with God as Father. When the creation went astray, man began to live more like an orphan than like a son. Orphans tend to be their own provider and protector. The Lord's Prayer is a dynamic prayer for reordering one's life and roles. The reconciliation of the cross restored us to the status of sons, and as such, we are called to learn His pattern of submission.

If you look closely, the Lord's Prayer is in direct opposition to the specific points mentioned in the temptation of Jesus (Our Father/If You are the Son; Give us bread/make bread for yourself; Thy Kingdom come/shown all the kingdoms of the world, etc.). Jesus came to destroy the works of the devil (1 John 3:8) and overthrow the systems of the world. He does this by redeeming man, and restoring us to sonship.

This is an invitation to walk in the bestowed favor of sons with access to heavenly places. It is a prayer of declared dependence, a forsaking of our own ways. Though we often pray this personally, it is corporate in nature (our, us). We move from worship, to intercession, to supplication, then confession. In these few simple words, God calls us home.

Question: Do you have this prayer memorized? Which part is most meaningful to you?

171. Lean Not on Your Own Understanding

"The Lord by wisdom founded the earth; by understanding He established the heavens."
~ Proverbs 3:19

Wisdom and understanding are often paired together in the scriptures, yet I have paid more attention to wisdom—I gave it more star power. The word itself seemed more tangible. Then I read Proverbs 3:19, *"The Lord by wisdom founded the earth; by understanding He established the heavens."* In the moment it took to read that simple verse, "understanding' began to give me a guided tour of its nature.

In Isaiah 11:2, the Spirit of God is described as the *"Spirit of wisdom and understanding, the spirit of counsel and strength, the spirit of knowledge and the fear of the Lord."* Three couplets partnered in word and work. Wisdom and understanding must work together for us to have full access to all the Lord would impart.

When Jesus walked among us, He spoke only what He heard the Father saying. His lips formed wisdom...once more Wisdom was lifting her voice in the noisy streets and calling to the naive and the foolish to turn to reproof (Proverbs 1:20-33). All could hear, but not all could understand. Indeed, understanding is a return to fluency.

Wisdom lures us to the veil between heaven and earth. Understanding is the portal.

Question: What is your initial response when you discover you lack understanding about the scriptures?

172. *Restoration to Identity and Fellowship*

"... go to My brethren, and say to them, I ascend to My Father and your Father, and My God and your God." ~ John 20:17

Though Jesus put on flesh and lived on earth as the Son of Man, He remained Son of God and never forfeited His identity or His fellowship with the Father. Before the great exchange on the cross when He became sin on our behalf, He lived with His identity and fellowship intact on earth.

Identity is based on who we are more than what we do. So often we identify ourselves by a list of tasks, which is more the identity of a slave than a son. Certainty over our identity allows us to be defined by our relationships, rather than our workload. Though Jesus was God in flesh appearing, He sustained and nourished His fellowship with His Father as He lived in complete dependence while among us. The salvation purchased for us at the cross restored our ability to be reconciled to Father God as sons, and to reclaim our own identity and fellowship with God. When the younger brother returns to his father's house in the story of the prodigal son, His father sees him coming, and runs to embrace and kiss him. There is a restoration of fellowship. The father wraps him in a robe, puts sandals on his feet, and a ring on his finger ... a restoration of identity. (Luke 15:11-32).

Question: What keeps you from living into the fullness of your identity as a son? What interrupts your fellowship with Him?

173. Earthly Role and Heavenly Role

"Although He was a Son, He learned obedience
from the things which He suffered. And having been
made perfect, He became to all those who obey Him
the source of eternal salvation, being designated by
God as a high priest according to the order of
Melchizedek." ~ Hebrews 5:8-10

While among us, Jesus modeled His earthly role as a Son. As He lived with His people Israel, His life was an illustration of the kind of relationship God had intended to have with His creation. He declared that His works, His words, and His ways were born of the Father, and not His own. He modeled for us the narrow way that leads to life in a restored relationship with Father. His life was a living blueprint for the sons He came to ransom. When He taught His disciples to pray (the Lord's Prayer), it was an invitation into our own sonship. Following the Ascension, Jesus was restored to His heavenly role as our High Priest. *"Since then we have a great high priest who has passed through the heavens, Jesus the Son of God, let us hold fast our confession. For we do not have a high priest who cannot sympathize with our weaknesses, but One who has been tempted in all things as we are, yet without sin. Let us therefore draw near with confidence to the throne of grace, that we may receive mercy and may find grace to help in time of need"* (Hebrews 4:14-16).

Question: *Since we are called to be a royal priesthood (1 Peter 2:9), what have you learned from Jesus about being a priest?*

174. Mature Son

*"And He went down with them, and came to
Nazareth; and He continued in subjection to them;
and His mother treasured all these things in her
heart." ~ Luke 2:51*

The goal of the Father is to raise mature sons who will bear His image and likeness. From the time Jesus was a child, His life was a reflection of what His Father was about. After being left behind in Jerusalem at the age of twelve, Jesus was found in the temple, *"sitting in the midst of the teachers, both listening to them, and asking them questions. And all who heard Him were amazed at His understanding and His answers"* (Luke 2:46-47). When His mother questioned Him, He responded, *"...Did you not know that I had to be in My Father's house?"* (Luke 2:49).

While yet a child, through subjecting His will to earthly parents (Luke 2:51), He learned the way of His Heavenly Father. *"And Jesus kept increasing in wisdom and stature, and in favor with God and men"* (Luke 2:52). From the Incarnation to the Crucifixion, Jesus lived a life of dependence, obedience, and wisdom, leaving us a pattern for learning maturity as sons.

Question: How did your upbringing by earthly parents prepare you for living as a son of the Heavenly Father? Did it set a good pattern, or a distorted one?

175. Symbol and Type

> *"Now if He were on earth, He would not be a priest at all, since there are those who offer the gifts according to the Law; who serve a copy and shadow of the heavenly things ..." ~ Hebrews 8:4-5*

God created in two realms: the natural, physical realm of earth, and the heavenly, spiritual realm. *"For by Him all things were created, both in the heavens and on earth, visible and invisible, whether thrones or dominions or rulers or authorities—all things have been created by Him and for Him"* (Colossians 1:16). Man, originally designed to access both realms, became confined to just the earthly realm after the fall. Since we were no longer able to perceive the true nature of all things, the Father began to describe the heavenly realms to us through the use of symbol and type. These symbols were *"a shadow of the good things to come and not the very form of things ..."* (Hebrews 10:1). The Old Testament displayed a shadow of the divine provision, so that when Jesus appeared in the flesh, He might be readily recognized as God's gift. As New Testament believers, these earthly illustrations help bring greater insight into the full identity of Jesus.

Question: What do we recognize when a shadow is seen?

176. Works Bear Witness

*"But the witness which I have is greater than that
of John; for the works which the Father has given
Me to accomplish, the very works that I do, bear
witness of Me, that the Father has sent Me."*
~ John 5:36

Because Jesus only did what He saw the Father doing, He
was a living witness on earth of all that was taking place in
the heavenly realm. The works that Jesus walked in were
works that were prepared beforehand, that He should walk
in them (Ephesians 2:10). Many of the things accomplished by
Christ were prophesied, thus indicating that the One who was
promised had come. *"The Spirit of the Lord God is upon me, because the Lord has anointed me to bring good news to the afflicted;
He has sent me to bind up the broken-hearted, to proclaim liberty to
captives, and freedom to prisoners; to proclaim the favorable year of
the Lord ..."* (Isaiah 61:1-2). First prophesied by Isaiah, centuries before Christ's appearing, these works were announced
before Jesus ever arrived to walk in them. After He was baptized, He entered the synagogue and read this same passage
from the scroll that was handed to Him, proclaiming that the
"scripture has been fulfilled in your hearing" (Luke 4:21). Jesus
would go on to fulfill every work prescribed for Him—and
on the day of His crucifixion be able to respond to His Father,
saying, *"It is finished"* (John 19:30). Every work and word was
complete; His works bearing witness that the Father had sent
the Son.

*Question: How do you discern what works the Father has entrusted to
your stewardship?*

177. *Receiving Discipline*

*"It is for discipline that you endure; God deals
with you as with sons; for what son is there whom
his father does not discipline? But if you are
without discipline, of which all have become
partakers, then you are illegitimate children
and not sons." ~ Hebrews 12:7-8*

Because the Father loved Jesus, He disciplined Him as a Son.
He who was without sin still required discipline. We often
confuse discipline with punishment. Punishment is what we
receive from the hands of man for past failures. Discipline is
what we receive from the Lord for future training. When God
spoke to Cain, in Genesis 4, He said, *"Why are you angry? And
why has your countenance fallen? If you do well, will not your
countenance be lifted up? And if you do not do well, sin is crouching
at the door; and its desire is for you, but you must master it."* He
attempted to bring correction to Cain, training him for future
worship. Cain perceived it as punishment and rejection, and
defied God. Jesus lived His life dependent on the Father's
instruction, daily disciplined in the regimens of sonship. He
offers us this same kind of discipline as we learn to walk
by the Spirit.

Question: *When did you learn to see discipline as a gift?*

178. Peacemaking

"Blessed are the peacemakers, for they shall be called sons [huios] of God." ~ Matthew 5:9

God has always been the one to initiate peacemaking. *"For God so loved the world, that He gave His only begotten Son, that whoever believes in Him should not perish, but have eternal life"* (John 3:16). It is out of the overflow of His love that He has paid the price for peace. *"But God demonstrates His own love toward us, in that while we were yet sinners, Christ died for us ... While we were enemies, we were reconciled to God through the death of His Son, much more, having been reconciled, we shall be saved by His life"* (Romans 5:8,10). This is the fullness of His grace, in which we now stand. Since we have been lavished with a love that has forgiven us our trespasses, we can now forgive those who have trespassed against us. This mature demonstration of His love can now be released through us. *"Now all these things are from God, who reconciled us to Himself through Christ, and gave us the ministry of reconciliation, namely, that God was in Christ reconciling the world to Himself, not counting their trespasses against them, and He has committed to us the word of reconciliation. Therefore, we are ambassadors for Christ, as though God were entreating through us; we beg you on behalf of Christ, be reconciled to God. He made Him who knew no sin to be sin on our behalf that we might become the righteousness of God in Him."* (2 Corinthians 5:18-21).

Question: *Where is the Lord asking you to serve someone in the midst of their conflict—with God or others?*

179. Father Loves the Son

*"The Father loves the Son, and has given all
things into His hand." ~ John 3:35*

God is love, and as such, He is the source of all love that exists within His creation. Our only capacity to genuinely love is because we have been loved first. *"We love, because He first loved us"* (1 John 4:19). So, as Jesus walked out a pure demonstration of the Father's love toward us, He first received, in order to give. This love is the basis for our identity, and has been conferred on us from love, rather than from our performance. Learning to live in the love of the Father is critical to our maturity as sons. If we fail to believe, we will continue to relate to Him based on our former identities, that of slaves or orphans. This love, that stirs up love, allows the gospel to access our hearts.

Question: Do you know someone who struggles to believe that they are loved? Be a living demonstration to them today.

180. Words of Spirit and Life

"Death and life are in the power of the tongue,
and those who love it will eat its fruit."
~ Proverbs 18:21

How do you judge what words should come out of your mouth? I have seen a poster that matches the letters in the word "think". Is it True? Is it Helpful? Is it Inspiring? Is it Necessary? Is it Kind? This grid is a good reminder, but it only serves to restrain our flesh. Scripture teaches us that the tongue is a place that demonstrates who we serve. *"So also the tongue is a small part of the body, and yet it boasts of great things. Behold, how great a forest is set aflame by such a small fire! And the tongue is a fire, the very world of iniquity; the tongue is set among our members as that which defiles the entire body, and sets on fire the course of our life, and is set on fire by hell...But no one can tame the tongue; it is a restless evil and full of deadly poison. With it we bless our Lord and Father; and with it we curse men, who have been made in the likeness of God"* (James 3:5-9).

How can we learn to speak by the Spirit? We must learn the nature of His voice, and then speak at His initiative. Jesus modeled the path for us. He only said what He heard the Father saying.

Question: Have you blessed someone with words of life this week?

181. In Community

*"I in them, and Thou in Me, that they may be
perfected in unity, that the world may know that
Thou didst send Me, and didst love them, even as
Thou didst love Me." ~ John 17:23*

Though Jesus was the fullness of deity in bodily form, He lived His years of ministry in the context of community. He purposed to demonstrate how the oneness of the Father, the Son, and the Spirit operate together. Following His ascension, He was manifested as the Head of the Body, His church—a people who are called to display covenant life together. Community is the only way man can accurately reflect the image and likeness of God. In Christ's priestly prayer, in John 17, He prayed that we would be one, even as He and the Father are one—that we would be perfected in unity. Sustaining oneness is the means God uses to perfect us. On the day two people marry, God makes the two into one. Their responsibility is to sustain oneness—which will bring about their maturity. When we are born again, the Lord places us into His church. We become members one of another. As we sustain that oneness, we mature.

*Question: Do you belong to a church community that is an accurate re-
flection of the oneness of the Godhead?*

Part 7

Fruit

182. New Commandment (1)

*"For the law of the Spirit of life in Christ Jesus
has set you free from the law of sin and of death."*
~ Romans 8:2

A lawyer once asked Jesus, *"Which is the greatest
commandment in the Law?"* Jesus replied, *"You shall love the
Lord your God with all your heart, and with all your soul, and with
all your mind. This is the great and foremost commandment. The
second is like it, 'You shall love your neighbor as yourself.' On these
two commandments depend the whole Law and the Prophets"*
(Matthew 22:35-40).

So, here is our question: Is this Old Covenant or New Covenant? Jesus states the two greatest commandments of the
Law; which He alone can satisfy. Consider why the Father
sent the Son: *"For what the Law could not do, weak as it was
through the flesh, God did: sending His own Son in the likeness of
sinful flesh and as an offering for sin, He condemned sin in the flesh,
in order that the requirement of the Law might be fulfilled in us,
who do not walk according to the flesh, but according to the Spirit"*
(Romans 8:3-4). No amount of walking in the strength of our
soul can ever satisfy the requirements of the Law. Once Jesus
applies the Law to our hearts, rather than our religious performance, we recognize our poverty. The Holy One, the Son
sent, purchased us by satisfying the Law with His own
blood—the price of redemption.

Question: Has the commandment to love changed your capacity to love?

183. New Commandment (2)

"By this all men will know that you are My
disciples, if you have love for one another."
~ John 13:35

Under the Old Covenant, the greatest commandments—to love God and our neighbor—is sourced from our own hearts. And try as we might, we fail to keep the Law, or to satisfy its righteous requirements. Through the death of Jesus Christ, the Old Covenant is fulfilled and then replaced by a New Covenant in His blood. With the New Covenant, comes a new law: *"A new commandment I give to you, that you love one another, even as I have loved you, that you also love one another"* (John 13:34). Instead of being the source of love, we must first be the recipients of His love; then we can be the distribution system of what we have received. Under the Law, when love was tested, we often failed. With the New Covenant Law being written on our hearts, we are able to obey from a place of living loved. You might well understand the work of the evil one in keeping us from believing we are loved, and thus unable to release what we have received. We love, because He first loved us (1 John 4:19).

Question: *Read I John 4:16-19. Have you come to know and believe the love God has for you?*

184. Know and Believe

"There is no fear in love; but perfect love casts out fear, because fear involves punishment, and the one who fears is not perfected in love." ~ I John 4:18

Fulfilling the New Covenant Law to "love one another, even as I have loved you," requires that we know and believe that we are loved. The Greek word for "know" is *ginosko* and it has three characteristics: relational, progressive, and effectual. We come to "know" this love because it is offered to us relationally. It is not just information to be believed, but an intimate relationship to be experienced.

It is progressive—you don't get it all at once, but continue to increase in capacity as His love enlarges your heart.

And last, it is effectual; it transforms the one who knows and believes this kind of love. Believing we are loved is the response to such a lavish gift, yet many struggle to receive this truth. Wounds to our soul, left untended, often result in an inability to receive the Father's love and form healthy trust relationships. Acknowledging the state of our heart, and inviting the Father to comfort us with His love, begins our process of maturing in our new birth.

Question: *What helped you come to know and believe that you were loved?*

185. Casts Out Fear

"In this is love, not that we loved God, but that
He loved us and sent His Son to be the propitiation
for our sins." ~ I John 4:10

Fear and anxiety are the sentries that many have trusted to watch over their hearts. Imbedded within their souls and dominating their thoughts and behaviors, these two invaders manage to steal peace, rob joy, and counteract faith. An entire generation has grown up believing that fear is a normal state, and that anxiety has no remedy. The Father knew that the antidote for fear was perfect love, and modeled this kind of love in the life of Jesus. He *"demonstrates His own love toward us, in that while we were yet sinners, Christ died for us"* (Romans 5:8). Based on His unmerited favor, this love is what awakens us to the freedom of the sons of God. Being rooted and grounded in His measure of love toward us, we are filled, freed, and fruitful.

Question: Does fear have any territory in your heart? Do you know why?

186. Accessing the Creation

"For God so loved the world, that He gave His
only begotten Son, that whoever believes in Him
should not perish, but have eternal life."
~ John 3:16

Following the rebellion of mankind, God chooses to access His creation again by the giving and receiving of love. The Lord designs a way to regain the hearts of man. This point of entry—a divine strategy of recovery—restores mankind to a love relationship with the Beloved. Rather than the performance of religious works, it is the work of the cross that the Son uses to reclaim His design for a race of sons. This love is visible and tangible and affords those who receive Him newness of life. His love is merciful—He knows who we are and loves us anyway. His love is good—He sees what is best for us and acts on our behalf. His love is fruitful—He bears His life from the midst of our brokenness. His love is expressed—abounding in His gifts and the fruit of His Spirit. His love is everlasting—He has promised to never leave or forsake us. His love is new every morning—We can experience more of Him as we trust in His love. His love *"bears all things, believes all things, hopes all things, endures all things ... never fails"* (1 Corinthians 13:7-8).

Question: *Has your heart ever been transformed by someone who loved you well?*

187. Return to Joy

*"Thou wilt make known to me the path of life; in
Thy presence is fullness of joy; in Thy right hand
there are pleasures forever."*
~ Psalm 16:11

One of the first skills that an infant begins to learn is how to return to joy. Born entirely dependent on others to meet their needs, an infant expresses a felt need through expressing a level of displeasure with current circumstances. If needs are met in a timely manner, the infant can be satisfied and then reorient their emotions to a place of joy. In the natural this is developed and sustained through committed love bonds. When people suffer—or their needs are repeatedly ne-glected—they begin to experience depression, anxiety, and despair, and are unable to return to a state of well-being or joy. The pleasure center of the brain becomes vulnerable, and whatever brings relief from discomfort becomes the pattern the child adopts in order to care for themselves. When we are born again, and become a part of the family of God, one of the first lessons in our spiritual journey is accessing the Holy Spirit, the God of all comfort. We must learn to reorient from old ways of relieving our sufferings to leaning upon the Com-forter for His ways.

Question: *Have you learned to access His presence to the point of re-stored joy?*

188. Happiness or Joy

"These things I have spoken to you, that My joy
may be in you, and that your joy may be made full."
~ John 15:11

What if joy is a place and not just an elusive emotion? What
if joy is the best way to describe the state of our being when
we have been reconciled with our God and with others?
When we consider how much depression, discouragement,
and despair thrive in broken relationships, you might agree
that I am on to something. So many of the Psalms indicate that
fullness of joy is realized when we have entered into His
presence and that pleasure is available at His right hand
(Psalm 16:11). Scripture also indicates that there is the
opportunity for a divine exchange to take place when we
encounter the presence of the Comforter. Though we have
"sown with tears—we shall reap with joyful shouting" (Psalm
126:5-6). The Comforter will *"turn mourning into joy, comfort*
them, and give them joy for their sorrow" (Jeremiah 31:13). As we
walk by the life of the Holy Spirit, relying on His presence
determines whether we are able to sustain joy or be tempted
in our sufferings.

Question: Is it possible to be the Lord's delivery system for joy? How has
this happened for you?

189. In His Presence—Joy

*"Then I will go to the altar of God, to God my
exceeding joy; and upon the lyre I shall praise Thee,
O God, my God." ~ Psalm 43:4*

If we consider joy to be a highly valued human emotion, we will miss the source it has in God Himself. If joy is a fruit of the Spirit—then it is a tangible demonstration of a quality that the Holy Spirit would like to express in you and through you. Joy is a quality that we find within the nature of God, Himself. Consider Zephaniah 3:17: *"The Lord your God is in your midst, a victorious warrior. He will exult over you with joy, He will be quiet in His love, He will rejoice over you with shouts of joy."* The Lord delights in expressing pleasure, letting man know what brings Him joy. The idea of expressing pleasure between two parties is seen in Zephaniah and again in Isaiah 35:5-10: *"Then the eyes of the blind will be opened, and the ears of the deaf will be unstopped, then the lame will leap like a deer, and the tongue of the dumb will shout for joy ... And the ransomed of the Lord will return, and come with joyful shouting to Zion, with everlasting joy upon their heads. They will find gladness and joy, and sorrow and sighing will flee away."*

Question: *Do you know any reason why joy could not remain sustainable in your life?*

190. Peace

"Therefore having been justified by faith, we have peace with God through our Lord Jesus Christ ..."
~ *Romans 5:1*

Oneness is one of the identifying characteristics of the Godhead and a description of what happens when our hearts are brought to a restored state of relationship. Peace is defined as the absence or end of strife; it is the opposite of war and dissension. In the Old Testament, the equivalent word for peace was *shalom*—a state of wholeness, soundness, health, and well-being. It was a state that restored God's blessing. There are two responses that mankind tends to make in order to achieve peace. One is peacekeeping—a way to keep people from attacking one another by erecting some kind of barrier. Peacekeepers try to keep people's emotions and tensions from arising and avoid conflict at any cost. Peacekeeping has an eroding quality to it, in that it maintains surface appearances of peace without addressing the issues that prevent it.

Peacemaking, on the other hand, is the process required to create true reconciliation and union between two parties that are separated. It is willing to navigate ill-will and painful responses to establish an enduring, sometimes hard-earned, restoration. The Beatitudes describe the work of mature sons as peacemakers (Matthew 5:9).

Question: Do you see the church model peacekeeping or peacemaking?

191. Reconciled to God

"So then let us pursue the things which make for
peace and the building up of one another."
~ Romans 14:19

In the absence of peace, mankind lives in a continual state of fear and anxiety. Our soul's response to human disarray is to become troubled and unsettled. Ephesians 2:14-16 is a description of the ultimate peace treaty, enacted by the Lord Himself: *"For He Himself is our peace, who made both groups into one, and broke down the barrier of the dividing wall, by abolishing in His flesh the enmity, which is the Law of commandments contained in ordinances, that in Himself He might make the two into one new man, thus establishing peace, and might reconcile them both in one body to God through the cross, by it having put to death the enmity."*

As we mature as sons of God, He entrusts the work of peacemaking to us: *"Now all these things are from God, who reconciled us to Himself through Christ, and gave us the ministry of reconciliation, namely, that God was in Christ reconciling the world to Himself, not counting their trespasses against them, and He has committed to us the word of reconciliation. Therefore, we are ambassadors for Christ, as though God were entreating through us; we beg you on behalf of Christ, be reconciled to God. He made Him who knew no sin to be sin on our behalf, that we might become the righteousness of God in Him"* (2 Corinthians 5:18-21).

Question: *Is there any territory in your life where fear and anxiety rob you of peace?*

192. Setting the Mind

*"Finally, brethren, whatever is true, whatever is
honorable, whatever is right, whatever is pure,
whatever is lovely, whatever is of good repute, if
there is any excellence and if anything worthy of
praise, let your mind dwell on these things."*
~ Philippians 4:8

When we make the Lord's will our fixed purpose, we have
the ability to continually walk in the Spirit. Galatians 5:17 tells
us, *"the flesh sets its desire against the Spirit, and the Spirit against
the flesh; for these are in opposition to one another, so that you may
not do the things that you please."* Both are at work in our lives,
and though we walk by the Spirit continually, we are never
free from the opposition of the flesh. The flesh will always
work to express its desires, and they often lead to the deeds
listed in Galatians 5:19-21. Our new discipline as believers is
found in Romans 8:6-8: *"For the mind set on the flesh is death,
but the mind set on the Spirit is life and peace, because the mind set
on the flesh is hostile toward God; for it does not subject itself to the
law of God, for it is not even able to do so; and those who are in the
flesh cannot please God."* Peace is a gift, but the practice of it is
a learned response to the Spirit.

Question: *What is the state of your thought life when you find yourself
unreconciled to someone?*

193. Longsuffering

*"Or do you think lightly of the riches of His
kindness and forbearance and patience, not knowing
that the kindness of God leads you to repentance?"*
~ Romans 2:4

Longsuffering is divinely regulated patience. It embraces steadfastness and staying-power and does not seek to express itself with anger or retribution. Longsuffering is the quality of endurance that comes when faced with trouble caused by people. Just like strength for running a race is developed by running, endurance is developed with the passage of time and pressure. This quality is produced in us when we turn to the Holy Spirit in the midst of a conflict, rather than resorting to behaviors that are based on the state of our emotions. As we learn to cooperate with the will of the Holy Spirit in relationships, we become those who display what covenant love looks like. Those who have developed the fruit of longsuffering can model extravagant grace, mercy, and forgiveness in the midst of a congregation.

Question: Who or what has helped sustain you in the midst of a long-term trial?

194. Sustaining Love

*"And thus, having patiently waited, he obtained
the promise." ~ Hebrews 6:15*

Mature love is not found in the absence of conflict, but in the ability to navigate conflict and return to oneness and unity. As we develop longsuffering in our own lives, we become those who have the capacity to contend for reconciliation for others. We are willing to believe all things, hope all things, endure all things, knowing that love never fails. There are times that the mature believers in a congregation are those, who through previous sufferings, have developed the ability to bear the weight of a season of turmoil with courage and faith for resolution. The key in this process of overcoming is being seated with Christ in heavenly places—above the fray. From this perspective we become aware of the long term results of contending for relational well-being.

Question: What is your motivation to contend for reconciliation in a long-term conflict?

195. Grace Meets Needs

*"Therefore, putting aside all malice and all deceit
and hypocrisy and envy and all slander, like
newborn babes, long for the pure milk of the word,
that by it you may grow in respect to salvation, if
you have tasted the kindness of the Lord."*
~ I Peter 2:1-3

Kindness is the delivery system for the love of God. God's love is demonstrated in a tangible way and meets real needs with excellence. His nature is displayed through graces that overcome our ideas of a harsh, austere God. Being able to see and believe the kindness of God is key for maturing in love, and enables us to be free from fear. There are many who struggle to believe in the kindness of Father God, while believing that the Son and the Spirit are kind. When our earthly parents fail to reflect the nature of our Heavenly Father, our understanding can be conflicted. Ongoing forgiveness and healing can restore us to an accurate perception. *"But God, being rich in mercy, because of His great love with which He loved us, even when we were dead in our transgressions, made us alive together with Christ (by grace you have been saved), and raised us up with Him, and seated us with Him in the heavenly places, in Christ Jesus, in order that in the ages to come He might show the surpassing riches of His grace in kindness toward us in Christ Jesus"* (Ephesians 2:4-7).

Question: *Where has the Lord demonstrated His kindness to you this week?*

196. Kindness Displayed

"But when the kindness of God our Savior and
His love for mankind appeared, He saved us, not on
the basis of deeds which we have done in
righteousness, but according to His mercy, by the
washing of regeneration and renewing
by the Holy Spirit ..." ~ Titus 3:4-5

Kindness is a means for Kingdom advancement, a vehicle to carry God's will into the circumstances we face. To walk in the fruit of kindness means more than restraining my fleshly response in a situation. It is a confident release of the character of Christ, and a dependence on Him to display His affection and will through me. It is the willing ability to display the love of God in an approachable way to those who need to know and believe His love. *"And so, as those who have been chosen of God, holy and beloved, put on a heart of compassion, kindness, humility, gentleness, and patience; bearing with one another, and forgiving each other, whoever has a complaint against anyone, just as the Lord forgave you, so also should you. And beyond all these things put on love, which is the perfect bond of unity"* (Colossians 3:12-14).

Question: *Who do you know that is a good example of Christ's kindness to others?*

216

197. Displaying His Goodness

"O taste and see that the Lord is good; how
blessed is the man who takes refuge in Him."
~ Psalm 34:8

In the days of creation, the Lord God used one word to describe His daily display: good. As God makes this pronouncement at the completion of each day, we discover His opinion of His handiwork, but also His authority to define goodness. Wrapped up in its meaning is the idea of sacrificial benevolence, a goodness for the sake of another. Having mankind in mind, all of creation was declared good. As the Garden story continues to unfold, two trees are introduced—the Tree of Life and the Tree of the Knowledge of Good and Evil. Of the latter tree, all aspects of this tree are evil. The fruit of this forbidden tree became the first bait that the evil one used to tempt Adam and Eve. The evil lure would place man in the position of deciding what was good; that being accomplished as we doubt His goodness and look for a better good that we can supply for ourselves. Pursuing a good apart from God, gaining information independently, is rebellion against Wisdom incarnate.

Question: *When are you most tempted to doubt God's goodness?*

198. Doubting God's Goodness

*"... Why do you call Me good? No one is good
except God alone." ~ Mark 10:18*

When we decide what is good or evil, one of the first things we forfeit, in the midst of a trial, is our trust and belief in the goodness of God. Once that lifeline is breached, we are isolated from our only source of recovery. We tend to put the Lord to the test then, instead of ourselves, and begin to negate Him—one quality and attribute at a time—until we have a God with the nature and attributes we could walk away from. If the father of lies can get us to doubt God's goodness, we will continually bear the fruit of our own fears.

As we learn to be led by the Holy Spirit in every thought, word, and action, we begin to be restored to the Tree of Life. Wisdom begins to flow to us relationally, and when we encounter various trials, we can consider it joy—as we receive the very counsel of God. (James 1:2-5).

Question: What is the outcome of choosing a good for your own sake?

199. Goodness Apart From God

*"Then Moses said, 'I pray Thee, show me Thy
glory!' And He said, 'I Myself will make all My
goodness pass before you, and will proclaim the
name of the Lord before you ...'"*
~ Exodus 33:18-19

"And the Lord God commanded the man, saying, 'From any tree
of the garden you may eat freely; but from the tree of the knowledge
of good and evil you shall not eat, for in the day that you eat from it
you shall surely die'" (Genesis 2:16-17). When mankind chose
to violate this command, we began to decide for ourselves
what is good and what is evil. Due to our self-orientation, this
is often decided through the grid of what we perceive to be
good for our own sake. In elevating ourselves, we elevate our
thoughts, feelings, and actions above the will of God. The
entire fallen creation now doubts the goodness of God, and
keeps pursuing knowledge to obtain a greater good. As
believers, when we allow the fruit of the Holy Spirit to
manifest in our lives, we turn from the Tree of the Knowledge
of Good and Evil and, instead, manifest the fruit of the Tree
of Life—His goodness.

Question: *How has the Lord expressed His goodness toward you?*

200. Faithful in Relationship

*"Now Moses was faithful in all his house as a
servant, for a testimony of those things which were
spoken later; but Christ was faithful as a Son over
His house whose house we are, if we hold fast our
confidence and the boast of our hope firm
until the end." ~ Hebrews 3:5-6*

Faithfulness is how God shows the nature of His covenantal love. Because He is from everlasting to everlasting, the nature of His love is displayed in His loyalty to love. Slaves will exhibit a level of faithfulness, but their motive is to receive a reward, and to gain their master's favor. Their loyalty is in order to avoid punishment. Those who relate to the Lord on the basis of sonship display the image and likeness of their Father in their daily lives. They know and understand the Father's will and purposes, and yield their own lives to display His faithfulness.

In the New Covenant, we realize that we must first receive His love in order to display it in our own lives. As He continues in steadfast love toward us, we are able to sustain and display faithful love toward others.

Question: How is faithfulness measured?

201. Faithfulness to the Task

"His master said to him, 'Well done, good and faithful slave; you were faithful with a few things, I will put you in charge of many things; enter into the joy of your master.'" ~ Matthew 25:21

Christ was continually *"faithful as a Son over His house whose house we are"* (Hebrews 3:6). He purposed to yield His body to do the Father's will in all things. He only said what He heard the Father saying; He only did what He saw the Father doing. He never acted on His own initiative. Since Israel continually turned from the Lord to pursue their own ways, Jesus came to be a living demonstration of Sonship. In the Old Testament, Joseph displayed faithfulness in his integrity. Nehemiah sustained his faithfulness in a season of great challenge and resistance. And Esther, as she modeled faithfulness to the King, through challenge and threat, overcame the purposes of the enemy toward Israel. As the church, we now bear a faithful witness and demonstration of the ways of God to a watching world.

Question: Who is a living model of faithfulness for you?

202. Fidelity in Relationship

*"Faithful is He who calls you, and He also will
bring it to pass." ~ I Thessalonians 5:24*

Samwise Gamgee, a friend and servant to Frodo Baggins in *The Lord of the Rings*, was a wonderful demonstration of fidelity in relationship. His willingness to suffer the same hardships that his friend endured, speaks of his loyalty and faithfulness. Jesus promises us a similar companionship in the Holy Spirit. Though betrayed Himself, Jesus promises an enduring love, never leaving or forsaking us (Deuteronomy 31:6). Marriage is supposed to be a visible demonstration of the relationship between Christ and His Church. As such, it is to be marked by faithfulness. When a husband and wife covenant their lives to each other, they are called to demonstrate faithfulness in love, word, and deed, so a rebellious world can see a narrow way that leads to life.

Question: How have you demonstrated faithfulness to a spouse or a friend?

203. Power Under Control

*"... with all humility and gentleness, with
patience, showing forbearance to one
another in love." ~ Ephesians 4:2*

Walking in the spiritual fruit of gentleness is to model meekness of divine origin. This gentle strength is an expression of power that is under authority, operating with reserve. It is a divinely balanced virtue that operates by our sustained obedience to the will of the Holy Spirit. Jesus demonstrated, from birth to the cross, a life restrained in His flesh, but fully alive to the ways of the Holy Spirit. He lived life with the same limitations that we are subject to, demonstrating the power of fully submitted humanity. *"For you have been called for this purpose, since Christ also suffered for you, leaving you an example for you to follow in His steps, who committed no sin, nor was any deceit found in His mouth; and while being reviled, He did not revile in return; while suffering, He uttered no threats, but kept entrusting Himself to Him who judges righteously ..."* (1 Peter 2:21-23). Yielded to the Holy Spirit, believers are able to endure injury and offense with patience and without resentment.

Question: Where have you seen the best model of gentleness?

204. Gentle toward Us

"... but sanctify Christ as Lord in your hearts,
always being ready to make a defense to everyone
who asks you to give an account for the hope that is
in you, yet with gentleness and reverence."
~ 1 Peter 3:15

Jesus invited us, weary and heavy laden, to come to Him to find rest. *"Take My yoke upon you, and learn from Me, for I am gentle and humble in heart; and you shall find rest for your souls. For My yoke is easy, and My load is light"* (Matthew 11:28-30). Our lives will be marked with weary effort if we try to follow the Lord while relying on our soul's strengths to accomplish it. Jesus lived in this yoked position as a lifestyle, rather than for the sake of an event. He willingly placed His life under the leadership of His Father, and invited us into a companionship of the Spirit that we learn when we live from His life instead of our own.

Question: How have you seen gentleness developed in your life?

205. Connected to the Will of the Father

*"... Behold, I have come to do Thy will, O God
..." ~ Hebrews 10:5-9*

Self-control has less to do with sin management and more to do with learning to mature in our free will. The words "self-control" imply self-mastery and restraint, in the realm of dominion or mastery within oneself. With self-control, we begin to master our desires, passions, and appetites. Mankind was formed to be an expression of the image and likeness of God. Since the Lord is sovereign, man was formed with free will. Apart from God, free will is self-serving and produces separation and independence; it is completely void of the ability to please God. This quality was built into our original design, to keep us continually connected to the will of the Father and displaying evidence of sustained intimacy. We needed to learn how to live with His will being done on earth, as it is in heaven. As sons, we have the privilege of relearning being led, and living a life that is an accurate reflection of His divine sovereignty.

Question: *What has God used to develop this fruit in your life?*

206. Freewill in Submission

*"For I have come down from heaven, not to do My
own will, but the will of Him who sent Me."*
~ John 6:38

In order to develop self-control, we must be put in situations where our free will learns to respond in submission at a heart level. Those who learn to follow the Lord from their heart are able to navigate both good and difficult circumstances with the assurance of the Father's goodness at all times and in all capacities. This is demonstrated to us in the life of Jesus, when He invites us into His yoke to learn the way of restraint and movement. He lived a life that was continually yoked to the Father's will and calls us to learn this same lesson from Him. After redemption, we are restored to divine image bearing, instead of walking in an old identity as slaves to sin and self. This fruit of the Spirit is especially important as we learn to navigate with the Lord's divine power and authority.

Question: Why does the liberty of the Spirit have more power than the works of the Law?

207. *No Place in Me*

"But put on the Lord Jesus Christ, and make no
provision for the flesh in regard to its lusts."
~ Romans 13:14

Jesus stated that the works that He accomplished bore witness that, *"the Father is in Me, and I in the Father,"* (John 10:38). and that His *"food is to do the will of Him who sent Me, and to accomplish His work"* (John 4:34). As He completed His work upon the cross, He was able to declare, *"It is finished"* (John 19:30). He lived a life that was a perfect representation of the will and work of the Father, on earth as it is in heaven. Through this life of obedience, the word of the Father, sown into the heart of the Son, bore the full fruit of the Spirit. This good soil yielded 100-fold and left no room for the corrupting work of the evil one to take hold. Jesus was able to confidently say, *"the ruler of the world is coming, and he has nothing in Me"* (John 14:30). This is a perfect demonstration of Galatians 5:16: *"But I say, walk by the Spirit, and you will not carry out the desire of the flesh."* This kind of fruit bearing is the result of abiding in the Father, and allowing the fullness of His life to abide in you.

Question: *Do you find any obstacles to the fruit of the Spirit being displayed in your life?*

227

208. Parable of the Soils

"Therefore take care how you listen; for whoever has, to him shall more be given; and whoever does not have, even what he thinks he has shall be taken away from him." ~ Luke 8:18

Within the nature of a seed is the capacity for full fruit. Built into creation's design was the sowing of seed and the bearing of a fruitful harvest. This rhythm of nature was a natural depiction of how the Word of the Lord operates, and its ability to access our hearts. God has in mind fruit bearing, but the parable of the soils (Matthew 13:3-23 and Luke 8:4-15) indicates that there are many obstacles to this process. The seed's failure to thrive is usually an indication of something hostile within its environment. Each of the soil types "hear" but then fail to bring forth fruit. The Gardener approaches each type of soil and deliberately speaks in a way that exposes what is resistant to His will. Hard, thorny, and rocky terrain are exposed and there is the opportunity to repent to hearing with faith.

Question: Are you able to recognize each soil type? In others? What about in yourself?

209. *Abiding*

"Just as the Father has loved Me, I have also loved you; abide in My love." ~ John 15:9

"I am the true vine, and My Father is the vine dresser. Every branch in Me that does not bear fruit, He takes away; and every branch that bears fruit, He prunes it, that it may bear more fruit…Abide in Me, and I in you. As the branch cannot bear fruit of itself, unless it abides in the vine, so neither can you, unless you abide in Me" (John 15:1-2,4). In the parable of the vine, the Lord presents to us the way of sustaining the life He has entrusted to us. We are to live a merged life with the Father, a merged life with the Son, and a merged life with the Holy Spirit. We are to draw our daily breath and sustenance from the vitally of this relationship, and His life will perform His will through us. Rather than performing good works for God, we become the means of His works being released through us. *"If you abide in Me, and My words abide in you, ask whatever you wish, and it shall be done for you"* (John 15:7). There is a holy participation God offers to His people in this parable. May we be those who believe and ask.

Question: When do you experience the greatest communion with the Lord?

---

210. In Famine

*"The righteous man will flourish like the palm
tree, he will grow like a cedar in Lebanon. Planted
in the house of the Lord, they will flourish in the
courts of our God." ~ Psalm 92:12-13*

It is promised in the book of Amos that *"… days are coming,
declares the Lord God, when I will send a famine on the land, not a
famine for bread or a thirst for water, but rather for hearing the
words of the Lord. And people will stagger from sea to sea, and from
the north even to the east; they will go to and fro to seek the word of
the Lord, but they will not find it"* (Amos 8:11-12). Famine is an
extreme scarcity of food which leads to starvation. It can be
brought about through crop failure, hostile weather
conditions, population imbalance, and government policies.
Lives are lost, and children perish in a time of famine.
Extreme disobedience to the way and will of God produced
these conditions in the Old Testament. While people find
themselves languishing in the spiritual poverty and famine
they are enduring, God invites us into the realms of His
Garden *"How blessed is the man who does not walk in the counsel
of the wicked … but his delight is in the law of the Lord, and in His
law he meditates day and night. And he will be like a tree firmly
planted by streams of water, which yields its fruit in its season, and
its leaf does not wither; and in whatever he does, he prospers"*
(Psalm 1:1-3).

*Question: Are you being spiritually sustained in the midst of whatever
situations you are currently suffering?*

211. Tree of Life

*"And by the river on its bank, on one side and on
the other, will grow all kinds of trees for food. Their
leaves will not wither, and their fruit will not fail.
They will bear every month because their water
flows from the sanctuary, and their fruit will be for
food and their leave for healing." ~ Ezekiel 47:12*

There is an image in the Genesis account of Creation that is
seen in its fullness at the completion of the book of Revelation.
The Tree of Life seems central to the story of God, and
especially as we see it fulfilled in Christ. After the fall and
mankind's exile from the Garden, cherubim were stationed to
guard the way to the Tree of Life. We might think it was God's
intention to permanently keep us from the Tree—instead, it
was to mark the path for our eventual return. During the final
chapters of scripture, the Tree of Life emerges as a central
focus of the Heavenly Kingdom. *"And He showed me a river of
the water of life, clear as crystal, coming from the throne of God and
of the Lamb, in the middle of its street. And on either side of the river
was the tree of life, bearing twelve kinds of fruit, yielding its fruit
every month; and the leaves of the tree were for the healing of the
nations"* (Revelation 22:1-2). This imagery describes a time
when we attain to our full spiritual maturity. Then we
continually bear His fruit and accomplish His purposes, not
just individually, but corporately. When the Spirit moves in a
multitude the result impacts nations.

*Question: Consider one way that the Lord is bearing His fruit in you and
through you. How is He sustaining that fruit?*

212. Life from the Stump

"Then a shoot will spring from the stem of Jesse,
and a branch from his roots will bear fruit."
~ Isaiah 11:1

A number of years ago, the Lord said to me, "If you will give up what you are satisfied with, I will give you what you are hungry for." This came in the midst of a very fruitful year, spiritually. At His direction, I left a ministry position in order to walk in obedience to Him, certain it would be a season of great blessing. Instead, the darkest season of my entire walk with Him commenced. I endured three months of silence in prayer, dryness in the scriptures, and darkness over my spirit. While away on retreat, I began to hear again through the voice of Job. *"For there is hope for a tree, when it is cut down, that it will sprout again, and its shoots will not fail. Though its roots grow old in the ground, and its stump dies in the dry soil, at the scent of water it will flourish and put forth springs like a plant"* (Job 14:7-9). I had not understood that when a death takes place to an old way, there is often a tomb time before the new life comes forth. When a seed is sown into the earth, the old covering has to die before new life is released. The stump had to wait for the scent of water, but it rose again to new life.

Question: Have you ever experienced a severe pruning from the Lord?

Part 8

Types

213. Puzzle Pieces

"Now these things happened as examples
for us...." ~ I Corinthians 10:6

From the beginning of Genesis to the fulfillment of Revelation, the Lord has sought to teach us His ways through the narrative of scripture. Using images, types, and symbols, God displayed Himself in the Old Testament in such a way that when He was "God in flesh appearing", He would be recognizable. Saint Augustine declared that the Old Testament was the New Testament concealed, and the New Testament was the Old Testament revealed. They are meant to be one merged revelation of God; companion volumes that are studied together.

There are a variety of children's games that are played by identifying where a "match" is for an image you turn up on a card. If you find and remember where each image is, then a match can be made and you win that hand. Scripture can be unfolded in a similar manner as we discover a story in the Old Testament that is fulfilled in Christ. And an identity that Jesus takes for Himself in the New Testament that was first seen in the Old Testament.

Question: What kind of learner are you?

214. Shadow of Divine Provision

"For the Law, since it has only a shadow of the
good things to come and not the very form of things,
can never by the same sacrifices year by year, which
they offer continually, make perfect those
who draw near." ~ Hebrews 10:1

The Old Testament is a copy and shadow of God's divine provision for redemption. Sometimes, if we take a closer look at the copy, we can understand, in fuller measure, all that was revealed in Christ. God displayed, in earthly patterns, clear and accurate pictures for Israel (and us) to understand. If you only study the New Testament, then you can miss much of the significance of seeing Jesus as the High Priest, or the Son of David, or as the Bread which came down from heaven. By looking at the Old Testament description of the Exodus from Egypt, we have a roadmap for our own spiritual journey. When we discover what the shadow points to, we will always have a fuller revelation of Christ and His ways.

Question: *How can you tell if something is symbolic, an element that is a type?*

215. Indwelling Spirit

*"And to know the love of Christ which surpasses
knowledge, that you may be filled up to all the
fullness of God." ~ Ephesians 3:19*

In the Old Testament the Holy Spirit came upon men—
working on them from above. In the New Testament, the
Spirit enters, abides, and indwells. When God demonstrated
the movement of His Spirit through the pillar of fire, and later
through the tabernacle and the temple, we saw the Lord functioning from above, and then within. Imagine the mindset of
the Jews listening to Jesus in John 14:16-17: *"And I will ask the
Father, and He will give you another Helper, that He may be with
you forever; that is the Spirit of Truth, whom the world cannot receive, because it does not behold Him or know Him, but you know
Him because He abides with you, and will be in you."* God was
holy, unapproachable, and set apart from man, and only the
priests were given access. Now He abide within the human
heart. With the giving of the Holy Spirit, and filling of the
church, man is restored to his original design. With the indwelling Spirit, God once more puts on flesh, and tabernacles
in our midst.

Question: *Have you placed any limitation on what the Holy Spirit can
do in your life?*

216. Two Ways

*"Enter by the narrow gate; for the gate is wide,
and the way is broad that leads to destruction, and
many are those who enter by it. For the gate is
small, and the way is narrow that leads to life, and
few are those who find it." ~ Matthew 7:13-14*

New Testament believers often throw off the Law, rather than display how Jesus completely fulfilled it. If the Law is only viewed as a list of do's and don'ts, we miss one of the ways the Father tried to demonstrate Himself to His children, and establish patterns for walking in Him. By taking a closer look at the Old Testament narrative, we begin to discover a pattern that shows up throughout Sripture. There are two ways. In Genesis, there were two trees in the Garden. One was forbidden and one was blessed. In the stories of the patriarchs, there was a blessed son, and one who rebelled or disappointed the father. In Proverbs, the wise are in contrast to the foolish. When Jesus taught, He declared that there was a wide way that led to destruction, and a narrow way that led to life. In the final chapters of Revelation, there is the destruction of the wicked woman of Babylon, and the exaltation of the Bride of Christ. When two ways are mentioned in scripture, it is often for the sake of contrast. In seeing the difference between the wicked and the righteous, we learn to be led.

Question: How did you learn to see Jesus in the Old Testament?

217. The Dove (1)

*"Thou dost send forth Thy Spirit, they are
created; and Thou dost renew the face
of the ground." ~ Psalm 104:30*

The first appearance of the Holy Spirit in the Old Testament takes place in Genesis 1:2: *"And the earth was formless and void, and darkness was over the surface of the deep; and the Spirit of God was moving over the surface of the waters."* While the creation was not yet fully formed, the Holy Spirit began to brood over the waters. Seven chapters later, during another time of desolation, the great flood, the dove appears once more as a type of the Spirit. As the flood comes to an end, Noah sends out two birds to see if dry land has appeared yet. The first bird released was a raven. It passed back and forth across the waters, but found no place for its foot; symbolizing evil in vain pursuit of rest. When the dove was later released, it returned with an olive branch in its mouth—as a symbol of peace between God and man. Under the Law, birds were classified as clean (dove) and unclean (raven). They are types of two kinds of spirits that access the heavenly places. As we discover the meaning of types, we have greater understanding of what pleases God.

Question: What can we learn about the nature of the Holy Spirit, knowing that He is illustrated by a dove?

218. The Dove (2)

"Like flying birds so the Lord of hosts will protect Jerusalem. He will protect and deliver it; He will pass over and rescue it." ~ Isaiah 31:5

The first appearance of the Holy Spirit in the New Testament is the dove at the baptism of Jesus. *"And after being baptized, Jesus went up immediately from the water; and behold, the heavens were opened, and he saw the Spirit of God descending as a dove, and coming upon Him ..."* (Matthew 3:16). The Holy Spirit is sent through an opening in heaven's window, and found a place for his foot to rest on the Son of Man. Just as the dove sent from the ark was looking for a place for its foot to rest and begin a new creation, the Spirit is sent from the Father to begin a new Kingdom. The Father finds in the life of His Son, the last Adam, a place for a new beginning. Jesus later sends forth His disciples with the instructions: *"... I send you out as sheep in the midst of wolves; therefore be shrewd as serpents and innocent as doves"* (Matthew 10:16). We go forth with the same mission and are to represent all that the Spirit was sent for.

Question: *What is the nature of the situation when the Lord sends a dove to symbolize His presence?*

219. Gentle and Pure

*"But the wisdom from above is first pure, then
peaceable, gentle, reasonable, full of mercy and good
fruits, unwavering, without hypocrisy."*
~ James 3:17

Two qualities of the Holy Spirit are underscored as we observe the dove. The first quality is purity. Being identified as a clean bird, the dove is the first to set foot on a cleansed creation. The second is the quality of gentleness, a meekness with divine origin. This gentle creature approaches the creation as the Comforter—tender, gentle, full of love, lowliness, and quietness. The Holy Spirit does not enter our lives in order to dominate. We are given the Spirit as a gift—to live a merged life with Him, receiving His companionship and leadership.

"But the Helper, the Holy Spirit, whom the Father will send in My name, He will teach you all things, and bring to your remembrance all that I said to you" (John 14:26). The Spirit does not come with a great flapping of wings, but finds that one who has quieted their soul to receive Him. This reflected beautifully in the Greek word translated "Helper": *parakletos*, one called alongside to help.

Question: *When or how do you find yourself most sensitive to the presence and movement of the Holy Spirit?*

220. First Breath

"By the word of the Lord the heavens were made,
and by the breath of His mouth all their host."
~ Psalm 33:6

In the Sermon on the Mount, Jesus tells the people to look at the birds of the air, and to consider the lilies of the field. There is instruction and wisdom available if we are able to see what God is saying to us. Turning once more to the creation story, we find a type of the Holy Spirit. In Genesis, the days of creation come after the moving of the Spirit of God. In Hebrew, the word for spirit is *ruah*. But it can also mean wind and, interestingly, breath. Each day of creation, God spoke. By His powerful and living Word (breath-spirit) all things came into being. Then, as Adam is formed of the dust, God breaths into his nostrils, and he is quickened to life. *"Then the Lord God formed man of dust from the ground, and breathed into his nostrils the breath of life; and man became a living being"* (Genesis 2:7). Life is transferred from deity to humanity by breath. Breath in equals life. Breath out equals death. When we are born from above, receiving the gift of salvation, we receive the Breath of God, His precious Holy Spirit. We are quickened to newness of life, becoming a new creation.

Question: You have heard the phrase, "to be out of breath". What does it mean to be spiritually out of breath?

221. New Breath

*"The wind blows where it wishes and you hear the
sound of it, but do not know where it comes from
and where it is going; so is everyone who is born of
the Spirit." ~ John 3:8*

Fallen creation clings to the visible realm, that is the seen,
the natural, physical realm, the known. For the Christian, new
birth is an exciting time of being sensitive once more to the
unseen, invisible realm. When Jesus breathes on His disciples
in John 20:22, He is once more God the Creator, speaking into
existence the formation of His Body. As Jesus breathes on
them, there is a fulfillment of the imagery given in Ezekiel's
prophecy concerning the valley of dry bones (Ezekiel 37:1-10).
The first breath, released over the dead bones, causes them to
rattle together into one body. The second prophecy releases a
wind/breath (*ruah*) that raises them into a mighty army. After
Jesus breathes on His disciples, He instructs them to wait to
receive power from the outpouring of the Holy Spirit—released as a mighty wind on the day of Pentecost. His first
breath makes us one, and His second breath fills us with His
life and power.

Question: *As you read the prophecy in Ezekiel, can you discover anything about the gift of the Holy Spirit to the church?*

222. Holy Breath

*"The Spirit of God has made me, and the breath of
the Almighty gives me life." ~ Job 33:4*

Two keys are gained as we consider the *breath* of God. God
is triune in His being and essence. When Jesus prays for us in
John 17:21-23, He is praying for oneness: *"... that they may all
be one; even as Thou, Father, art in Me, and I in Thee, that they also
may be in Us; that the world may believe that Thou didst send Me.
And the glory which Thou has given Me I have given to them; that
they may be one, just as We are one; I in them, and Thou in Me, that
they may be perfected in unity, that the world may know that Thou
didst send Me, and didst love them, even as Thou didst love Me."*
This prayer for oneness was designed to return us to our original design, our means for walking with God. As Jesus
breathes upon His disciples, they are brought into this union
with the Godhead. The second breath, on Pentecost, released
the power of God to indwell and move through His Body, an
exceeding great army.

*Question: What have you been taught about the baptism of the Holy
Spirit? Did you experience any power as the result of your baptism?*

223. The Fire of God

"For behold, the Lord will come in fire and His
chariots like the whirlwind, to render His anger
with fury, and His rebuke with flames of fire."
~ Isaiah 66: 15

There is a type of the Holy Spirit found in Exodus that is directly linked to our own spiritual journey. God expresses Himself visibly through fire in Exodus. He appears as the burning bush which is aflame but not consumed, the pillar of fire and cloud, fire on the Mount, and the lamp of His presence in the tabernacle. Fire, throughout the scriptures, symbolizes the presence and power of God. Fire is an agent of purification: *"… each man's work will become evident; for the day will show it, because it is to be revealed with fire; and the fire itself will test the quality of each man's work"* (1 Corinthians 3:13). It is used to test and to refine. It is also a source of light. As we learn to be led by the Holy Spirit, He will be our teacher, bringing us into the ways of God. He will serve as an agent of purification for our own hearts and minds. He will enlighten our hearts, so we can learn how to walk by the Spirit.

Question: What worship experience has been holy ground for you?

224. Burning Bush

*"... And with the choice things of the earth and
its fullness, and the favor of Him who dwelt
in the bush ..." ~ Deuteronomy 33:16*

From the time he was an infant, Moses was raised in the house of Pharaoh, educated in all the learning of the Egyptians. When he approached the age of forty, *"it entered his mind to visit his brethren, the sons of Israel"* (Acts 7:23). God was stirring in the heart of Moses as he looked upon his brethren. Though God would one day use His servant as a great prophet and deliverer, Moses would still need to learn that deliverance would not come from his own hands. After attempting deliverance by his own strength, he fled to Midian, where he lived as an exile for the next forty years. For forty years, he was raised to think like the world; then, for another forty years he unlearned his former ways. *"And after forty years had passed, an angel appeared to him in the wilderness of Mount Sinai, in the flame of a burning thorn bush"* (Acts 7:30). Turning aside to see this wonder, he heard the Lord speak: *"Take off the sandals from your feet, for the place on which you are standing is holy ground"* (Acts 7:33). An encounter with God changes everything. Where He is, is holy ground. Moses is told to remove his shoes in order stand in God's presence. He is to adopt a posture of humility; make himself vulnerable. It is as though the only way to appear before God is naked.

Question: Have you ever had a burning bush experience in your life?

225. Pillar of Fire

"And with a pillar of cloud Thou didst lead them
by day, and with a pillar of fire by night to light for
them the way in which they were to go."
~ Nehemiah 9:12

At the time of creation, we were entrusted with a free will, but we were designed to be led. Following the exile from the Garden of Eden, humanity lived lost. Without the Spirit to navigate life, each turned to their own ways, until the Lord intervened. Later, Israel came to represent all humankind as God ransomed His people from the cruel bondage of Egypt, and then began to lead them on a journey to the Promised Land. Numbers 9:15-23 rehearses the instruction for God's people to follow: *"... So it was continuously; the cloud would cover it by day, and the appearance of fire by night ..."* When the pillar moved, the people moved. When the pillar remained in one place, the people remained camped. Whether it was for a day, or a month, or a year, when the pillar moved, the people moved. They needed to practice following. This visible manifestation was what God chose to reorient His children to His commands. Jesus instructs us in following the movement of the Holy Spirit by only saying what He heard the Father saying, doing what He saw the Father doing, and never acting on His own initiative. Now it is our turn. Come, and follow.

Question: How do you as an individual, a family, or a congregation, apprehend and follow the movement of the Holy Spirit?

226. Fire on the Mount

*"And to the eyes of the sons of Israel the
appearance of the glory of the Lord was like a
consuming fire on the mountain top."*
~ Exodus 24:17

When God called His people from Egypt to Himself, they followed the pillar to Mount Sinai. This became the place where heaven and earth would meet. In this initial call to worship, the entire congregation was invited to become a nation of priests. *"You yourselves have seen what I did to the Egyptians, and how I bore you on eagles' wings, and brought you to Myself. Now then, if you will indeed obey My voice and keep My covenant, then you shall be My own possession among all the peoples, for all the earth is Mine; and you shall be to Me a kingdom of priests and a holy nation"* (Exodus 19:4-6). God appeared to Moses on the mountain in fire and smoke that ascended like a furnace. *"And the Lord came down on Mount Sinai, to the top of the mountain; and the Lord called Moses to the top of the mountain, and Moses went up"* (Exodus 19:20). The Law was given on the mountain, and before Moses reached the bottom, the covenant was violated with the idol of the golden calf. The priesthood was transferred to one tribe and remained so until God made a New Covenant with man. With this new agreement, we are once more called into our identity as a nation and a priesthood for Him.

Question: *Do you see God's holiness and His desire for holiness as a burden or a gift?*

---

227. Above the Tent

*"And there appeared to them tongues as of fire
distributing themselves, and they rested on each one
of them." ~ Acts 2:3*

When Israel created the tabernacle in the wilderness according to the likeness shown to Moses on the mount, the Lord blessed it with His presence. *"And it came about when the priests came from the holy place, that the cloud filled the house of the Lord, so that the priests could not stand to minister because of the cloud, for the glory of the Lord filled the house of the Lord"* (1 Kings 8:10-11). This tent of meeting was a place of communion with the God, pitched outside the camp. It was set apart for the sake of His holiness, so the people had to separate themselves from the camp to draw near with sacrifice. From Mount Sinai onward, Israel preferred Moses drawing near to God and listening on their behalf (Deuteronomy 5:24-27, Exodus 33:9-11). In Christ, we are called to be worshippers, to draw near to the throne of grace, and meet with our God. He is holy and has made us holy through the blood of His Son. On the day of Pentecost, His new tabernacle, the Body of Christ, was set apart as Holy to the Lord, with tongues of fire marking us—the new place for His glory to dwell.

Question: *Considering the four ways God demonstrated His presence with fire (burning bush, pillar of fire, fire on the mountain, and the lamp of his presence), which one is most like your current walk with Him?*

228. Glory Withdrawn and Restored

*"But we all, with unveiled face beholding as in a
mirror the glory of the Lord, are being transformed
into the same image from glory to glory, just as
from the Lord, the Spirit." ~ 2 Corinthians 3:18*

When Adam and Eve sinned, they found themselves naked
and ashamed. Sensing that they were uncovered, they hid
from God. When their connection to the Father was disrupted
His glory was withdrawn, and they were responding to His
absence. Prior to God's glory being a visible covering for the
tabernacle, it had covered His intended residence: man. When
Moses was exposed to the glory of God, he had to veil His
face, due to the residual effects from the exposure. *"... Moses
used to put a veil over his face that the sons of Israel might not look
intently at the end of what was fading away"* (2 Corinthians 3:13).
He represented the Law, described in 2 Corinthians 3:7-11:
*"But if the ministry of death, in letters engraved on stones, came
with glory, so that the sons of Israel could not look intently at the
face of Moses because of the glory of his face, fading as it was, how
shall the ministry of the Spirit fail to be even more with glory? For
if the ministry of condemnation has glory, much more does the ministry of righteousness about in glory. For indeed what had glory, in
this case has no glory on account of the glory that surpasses it. For
if that which fades away was with glory, much more that which remains is in glory."*

Question: *Do you recognize any ways in yourself that you live like the
Old Covenant, rather than the New Covenant?*

249

229. Living Water

*"... Whoever drinks of the water that I shall give
him shall never thirst; but the water that I shall give
him shall become in him a well of water springing
up to eternal life." ~ John 4:14*

When Jesus passed through Samaria, He paused for a drink at the village well and had a conversation with a thirsty woman. *"If you knew the gift of God, and who it is who says to you, 'Give Me a drink,' you would have asked Him, and He would have given you living water"* (John 4:10). In this small exchange, Jesus alludes to a type of Himself from the Exodus journey from Egypt. To quench the thirst of the nation in the desert, Moses was instructed to take his staff and strike a rock to bring forth water to drink. God stands on that rock, so when the rock is struck by the staff of God, God Himself is struck. Water pours forth and the nation drinks. Later, when the people needed water, Moses in anger struck the rock again, though he had been instructed to speak to the rock to release the water this time. For this breech of obedience, Moses was forbidden entry to the Promised Land. Why? Striking the rock—and thus God—the first time, brought forth life for the people to drink. After Christ was struck once on our behalf, we only need to ask for His living water to be released. At the well in Samaria, Jesus offered the opportunity for the Samaritan woman to ask for a drink, and receive the gift of Living Water—Christ the Lord.

Question: *Do you ever assume you know the will of God concerning a situation?*

230. The Anointing

*"And you shall put the holy garments on Aaron
and anoint him and consecrate him, that he may
minister as a priest to Me." ~ Exodus 40:13*

Oil was used in the Old Testament for anointing, which was a time when priests would rub oil on someone to set them apart for ministry, to consecrate them for service, or as an action following a prayer for healing. This oil represents the Spirit's work being released to and through the life of the anointed individual. When the Spirit came forth from heaven and rested on Jesus, following His baptism, the Father declared that He was well-pleased with His Son. This moment of anointing brought to fruition the prophecy concerning Jesus in Isaiah 61. *"The Spirit of the Lord is upon Me, because He anointed Me to preach the gospel to the poor. He has sent Me to proclaim release to the captives, and recovery of sight to the blind, to set free those who are downtrodden, to proclaim the favorable year of the Lord"* (Luke 4:18-19, quoting Isaiah 61:1-2). Set apart and empowered from on high, the Lord lived in the fullness of His Father's anointing.

Question: *Have you had prayer to set you apart for the ministry God is entrusting to you?*

231. Bread of God

"Jesus said to them, 'I am the bread of life; he who comes to Me shall not hunger, and he who believes in Me shall never thirst.'" ~ John 6:35

Bread is the sustenance for every civilization, and is also a type of Christ. The manna in the wilderness (Exodus 16:4), the fine flour in the offerings (Leviticus 2:4), and the showbread on the altar of the tabernacle (Exodus 25:30), were all prophetic pictures of Jesus and all that He would accomplish. Jesus spoke to those who sought Him for a sign, *"Truly, truly, I say to you, it is not Moses who has given you the bread out of heaven, but it is My Father who gives you the true bread out of heaven. For the bread of God is that which comes down out of heaven, and gives life to the world"* (John 6:32-33). He describes the nature of His relationship with the disciples in terms of bread. *"I am the bread of life. Your fathers ate the manna in the wilderness, and they died. This is the bread which comes down out of heaven, so that one may eat of it and not die. I am the living bread that came down out of heaven; if anyone eats of this bread, he shall live forever; and the bread also which I shall give for the life of the world is My flesh ... he who eats My flesh and drinks My blood has eternal life, and I will raise him up on the last day. For My flesh is true food, and My blood is true drink. He who eats My flesh and drinks My blood abides in Me, and I in him"* (John 6:48-51, 54-56). We are invited into the fulfillment of this declaration every time we participate in the Lord's Table.

Question: *In what ways is the church called to be a demonstration of bread for a hungry world?*

232. Feasts

"These are the appointed times of the Lord, holy convocation so which you shall proclaim at the times appointed for them." ~ Leviticus 23:4

Holiday feasts in our country are built around food, while the feasts of the Lord were built around worship. Each of the seven feasts of the Lord had specific instructions for how they were to be celebrated. The Hebrew word for feasts means "appointed times", and so their timing and frequency were significant opportunities to meet with God. Each of these feasts pointed to a spiritual reality to be fulfilled in Jesus. Therefore, their meaning, and what they celebrated, tell the story of God's redemption in Christ. Four of the seven holidays take place in the spring of the year. They were fulfilled in the first coming of the Messiah. Every minute detail included in the celebrating of each feast was satisfied in the way that Jesus fulfilled them. The last three take place in the fall, at the time of harvest, and will be fulfilled at His second coming. Passover, the Feast of Unleavened Bread, the Feast of Firstfruits, and Pentecost have all seen their fulfillment. Rosh Hashanah (the Feast of Trumpets), Yom Kippur, and the Feast of Tabernacles, are all still dress rehearsals—waiting for their finale.

Question: *How can the Feasts of the Lord be integrated into the practices of the church?*

233. Rock in the Desert

"And they remembered that God was their rock,
and the Most High God their Redeemer."
~ Psalm 78:35

Twice, during the Exodus journey through the wilderness to the Promised Land, God provided water from a rock. In Exodus 17, Moses struck the rock, and abundant water came forth, providing drink for all. In the second incident, in Numbers 20, Moses was instructed to speak to the rock, and water would be released. Due to his anger with the people, Moses struck the rock, as he had the first time. God released water, but disciplined Moses for his disobedience. Moses marred the imagery of these two events by failing to follow the instructions of the Lord. Jesus would be struck once, releasing a river of Life to fallen man. Following His sacrifice, we may *speak* to the Rock, and request living water for our thirst. *"...If any man is thirsty, let him come to Me and drink. He who believes in Me, as the Scripture said, 'From his innermost being shall flow rivers of living water'"* (John 7:37-38). Jesus is the fulfillment of this holy rock. *"... and all drank the same spiritual drink, for they were drinking from a spiritual rock which followed them, and the rock was Christ"* (1 Corinthians 10:4).

Question: Have you ever found yourself in a spiritual desert? How did Jesus become a well for you there?

234. *Mountain of the Lord*

"Even those I will bring to My holy mountain,
and make them joyful in My house of prayer … for
My house will be called a house of prayer for all the
peoples." ~ Isaiah 56:7

From creation onward, the Lord has used mountains and high places to establish authority and invite man to commune with Him. Satan recognized high places as valuable territory for worship. With these words, he described his intention to rival Almighty God, *"I will ascend to heaven; I will raise my throne above the stars of God, and I will sit on the mount of assembly in the recesses of the north"* (Isaiah 14:13). In the book of Daniel, there is a story about the king of Babylon, Nebuchadnezzar, who had a dream about future kingdoms: Babylon, Persia, Greece, and Rome. Then there is a description of a future divine kingdom—a stone cut from a mountain—that would overthrow all the others (Daniel 2:44-45). Both Isaiah (Isaiah 2:2) and Micah referred to this same mountain. Micah 4:1-2 states, *"And it will come about in the last days that the mountain of the house of the Lord will be established as the chief of the mountains. It will be raised above the hills, and the peoples will stream to it. And many nations will come and say, 'Come and let us go up to the mountain of the Lord and to the house of the God of Jacob, that He may teach us about His ways and that we may walk in His paths.'"* The transfiguration of Jesus is our opportunity to see this type fulfilled.

Question: Have you had a " mountain top" spiritual experience?

235. Names of Places

"... but at the place where the Lord your God
chooses to establish His name ..."
~ Deuteronomy 16:6

Names of places in the Scripture often reflect more than a physical description of the territory. If we look a little deeper, there are spiritual truths to be mined. Let's look at Gilgal and how it was named. Upon entering the Promised Land, Joshua circumcised the sons of Israel. *"Now it came about when they had finished circumcising all of the nation, that they remained in their places in the camp until they were healed. Then the Lord said to Joshua, 'Today, I have rolled away the reproach of Egypt from you.' So the name of that place is called Gilgal to this day"* (Joshua 5:8-9). Gilgal was a place for judgment of the flesh and became associated with power over evil. This is the very location where Saul forfeited his leadership. He was to wait for Samuel there, but grew impatient, took the role of the priesthood upon himself, and offered the burnt sacrifice. He was exposed as a fleshly leader, and could not keep the kingdom. Throughout Israel's history, Gilgal became a testing ground for following the Lord.

Question: *Do you know what your name means? Does it have any family significance? Any spiritual significance?*

236. Circumcision—Flesh and Heart

*"… for we are the true circumcision, who worship
in the Spirit of God and glory in Christ Jesus and
put no confidence in the flesh …" ~ Philippians 3:3*

In the Old Testament, God revealed through circumcision His plan to restore the hearts of man. Circumcision was the action of "cutting away the flesh", and was a part of the covenant that God made with Abraham. It was a picture of removing our covering of flesh, allowing our hidden places to be exposed, and an act of submission to an authority beyond ourselves. *"… and in Him you were also circumcised with a circumcision made without hands, in the removal of the body of the flesh by the circumcision of Christ; having been buried with Him in baptism, in which you were also raised up with Him through faith in the working of God, who raised Him from the dead. And when you were dead in your transgressions and the uncircumcision of your flesh, He made you alive together with Him, having forgiven us all our transgression…"* (Colossians 2:11-13). Paul also explains in Romans 2:28-29, *"For he is not a Jew who is one outwardly; neither is circumcision that which is outward in the flesh. But he is a Jew who is one inwardly; and circumcision is that which is of the heart, by the Spirit, not by the letter; and his praise is not from men, but from God."*

Question: *What has the Lord used to cut away old things from your life?*

237. Clothed from Above

"And behold, I am sending forth the promise of
My Father upon you; but you are to stay in the city
until you are clothed with power from on high."
~ *Luke 24:49*

We were designed to dwell in oneness; a merged life with the Living God. Apart from Him, Adam (mankind) immediately recognized that he was naked and hid himself, hiding among leaves rather than being wrapped in glory.

Lesser things continued to cover man until the Spirit was poured out at Pentecost. Glory from heaven could once more rest upon men. Whether they recognize it or not, all of mankind has a longing to live into our original design. *"For we know that if the earthly tent which is our house is torn down, we have a building from God, a house not made with hands, eternal in the heavens. For indeed in this house we groan, longing to be clothed with our dwelling from heaven; inasmuch as we, having put it on, shall not be found naked. For indeed while we are in this tent, we groan, being burdened, because we do not want to be unclothed, but to be clothed, in order that what is mortal may be swallowed up by life"* (2 Corinthians 5:1-4).

Question: Do you struggle with shame? Do you have any hiding strategies?

238. Ark of His Presence

"But when Christ appeared as a high priest of the
good things to come, He entered through the greater
and more perfect tabernacle, not made with hands,
that is to say, not of this creation." ~ Hebrews 9:11

In the Old Testament, the ark of the covenant was the place of God's presence. He was among His people, yet separate from them due to their sin and His holiness. The protocol for sacrifice, service, and worship allowed Him to abide with Israel. When Israel became apostate, God withdrew, and also withdrew His glory.

The imagery of God 'tabernacling' among men was fulfilled when the Son of God put on flesh and dwelt among us. While Mary carried the Word in her womb, she served as the ark of His presence once more among His people. *"Now all this took place that what was spoken by the Lord through the prophet might be fulfilled, saying, 'Behold, the virgin shall be with child, and shall bear a son, and they shall call His name Immanuel,' which translated means, 'God with us'"* (Matthew 1:22-23). *"And the Word became flesh, and dwelt (tabernacled) among us, and we beheld His glory, glory as of the only begotten from the Father, full of grace and truth"* (John 1:14). Following the crucifixion, resurrection, and ascension of Jesus, God poured out His Spirit upon a Body formed to carry His holy presence into the world.

Question: Does the church look more like the Temple or the Tabernacle in the world today?

---

239. Baptism

"He saved us, not on the basis of deeds which we
have done in righteousness, but according to His
mercy, by the washing of regeneration and
renewing by the Holy Spirit ..." ~ Titus 3:5

When John the Baptist called for people to express their repentance through baptism, he introduced a different pattern to Israel for the cleansing of their sin. His father, Zacharias, had prophesied, *"And you child, will be called the prophet of the Most High; for you will go on before the Lord to prepare His ways; to give to His people the knowledge of salvation by the forgiveness of their sins ..."* (Luke 1:76-77). Sin offerings were required at the temple in Jerusalem, where gifts were offered according to the Law. *"For the Law, since it has only a shadow of the good things to come and not the very form of things, can never by the same sacrifices year by year, which they offer continually, make perfect those who draw near. Otherwise, would they not have ceased to be offered, because the worshippers, having once been cleansed, would no longer have had consciousness of sins?"* (Hebrews 10:1-2). As John the Baptist stood in the Jordan, he illustrated a new pattern for the people of God modeled after the Old Testament tabernacle. In the temple was a large basin on a pedestal containing water for the cleansing of the priests and sacrifices. It was called the *laver.* Baptism is the new laver, inviting a priesthood of believers to draw near.

Question: What is one of the first things you remember about stepping into newness of life?

240. Wilderness and Promised Land

"Now these things happened as examples for us ...." ~ I Corinthians 10:6

The deliverance of Israel from Egypt and their journey to the Promised Land, is an illustration of our own spiritual journey. We too, were held in cruel bondage under a wicked ruler, before our deliverance from the captivity of sin. The Lord exercised His power and authority at the cross, triumphing over the ruler of this world, that He might serve as our Passover Lamb. As His blood is applied to our hearts, the angel of death passes over, and we are liberated. We are set free from one kingdom and transferred to another. The Holy Spirit is given, and like the pillar of fire, leads us on our journey toward the Kingdom. Leaving Egypt is not the same as entering the Promised Land. There is a process of learning to repent from (leave Egypt) and how to repent to (enter the Promised Land). Walking by the Spirit is the lesson that must be learned. Failure to learn how to follow could keep us wandering in the wilderness—and thinking the desert is the Kingdom.

Question: Do you recognize an area where the Lord is teaching you how to "repent to"?

241. Sand and Stars

*"... in order that in Christ Jesus the blessing of
Abraham might come to the Gentiles, so that we
might receive the promise of the Spirit
through faith." ~ Galatians 3:14*

One of the ways that a type is recognized is that it takes a natural illustration and gives it spiritual significance. This is true for the promise made to Abraham, that his descendants would be as numerous the "dust of the earth" (Genesis 13:16), and as the "stars of the heavens" (Genesis 15:5). He is promised heirs that will be born through his natural life, with Sarah, too old to conceive, miraculously becoming pregnant and giving birth. From the giving of this promise, to the present, Israel has multiplied, filling the earth as its "dust".

We also see that father Abraham became the father of faith. *"Even so Abraham believed God, and it was reckoned to him as righteousness. Therefore, be sure that it is those who are of faith who are sons of Abraham. And the scripture, foreseeing that God would justify the Gentiles by faith, preached the gospel beforehand to Abraham, saying, 'All the nations shall be blessed in you.' So then those who are of faith are blessed with Abraham, the believer"* (Galatians 3:6-9). We are participants in the second promise being satisfied—those counted as the stars of the heavens.

Question: *Has God made a promise to you that will affect others in your life?*

242. Altars

*"We have an altar, from which those who serve
the tabernacle have no right to eat ... through Him
then, let us continually offer up a sacrifice of praise
to God, that is, the fruit of lips that give thanks to
His name." ~ Hebrews 13:10, 15*

Altars are specific locations set apart for worship and sacrifice. In the Old Testament, they were a place of communion (intimacy and friendship) between God and people. They were often built in places where God stepped into time and met with man. Altars were also a place of consecration. The tabernacle contained several altars, representing atonement and worship.

When God's people gather to pray, they are establishing an invisible altar, where they can offer their lives as a living sacrifice. In the book of Acts, we read about the church gathering to fast and pray—making their hearts an altar to God. They presented their lives as their reasonable service of worship (Romans 12:1). Commissioning of the first missionaries was the result. I Peter 2:9 states, *"But you are a chosen race, a royal priesthood, a holy nation, a people for God's own possession, that you may proclaim the excellencies of Him who has called you out of darkness into His marvelous light ..."* A priesthood has now been gathered—the people of God set apart to worship and serve at the altar of the Living God.

Question: *Are there any physical locations that have been particularly significant in your spiritual journey?*

263

243. Wells

"I am the bread of life; he who comes to Me shall not hunger, and he who believes in Me shall never thirst." ~ John 6:35

Throughout Scripture, wells were a place of life and sustenance; a place of refreshment and quenched thirst. The first mention of a well in the Old Testament is in the story of Hagar. After she fled the presence of her mistress, Sarah, she was found by the angel of the Lord near a spring of water in the wilderness. He prophesied over her, and she proclaimed, *"Thou art a God who sees"* (Genesis 16:7-14). The well in the wilderness was named for this encounter: *Beer-Lahaina-roi*, which means "the well of the Living One who sees me".

Throughout the Old Testament, wells were contended for because they were central to daily living. In the New Testament wells are still important, but now wells are people. Jesus offered Himself as the drink to the woman who came to the well in Samaria, and declares over us, *"If any man is thirsty, let him come to Me and drink. He who believes in Me, as the scripture said, 'From his innermost being shall flow rivers of living water'"* (John 7:37-38). Just as our hearts are an altar as we minister to the Lord, our lives are living wells as we minister to people.

Question: Have you engaged with the Holy Spirit in such a way that you can be a source for His Life—that the Water of Life might flow from you to others who are thirsty?

Part 9

Submission

244. Introduced to Submission

"For He has put all things in subjection under His feet ..." ~ I Corinthians 15:27

A number of years ago, I was urged from multiple directions to write a book. Even in prayer, I sensed the Lord urging me toward this assignment. I finally yielded to this idea, and hoped that the Lord would be pleased with my response to Him. But I sensed that He wasn't. As I walked and prayed, I asked what was "off" — since I had agreed to do what He had asked of me. I heard His response to my prayer, "You didn't ask Me what the book was about." I thought I knew. I had been doing a significant amount of teaching on intimacy with Christ, so assumed the topic was clear. So, I asked Him, "What is the book supposed to be about?" I heard: "Submission." My response was, "I don't know anything about that." His response: "I know." A learning journey began that unfolded His intention for His creation. Submission is the state of our original design.

Question: What has the Lord used in your life to teach you about submission?

245. *The Way We Learn*

"And when all things are subjected to Him, then
the Son Himself also will be subjected to the One
who subjected all things to Him, that God may be
all in all." ~ I Corinthians 15:28

Most lessons about submission are aimed at women and children, but submission is for the entire church. This topic is so critical for our understanding that the Lord Himself came to demonstrate its power for us. *"Therefore, when He comes into the world, He says, 'Sacrifice and offering Thou hast not desired, but a body Thou hast prepared for Me; in whole burnt offerings and sacrifices for sin Thou hast taken no pleasure.' Then I said, 'Behold, I have come (in the roll of the book it is written of Me) to do Thy will, O God"* (Hebrews 10:5-7). We were created to be led by His Spirit. After living lives that had gone so far astray, we needed a living model of what submission looked like for sons. Christ's willingness to humble Himself and only say what He heard the Father saying, only do what He saw the Father doing, and to refrain from doing anything from His own initiative, was in stark contrast to the independence of His rebellious creation. This re-ordering of the world is what submission is all about.

Question: When do you find it most difficult to live in submission to someone?

---

246. Submission as Children

"Children, obey your parents . . . for this is right.
Honor your Father and Mother (which is the first
commandment with a promise), that it may be well
with you ...." ~ Ephesians 6:1-3

Luke tells us the story of how Jesus stayed behind in Jerusalem after traveling there with his parents to celebrate the Passover. His parents, discovering He was wasn't with them, return to Jerusalem to look for Him. When they find Him in the Temple, Jesus responded, *"Why is it that you were looking for Me? Did you not know that I had to be in My Father's house?"* Luke goes on, *"... and He went down with them, and came to Nazareth; and He continued in subjection to them; and His mother treasured all these things in her heart. And Jesus kept increasing in wisdom and stature, and in favor with God and men"* (Luke 2:49-52). Jesus' detour to the temple reflects the singular passion of His life and then places His zeal in the context of submission. He patiently explains His actions to His parents, then goes home and lives obediently. The God of the universe submitted to His human guardians.

Our relationship with our parents is where we first learn submission. From them, we learn how to yield to a will other than our own. A healthy understanding of that kind of yielding only comes when trust has developed between the parent and the child. As a result of living in submission to human parents, Jesus grew in wisdom and stature. That early training taught Him how to harmonize His behavior with the will of His Heavenly Father.

Question: *Did the discipline you received as a child accurately reflect the nature of the Heavenly Father?*

247. As a Servant

*"... My food is to do the will of Him who sent Me,
and to accomplish His work." ~ John 4:34*

As a Son, Christ demonstrated how to act like the Father, but Christ the servant teaches how to act on behalf of the Father. The role of the son draws life from "being," while the servant learns to defer his own purposes to those of another. The will of the master is the duty of the slave. Slaves must prepare themselves for the work and be consistently available to the master, ready to act on the work entrusted to them. The focus of the slave becomes how he spends his time, and on what.

A servant submitted to God is not a slave by compulsion, but a bond servant—one willingly indentured in a covenant of love. It is from this foundation and heart attitude that Christ-like ministry flows. As Jesus knelt before the disciples, washing their feet, a powerful demonstration for servant leadership was modeled. *"If I then, the Lord and the Teacher, washed your feet, you also ought to wash one another's feet. For I gave you an example that you also should do as I did to you. Truly, truly, I say to you, a slave is not greater than his master; neither is one who is sent greater than the one who sent him. If you know these things, you are blessed if you do them"* (John 13:14-17).

Question: Where have you seen a good example of servant leadership? In the church? In business? In government?

248. Bridal Submission

"... and be subject to one another in the fear of Christ. Wives, be subject to your own husbands, as to the Lord. For the husband is head of the wife, as Christ also is head of the church, He Himself being the Savior of the body. But as the church is subject to Christ, so also the wives ought to be to their husbands in everything."
~ Ephesians 5:21-24

The original intention of Creation was for mankind to participate in the triune fellowship at the center of the Kingdom of God. When Adam and Eve disobeyed, this fellowship became a mystery to mankind, not understood and not experienced. The resulting chaos has marred the connection between Creator and creation; and muddled the relationship between men and women. The blunder of Eden was forsaking submission to the only Being to whom it is rightfully due. When Eve was deceived toward independence and self-rule, unity was destroyed.

> *Through the Holy Spirit, man can make himself available to God, and through the Holy Spirit, God is prepared to make Himself available to man. The Spirit becomes the agent of mutual interavailability. All there is of God is available to every human being who is available to all there is of God...*
>
> *Major Ian Thomas*

This marked the beginning of rivalries, the introduction of rebellion, and the loss of intimacy.

This initial error on the part of Eve has been replayed ever since. Both Adam and Eve found themselves in rebellion. Eve turned her attention toward the serpent, away from her husband, and away from God. Adam turned his attention away from God and turned toward his wife. Turned away from the headship of Creator God, they began a pattern of self-will that still persists: woman not rightly related to man, man not rightly related to God, soul disconnected from spirit, and creation unsubmitted to Creator. God is calling for an about face—reversing our attitude and direction, and restoring order in His creation. Women have the privilege of modeling the role of the Bride in an earthly marriage, which, when rightly portrayed, allows both men and women to learn their role as the Bride of Christ.

Question: What objections rise in your heart when the topic of submission in marriage is discussed?

---

249. Submission Defined

"Greater love has no one than this that one lay down his life for his friends." ~ John 15:13

Submission is about rightly ordering the creation so the rule of God might be facilitated through His church. It does not place a higher value on one gender over another, on one race over another, one culture over another, or age, or gifting, or calling over another. Submission is to order ourselves in such a way that all our words, behaviors, and relationships display the Lordship of Christ. If we live rightly before Him, we will be an accurate display of heavenly matters to a watching world.

This lesson is so potent and powerful that the Lord Himself came and modeled submission as a child, as a servant, and as the Bridegroom. The word "Islam" means submission, but lends itself to a different definition than what is biblically called for. For too long, the church has held to the same bent understanding. We have allowed the meaning to default to domination and passivity; failing to lay hold of its true nature and power to recover our creation design.

Question: *Where have you seen domination and passivity partner together?*

250. Conformation

"For while we were in the flesh, the sinful
passions, which were aroused by the Law, were at
work ... to bear fruit for death. But now we have
been released from the Law, having died to that by
which we were bound, so that we serve in newness
of the Spirit and not in oldness of the letter."
~ Romans 7:5-6

Once you are born again, you are not suddenly overpowered, unable to walk at your own will. Now that you are spiritually alive, you have the opportunity to learn how to follow the Lord. Sometimes, we attempt to change our lives through conformation. Conformation comes from the exertion of outside pressure; it is a force applied to bring about inward change. This is the general idea behind penitentiaries. The focus of conformation is your strengths being perfected. It teaches people how to respond to guilt and shame—trying to keep the Law, but with the inability to do so. Any change of behavior usually comes from the influence of an outside authority, encouraging external behaviors rather than internal attributes, that is, a real change of heart. With conformation, there is the tendency to hide, or cover up our weaknesses and deficiencies, and walk in strength of soul. This produces pride. These are fleshly ways and do not reflect the nature of the indwelling Spirit of God. Conversion from old life to new life is our means of true change.

Question: Have you ever tried to change one of your behaviors by keep-
ing the rules? Was this effective?

251. Transformation

*"... that, in reference to your former manner of
life, you lay aside the old self, which is being
corrupted in accordance with the lusts of deceit, and
that you be renewed in the spirit of your mind, and
put on the new self, which in the likeness of God has
been created in righteousness and holiness
of the truth." ~ Ephesians 4:22-24*

While conformation relies on external pressure for change, transformation is a change from within that begins to radiate new life from the inside out. The focus of transformation is on the Lord and His abilities. The word means to change form, appearance, or character. It is about inner changes and embracing hearing with faith. The goal is for us to learn to function by the life of the indwelling Spirit of Christ. We can then respond with, "Thy will be done".

Too often as Christians we have treated salvation as a debt payment, then attempted to live new life with our same old flesh. Transformation allows someone to respond to the parameters of the life of the Spirit rather than the dictates of the culture. It is about desiring to release the nature of our God through our lives, rather than just hindering our human nature. Transformation is like a caterpillar becoming a butterfly, while conformation is like gluing wings on a caterpillar.

Question: Do you find yourself in the midst of a trial? How can you be transformed by the Holy Spirit as you move through it?

252. Sin Management

*"Now those who belong to Christ Jesus have
crucified the flesh with its passions and desires."*
~ Galatians 5:24

It you have been living your life in Christ as though it were
a course in sin management, I expect you are becoming
weary. But, what if 2 Corinthians 5:17 is the best description
of what has taken place? *"Therefore if any man is in Christ, he is
a new creature; the old things passed away; behold, new
things have come."*

The sacrifice of Christ on the cross not only purchased a new
life, it purchased a new way of life. Our unfamiliarity with
this new lifestyle requires that we relearn it by observing
Jesus model life with His Father. It is impossible to follow the
Lord in this way in the strength of soul. We cannot depend on
our mind, will, or emotions to free us from our old life, and
they have no ability to walk in the new life. *"But I say, walk by
the Spirit, and you will not carry out the desire of the flesh. For the
flesh sets its desire against the Spirit, and the Spirit against the
flesh; for these are in opposition to one another, so that you may not
do the things that you please"* (Galatians 5:16-17).

*Question: Was there a particular realm of sin that was difficult to break
free from? What was the turning point?*

253. Led by What We Love

"... the one who says he abides in Him ought
himself to walk in the same manner as He walked."
~ I John 2:6

What if we live more from what we love than from what we believe? Then it would make sense that the two greatest commandments in the Law were about loving. As we work to relearn how to sustain a love relationship from the heart, what we focus on can encourage or interrupt that process. Paul prayed that the *"eye of your heart may be enlightened, so that you may know what is the hope of His calling, what are the riches of the glory of His inheritance in the Saints ..."* (Ephesians 1:18). Under the Old Covenant, we were the source of love and were required to demonstrate it with all of our being to God and others. Under the New Covenant, we are the recipients of a love we can then give away. It is all about receiving with the heart and then responding from the heart. Our affections must be continually reoriented to the One we call our Beloved. When we fasten our gaze upon Him our footsteps can be properly ordered.

Question: Do you ever find yourself speaking one thing about the Lord with your lips, while your heart is far from Him?

254. Living in Oneness

"If therefore there is any encouragement in Christ,
if there is any consolation of love, if there is any
fellowship of the Spirit, if any affection and
compassion, make my joy complete by being of the
same mind, maintaining the same love, united in
spirit, intent on one purpose." ~ Philippians 2:1-2

The Triune God is One God, therefore a display of His image and likeness among men requires a community that also operates in oneness. There are two arenas where God forms this bond for us and then trusts us to preserve it. The first area is marriage. God takes a man and a woman, diverse in physical, emotional, and spiritual giftings, and merges their lives on their wedding day. Jesus prays in John 17:23, *"that they may be perfected in unity"*. This phrase is not requesting that we finally attain to unity one day, but that we would become mature as we maintain such a gift.

The other arena where the Lord gives His gift of oneness is the church. *"For even as the body is one and yet has many members, and all the members of the body, though they are many, are one body, so also is Christ. For by one Spirit we were all baptized into one body, whether Jews or Greeks, whether slaves or free, and we were all made to drink of one Spirit. For the body is not one member, but many"* (1 Corinthians 12:12-14). As we become the delivery system for God's love, we both receive and pour forth all that is necessary for the church to mature in oneness.

Question: Has your experience of unity in the church been a reflection of the kind of unity that the Triune God shares?

255. Called as Followers

*"And He said to them, 'Follow Me, and I will
make you fishers of men.' And they immediately left
the nets, and followed Him."*
~ Matthew 4:19-20

It is very purposeful that Jesus' first disciples were called followers. A follower is a person who moves or travels behind someone, one who accepts the guidance, command or leadership of another. As we purpose to walk in this way, we are learning to respond to the voice of the Spirit rather than keeping a rule. Hearing brings faith, and faith sees what is yet unseen to the natural eye. By keeping it relational, we discover a deep communion rather than religious dogma. We are learning how to transition from being the initiators, to being the responders.

This is a particularly hard lesson for people who are often in a role of leadership who are used to "making things happen." Jesus said, *"I can do nothing on My own initiative ... I do not seek My own will, but the will of Him who sent Me"* (John 5:30). Jesus operated in meekness (great strength under control), and humility (dependence on a strength outside of Himself). This retraining in Godly submission is God's way of restoring His power and authority to the church. Submitted followers are a visible witness to the rule of God.

Question: Do you recognize a leader who is well-led by Christ?

256. Transition of Power

*"For the kingdom of God does not consist in
words but in power." ~ I Corinthians 4:20*

In the upside down way of the Kingdom of God, true spiritual authority is gained by wholehearted submission. Willingness to follow is the basis for Christian leadership. When Jesus stepped down from His heavenly reign to model submission among men, He operated in the opposite Spirit from the *Kosmokrater*, the ruler of this world. Living with a submitted will, Jesus carried the word and will of the Father into every encounter and situation. That response released the full power and authority of the Living God into each moment of His humanity. When it was time for Him to ascend once more to the Father, Jesus invited His disciples to wait in Jerusalem until they received the gift of the Holy Spirit. He was outfitting the church to carry His power and authority through their willingness to live in submission. Forfeiture of self-will restores God's people to their original design.

*Question: How have you experienced God's power toward you?
Through you?*

257. Domination and Passivity

"... and be subject to one another in the
fear of Christ." ~ Ephesians 5:21

A misunderstanding of submission is to believe that it is displayed though domination and passivity. These are two imposters to the true meaning of the word, and they work in partnership with one another. This false definition is often the default understanding of the church.

Humility and devotion are the qualities that give life to submission, not hostility and suppression. The reason domination and passivity are so opposed to the ways of God is because they take away a person's right to choose—in fact, they take away a person's responsibility to choose. True submission can only take place when someone is exercising their free will because submission is the appropriate exercise of God's gift of choice. This is why God is opposed to one gender dominating another. He is opposed to one race, one gift, one age, or one status being dominant. Dominance is a false form of leadership and is displayed by those who have no true spiritual authority.

Question: *Are there any ways, as a church, that we promote domination and passivity?*

258. Taming the Soul

*"For those who are according to the flesh set their
minds on the things of the flesh, but those who are
according to the Spirit, the things of the Spirit."*
~ Romans 8:5

At creation, God made man so that he would be perfectly
suited to his environment. He was given a physical body to
dwell in, a soul to comprehend with, and a spirit to commune
with the Lord. Since God created man with a free will, it was
necessary to be trained in its use. The spirit was God's means
of leading and impressing this first Adam in His ways. At the
fall when God withdrew His Spirit, man was left to navigate
with only his body and soul. Rather than being oriented
toward God, the creation began to orient toward self. *"For
even though they knew God, they did not honor Him as God, or give
thanks; but they became futile in their speculations, and their foolish
heart was darkened. Professing to be wise, they became fools"*
(Romans 1:21-22). Without the leading of the Spirit, man
compensated by operating from the strength of his soul—
mind, will, and emotions. Every choice then, was a matter of
what he thought, felt, or wanted. As Christians who are now
endowed with the gift of the Holy Spirit, we must learn to be
led by the Spirit and to bring our flesh into submission.

Question: *Have you learned to discern the difference between your soul
and spirit?*

259. For the Bride

"Nevertheless let each individual among you also love his own wife even as himself; and let the wife see to it that she respect her husband."
~ Ephesian 6:33

Submission is not just for women anymore—it never was. Learning to bring our lives into order under the headship of Christ is a lesson for the Bride. In order for the man to be the groom to the bride, he must first be the bride to the Groom. God uses certain roles to teach His people His ways. Two of these are less gender specific than we might think. *"For you are all sons of God through faith in Christ Jesus. For all of you who were baptized into Christ have clothed yourselves with Christ. There is neither Jew nor Greek, there is neither slave nor freeman, there is neither male nor female; for you are all one in Christ Jesus"* (Galatians 3:26-28). In Christ, we all learn submission as sons. Then in Ephesians 5:31-32, we are called to display our relationship with Jesus in another role: *"For this cause a man shall leave his father and mother, and shall cleave to his wife; and the two shall become one flesh. This mystery is great; but I am speaking with reference to Christ and His church."* In the natural, women are invited to display what submission looks like in an intimate relationship. Through careful observation Men get to learn how to be led.

Question: Have you seen an observable model of submission that helped you learn how to walk in the Spirit?

260. Taming the Tongue

*"The good man out of the good treasure of his
heart brings forth what is good; and the evil man
out of the evil treasure brings forth what is evil; for
his mouth speaks from that which fills his heart."*
~ Luke 6:45

The tongue is set among the members of our body as a measure of our submission. This very small part has the ability to display Jesus with maturity or defy Him with insubordination. The tongue gives an x-ray of our heart, disclosing the true state of our spirituality. *"... the tongue is a small part of the body, and yet it boasts of great things. Behold, how great a forest is set aflame by such a small fire! And the tongue is a fire, the very world of iniquity; the tongue is set among our members as that which defiles the entire body, and sets on fire the course of our life, and is set on fire by hell ... no one can tame the tongue; it is a restless evil and full of deadly poison. With it we bless our Lord and Father; and with it we curse men, who have been made in the likeness of God; from the same mouth come both blessing and cursing. My brethren, these things ought not be this way"* (James 3:5-6; 8-10). Since it is out of the abundance of the heart that the mouth speaks, may we bring both into submission to Christ.

Question: *Would the Lord be offended with any conversation that you participated in this week?*

261. Law vs. Led

"It was for freedom that Christ set us free;
therefore keep standing firm and do not be subject
again to a yoke of slavery." ~ Galatians 5:1

I had a conversation once with a young man who believed the only way to mature as a Christian was to become a Law-abiding citizen of the Kingdom of God. His ideas concerning legalism would have been familiar to the Galatians. *"You foolish Galatians, who has bewitched you, before whose eyes Jesus Christ was publicly portrayed as crucified? This is the only thing I want to find out from you: did you receive the Spirit by the works of the Law, or by hearing with faith? Are you so foolish? Having begun by the Spirit, are you now being perfected by the flesh?"* (Galatians 3:1-3). Having begun by the Spirit, we attempt to produce maturity within ourselves by adopting the Hebrew Law as our means to resist the flesh. Instead, Paul stated, *"... walk by the Spirit, and you will not carry out the desire of the flesh ... if you are led by the Spirit, you are not under the Law"* (Galatians 5:16, 18). Rather than a script to be satisfied, we follow the Spirit's leading. Rather than a rule to keep, there is a reliance on His indwelling Spirit to will and work through us.

Question: Once legalism is exposed, why do you think people tend to turn back to it?

262. Nature of Rebellion

"For rebellion is as the sin of divination, and
insubordination is as iniquity and idolatry."
~ I Samuel 15:23

At the core of rebellion is a prideful heart that refuses humility and submission. Such is the nature of Lucifer, the fallen angel who led a company of angelic beings into war in the heavenly places. That conflict spilled over into the earthly realm through the garden. Had Adam and Eve remained submitted to the will of the Creator, the rebellion in this dimension would have been over. Instead, this rebellion introduced sin that flooded creation with its corruption. With sin as the governor, rebellion became the result of every independent thought, word, and deed of mankind. Once, when sin and rebellion reached climactic proportions, God sent a flood that both cleansed the earth and reset the boundaries between the earthly and the heavenly dimensions. As we move toward the end of the age, wickedness, like a tare, is producing much fruit. On the other hand, submission—God's gift to man— bears the fruit of righteousness.

Question: Where or when does submission in the natural realm result in a triumph for God?

263. Potency of Submission

"And being found in appearance as a man, He humbled Himself by becoming obedient to the point of death, even death on a cross." ~ Philippians 2:8

Submission was never designed to be the means of keeping one part of the body under the control of another part. At all times, it is about learning to live in a coordinated obedience under the headship of Christ. This particular lesson is so important to the recovery of our original design, that Jesus Himself came and modeled it for us. In His obedience, Jesus destroyed the idea that submission is about domination and passivity. As the One who modeled humility in every aspect of His life, He never displayed a passive response. From the time He was a child, He demonstrated how to follow the leadership of the Spirit. *"... although He existed in the form of God, did not regard equality with God a thing to be grasped, but emptied Himself, taking the form of a bond-servant, and being made in the likeness of men"* (Philippians 2:6-7).

The power and authority of the Father were shown through each word that Jesus spoke, and each action that He took. Through His observable Sonship, Jesus disclosed the Father's path to true spiritual authority and divine power.

Question: What effect does insubordination have within a marriage? A family? A church? A nation?

264. When Tares Mature

*"But while men were sleeping, his enemy came
and sowed tares also among the wheat,
and went away ..." ~ Matthew 13:25*

There comes a point in time when the cumulative effects of sin reach a climax, and the boundaries of wickedness are reached. Once before, in the history of the world, evil hit its high mark and reaped the consequences of sin. *"Then the Lord saw that the wickedness of man was great on the earth, and that every intent of the thoughts of his heart was only evil continually. And the Lord was sorry that He had made man on the earth, and He was grieved in His heart. And the Lord said, 'I will blot out man whom I have created from the face of the land, from man to animals to creeping things and to birds of the sky; for I am sorry that I have made them'"* (Genesis 6:5-7). The evil one continues to sow seed for a harvest of wickedness. The parable of the tares teaches us that God will allow the tares to grow up with the wheat until the time of the harvest—and then harvest each to their own end (Matthew 13:24-30). Keeping our hearts fertile to the word of God and then acting on what we learn brings forth fruit. It is that which glorifies Him and remains.

Question: *What fruit of the Holy Spirit is being produced in your life right now?*

265. Rebellion to Anarchy

*"Therefore everyone who hears these words of
Mine, and acts upon them, may be compared to a
wise man, who built his house upon the rock. And
the rain descended, and the floods came, and the
winds blew, and burst against that house; and yet it
did not fall, for it had been founded upon the rock."*
~ Matthew 7:24-25

When rebellion overtakes men's hearts and is openly flaunted, the moral integrity of a people is destroyed. Psalm 11:3 asks a question that is immediately appropriate for the hour we live in: *"If the foundations are destroyed, what can the righteous do?"* How can we respond with love and truth, wisdom and strategic thinking, acting as wise as serpents and as innocent as doves as we experience a cultural climate change? A foundation built on the identity of Christ alone is our means of survival in the threat of the coming storm. A life built on traditions of men, identification with church, or reliance on strength of soul will be insufficient to face this hour. In order to prevail against wickedness, our foundation must not contain mixture. Christianity cannot be combined with any lesser "ism" (i.e. individualism, nationalism, etc.) and stand firm. God is always purposeful in the ways that He prepares His people, whether through conviction, confession, prophets, or trials. Knowing He is available to discipline us as sons should encourage our quick responsiveness to His shaking.

Question: When was the last time you were chastised by the Lord? What did it concern?

266. Antichrist Seats Himself

"… which He brought about in Christ … and
seated Him at His right hand in the heavenly places,
far above all rule and authority and power and
dominion, and every name that is named, not only
in this age, but also in the one to come."
~ Ephesians 1:20-21

One of the signals of the end of the age is when *"the man of lawlessness is revealed, the son of destruction, who opposes and exalts himself above every so-called God or object of worship, so that he takes his seat in the temple of God, displaying himself as being God"* (2 Thessalonians 2:3-4). When the tares of the evil one come to maturity, they will display the willful likeness of their progenitor, the devil. In the final days, the seed of Satan will embody in the natural realm what the father of lies had attempted previously in the spiritual realm. *"I will ascend to heaven; I will raise my throne above the stars of God, and I will sit on the mount of assembly in the recesses of the north. I will ascend above the heights of the clouds; I will make myself like the Most High. Nevertheless you will be thrust down to Sheol, to the recesses of the pit"* (Isaiah 14:13-15). The longing for worship was recognized as the evil one tempted Jesus in the wilderness. The presumption of worship is prophesied for the close of the age. A call to worship comes to the church in this hour that we might be found in the presence of the Lord Jesus, seated at the right hand of the Father, in heavenly places.

Question: What qualities of the antichrist do you observe in our culture today?

267. Submission to One Another

"Do nothing from selfishness or empty conceit,
but with humility of mind let each of you regard one
another as more important than himself."
~ Philippians 2:3

God's design for creation was more of an *"heir*archy" than a hierarchy. Our differing gifts and roles bring diversity to the body rather than establishing our value. As the body is not one member but many, we cannot fully express the image of God without one another. Designed to cooperate together under the headship of Christ, we must learn how to submit together in love. *"... but speaking the truth in love, we are to grow up in all aspects into Him, who is the head, even Christ, from whom the whole body, being fitted and held together by that which every joint supplies, according to the proper working of each individual part, causes the growth of the body for the building up of itself in love"* (Ephesians 4:15-16). This way of holy submission was modeled for us by the Lord. He demonstrated His humility through His dependence, His love through submission of His preferences, and His leadership through His sacrifice.

Question: Other than your immediate family, where have your choices expressed your submission to another?

268. Take My Yoke

"Be imitators of me, just as I also am of Christ."
~ I Corinthians 11:1

Jesus used a familiar image to teach His disciples about submission. *"Come to Me, all who are weary and heavy-laden, and I will give you rest. Take My yoke upon you, and learn from Me, for I am gentle and humble in heart; and you shall find rest for your souls. For My yoke is easy, and My load is light"* (Matthew 11:28-30). This is not just a momentary illustration that Jesus is willing to model for us but the demonstration of His entire earthly lifestyle. From the time of His incarnation, He placed Himself under complete submission to the Father, harnessed His will to the Divine, and found rest for the work of His soul. He didn't make it His ambition to throw off the constraint and pursue His own way. He found His rest, and in turn, offers us ours. His gentleness is demonstrated in a grace that pervades His whole nature, and His humble heart is seen as He models complete dependence on the Holy Spirit. We are invited to join Him.

Question: Has submission been a burden or a gift in your life?

269. Can't Serve Two Masters

"No one can serve two masters ... You cannot
serve God and mammon." ~ Matthew 6:24

During the days of King Ahaz of Judah and King Hoshea of Israel, Israel was taken captive by Assyria. They had greatly sinned and no longer knew the ways of the Lord. They worshipped in the high places and served idols. God raised up a priest to teach the people to fear and revere Him. The people responded by fearing the Lord and *"appointed from among themselves priests of the high places, who acted for them in the houses of the high places. They feared the Lord and served their own gods according to the custom of the nations from among whom they had been carried away into exile"* (2 Kings 17:32-33). God reminded them about His covenant, saying, *"And the covenant that I have made with you, you shall not forget, nor shall you fear others gods. But the Lord your God you shall fear; and He will deliver you from the hand of all your enemies. However, they did not listen, but they did according to their earlier custom. So while these nations feared the Lord, they also served their idols; their children likewise and their grandchildren, as their fathers did, so they do to this day"* (2 Kings 17:38-41). Fearing the Lord and serving our idols continues in the cultures of the world. Syncretism of Spirit and flesh—combining man's ways and God's ways—does not create greater influence, it only produces a hybrid gospel.

Question: *Can you see any places where the church practices the traditions of men (a practice that is revered, but not biblical)?*

270. Power of Pride

"Be devoted to one another in brotherly love; give
preference to one another in honor; not lagging
behind in diligence, fervent in spirit,
serving the Lord." ~ Romans 12:10-11

To turn toward oneself is to turn from God. To elevate that self with such recognition is egotism and pride. Pride is confidence in self and the rejection of anything other than self. It is resistant to submission. Perhaps, then, our propensity toward independence and individualism is also an indication of our vulnerability to prideful thinking and behavior. Part of the course work of learning to live submitted lives is to give preference to others in honor and turn away from selfishness and empty conceit. Egotism is an exaggerated sense of self-importance—the feeling or belief that you are better, more talented, and above other people. This is a subtle form of self-worship. It obstructs the Holy Spirit's gift of conviction and cripples our capacity to repent.

Question: *Do you recognize any areas of your life where you are tempted to prideful thinking or actions?*

271. In Submission to the Head

"And He is before all things, and in Him all things hold together. He is also head of the body, the church; and He is the beginning, the first-born from the dead; so that He Himself might come to have first place in everything."
~ Colossians 1:17-18

Every muscle in our bodies is intricately connected to the movement of the head. In fact, there is a saying: "where the head goes, the body will follow." This is not only true in our natural bodies. It is demonstrated in Christ's body, the church, as well. There are two ways that God chooses to demonstrate oneness on earth as it is in heaven. The first is through the marriage relationship. Marriage is designed to demonstrate the oneness of Christ and His church. The second, is His Body, the church which is designed to display a people group who have learned submission to the Spirit and submission to one another. Limbs that move independent of the will of the Head is not a condition of health but a symptoms of some neurological disorder. For us to live in a cooperative relationship with one another we must remain continually in a submitted relationship to the Head. Sustaining maturity in our image and likeness of Christ requires a cooperative submission to the Father so that we can learn to be led corporately by the Holy Spirit.

Question: Have you ever needed a chiropractor? What was the reason? Have you ever needed a spiritual adjustment? How was this accomplished?

272. Don't Rival His Rule

*"... then comes the end, when He delivers up the
kingdom to the God and Father, when He has
abolished all rule and all authority and power."*
~ I Corinthians 15:24

Ministry done in the name of Jesus is ministry that releases His power and authority. Preaching the word of God and evangelization needs the anointing of the Holy Spirit in order to be effective. Healing the sick and casting out demons requires a power greater than ourselves. To accomplish the *"works which God prepared beforehand, that we should walk in them"* (Ephesians 2:10). we must carry His indwelling presence. Only this releases His supernatural life. Paul, in Ephesians 1:19, prays that we would know *"what is the surpassing greatness of His power toward us who believe. These are in accordance with the working of the strength of His might which He brought about in Christ ..."* (Ephesians 1:19-20). While we are freely granted, and encouraged to operate in, His power and authority, we are not to rival His rule. There is *"one God and Father of all who is over all and through all and in all"* (Ephesians 4:6).

Question: *How do you remain in submission to Christ when His will opposes yours?*

273. Overthrowing Governments

*"But with righteousness He will judge the poor,
and decide with fairness for the afflicted of the earth;
and He will strike the earth with the rod of His
mouth, and with the breath of His lips He will slay
the wicked." ~ Isaiah 11:4*

There are seasons of time when governments are overthrown and new parties take office. Whether through uprising or disassembling structures, one form of government steps in to replace another. In the book of Daniel a meta narrative of this kind of upheaval was prophesied in Nebuchadnezzar's dream. With the vision of the large statue in chapter two, we are given foreknowledge of world history. One kingdom after another would rise and fall until a final kingdom comes forth. *"And in the days of those Kings the God of heaven will set up a kingdom which will never be destroyed, and that kingdom will not be left for another people; it will crush and put an end to all these kingdoms, but it will itself endure forever"* (Daniel 2:44).

Isaiah explains this kingdom that will never be destroyed. *"For a child will be born to us, a son will be given to us; and the government will rest on His shoulders; and His name will be called Wonderful Counselor, Mighty God, Eternal Father, Prince of Peace. There will be no end to the increase of His government or of peace, on the throne of David and over his kingdom, to establish it and to uphold it with justice and righteousness from then on and forevermore. The zeal of the Lord ... will accomplish this"* (Isaiah 9:6-7).

Question: What qualities of God's government can we model in our congregations?

Part 10

Eyes to See

274. How the Eye Operates

*"And from the throne proceed flashes of lightning
and sounds and peals of thunder. And there were
seven lamps of fire burning before the throne, which
are the seven Spirits of God." ~ Revelation 4:5*

The human eye is an exquisite display of God's creative capacity. The Lord uses the eye to explain who He is and how He functions. *"The lamp of the body is the eye; if therefore your eye is clear, your whole body will be full of light. But if your eye is bad, your whole body will be full of darkness. If therefore the light that is in you is darkness, how great is the darkness!"* (Matthew 6:22-23). We think we know what an eye is, so we assume that the natural eye is the lamp of the body. From the early days of Sunday School, children are taught the song, "Oh, be careful little eyes what you see ... the Father up above is looking down in love, so be careful little eyes what you see." Yet, the way an eye operates is more like a window than a lamp, which is a source of light. Another verse from the Old Testament is our key for understanding. *"The spirit of man is the lamp of the Lord, searching all the innermost parts of his being"* (Proverbs 20:27). Knowing that the spirit is the lamp—and the lamp of the body is the eye—we learn that the Lord is giving us a new eye to see and operate from—His Spirit.

Question: Without the use of the human eye, are there other ways we learn to see?

275. *Lamp is the Eye*

"But blessed are your eyes, because they see; and your ears, because they hear." ~ Matthew 13:16

When we link Matthew 6:22-23 together with Proverbs 20:27, we discover that the Spirit is the Lord's lamp, and this is now our new means of seeing—our eye. To truly see, as we were intended to see, and to truly hear as we were designed to hear, we must receive the indwelling lamp of the Spirit of God, and then learn to operate from His light. This entails converting from one power source to another, in order to receive what He desires to convey to us and through us. We have to decide which eye we will trust; especially since we are most familiar and trained in one way of perceiving. *"Therefore I speak to them in parables; because while seeing they do not see, and while hearing they do not hear, nor do they understand ... for the heart of this people has become dull, and with their ears they scarcely hear, and they have closed their eyes lest they should see with their eyes, and hear with their ears, and understand with their heart and return, and I should heal them" (Matthew 13:13,15).*

Question: *Have you substituted or compensated, in any way, for a lack of spiritual seeing and hearing?*

276. *Lamp is the Spirit*

"And the city has no need of the sun or of the
moon to shine on it, for the glory of God has
illumined it, and its lamp is the Lamb."
~ Revelation 21:23

When we read in the book of Revelation about the throne of God, we learn more about the lamp representing the Spirit. *"And there were seven lamps of fire burning before the throne, which are the seven Spirits of God"* (Revelation 4:5). The book goes on to describe the nature of the Lamb of God, *"... having seven horns and seven eyes, which are the seven Spirits of God, sent out into all the earth"* (Revelation 5:6). These verses tie together a powerful illustration for how the indwelling life of the Holy Spirit operates in our lives today. Before coming to Christ, we were dead in our sins and only able to operate in this world by our fleshly capacities. At new birth we receive the Holy Spirit to be the lamp of our human body, which allows us to see by the Spirit and hear by the Spirit, according to God's original design.

Question: *Has the Lord ever shown you something—that your natural eye was unaware of?*

277. Seeing by the Spirit

*"Although the Lord has given you bread of
privation and water of oppression, He, your Teacher
will no longer hide Himself, but your eyes will
behold your Teacher. And your ears will hear a
word behind you, 'This is the way, walk in it,'
whenever you turn to the right or to the left."*
~ Isaiah 30:20-21

In order to learn how to walk by the Spirit, we must learn how to be led. To move at the impulse of His Spirit, rather than operating from the inclinations of our soul, we must be trained to perceive and apprehend the Spirit of God. We are given the Holy Scriptures to check whether what we are perceiving is accurate. When Adam stepped out of dependence into rebellion, he lost his capacity to discern God's will. When Jesus purchased our redemption at Calvary, we were restored to sonship, and regained our spiritual hearing and sight. With a natural ability to see and a renewed spiritual capacity, we are caught in a conflict. These two ways of seeing are often opposed to one another. *"For the flesh sets its desire against the Spirit, and the Spirit against the flesh; for these are in opposition to one another, so that you may not do the things that you please"* (Galatians 5:17). It would appear that we are never free from the conflict between our natural means of seeing and our spiritual means of seeing. This is the place where we begin to walk by faith.

Question: Have you ever experienced an internal conflict between your reasoning mind and what you sense to be the voice of the Spirit?

278. *Instrument Rated*

"Commit your way to the Lord, trust also in Him,
and He will do it." ~ Psalm 37:5

There are two different types of licenses that a pilot can apply for: standard and instrument rated. One allows you to fly in good weather, during daylight hours, and requires far fewer hours of training than the other. Being instrument rated means you have learned to rely on the instrument panel for navigation, rather than your natural sight. It takes longer to acquire, since you are learning to navigate in darkness and stormy weather. Walking by the Spirit is learning to walk by our new instrument panel, rather than by the information that our natural sight conveys. It takes practice to live this verse, *"Trust in the Lord with all your heart, and do not lean on your own understanding. In all your ways acknowledge Him, and He will make your paths straight"* (Proverbs 3:5-6). As the days grow darker, and civilization stormier, may the church be those who have learned to navigate by the eye of the Spirit.

Question: When there is a conflict between your mind and the Spirit, how do you test your response?

302

279. *Visible and Invisible*

"For to us God revealed them through the Spirit;
for the Spirit searches all things, even the depths of
God." ~ I Corinthians 2:10

With a new capacity to hear and see by the Spirit, we are on a learning journey of walking by faith and not sight. We are able to uncover the complete nature of things—both visible and invisible. *"And He is the image of the invisible God, the first-born of all creation. For by Him all things were created, both in the heavens and on earth, visible and invisible, whether thrones or dominions or rulers or authorities—all things have been created by Him and for Him"* (Colossians 1:15-16). Since the beginning of creation God's design was for a people who could navigate both the visible and invisible realm; who could comprehend the nature of the heavenlies and live into that likeness upon the earth. In the Old Testament, prophets saw the spiritual realm and conveyed it in ways that natural man could understand. In our day, we have the scripture to help interpret what the Spirit conveys to us through His presence and His gifts.

Question: Has the Lord shown you something that was taking place in the invisible realm lately?

---

280. *Old Testament Prophets*

*"Then I heard the voice of the Lord, saying,
'Whom shall I send, and who will go for Us?' Then
I said, 'Here am I. Send me!'" ~ Isaiah 6:8*

Before God poured out His Spirit upon all flesh on Pentecost, He uniquely rested on some individuals in the Old Testament, who were called prophets. These men heard the voice of the Lord, and responded by translating what they heard to the nation of Israel. Each one was asked to go and communicate a message of correction, rebuke, warning, or comfort. Because God's people were prone to go astray, distancing themselves from God in the process, the Lord would raise up a prophet to remind them of who He was and who they were. Israel's religious life was oriented around a priesthood, but they too, were often corrupt in their personal life, allowing God's people to drift toward idolatry. Called from a variety of backgrounds, they brought their message, relaying God's will and warning. Moses and Amos were shepherds. Jeremiah and Ezekiel were priests. Deborah was a judge. The task given by God became their priority.

Question: Who is God using today to warn His people concerning His ways?

281. Listening Instructions

*"And all your sons will be taught of the Lord; and
the well-being of your sons will be great."*
~ Isaiah 54:13

The Old Testament prophets heard from the Lord on behalf
of the people. Their words give us additional instruction on
how to listen for His voice. *"The Lord God has given me the
tongue of disciples, that I may know how to sustain the weary one
with a word. He awakens me morning by morning, He awakens my
ear to listen as a disciple. The Lord has opened my ear; and I was not
disobedient, nor did I turn back"* (Isaiah 50:4-5). It begins with a
call; the Lord is the one who initiates, and we must become
sensitive enough to respond. The picture we are given is of
one who is awakened from a place of slumber, whether phys-
ically or spiritually. He is the one who develops my capacity
to hear by daily arousing my attention to His presence and
intentions. Our hearing is for the sake of activation—that we
might know how to sustain the weary with the word we have
heard. This lesson is required for fruitful ministry.

---

*Question: What does your morning routine look like? Is there any room
for listening?*

282. *Alertness*

"Be still, and know that I am God ..."
~ Psalm 46:10

As we continue to consider Isaiah 50:4, we realize that the Lord is actively engaged in our learning to listen and speak by the life of the Spirit. He is the one who draws us out of spiritual dullness into being a fully attentive and alert disciple, who has become practiced in discernment. *"For though by this time you ought to be teachers, you have need again for someone to teach you the elementary principles of the oracles of God, and you have come to need milk and not solid food. For everyone who partakes only of milk is not accustomed to the word of righteousness, for he is an infant. But solid food is for the mature, who because of practice have their senses trained to discern good and evil"* (Hebrews 5:12-14). Those who receive all of their spiritual nourishment through the life of another are still babes in Christ. When a child moves from milk to solid food it is no longer considered an infant. Those who wake up to Him and begin to respond to His voice, are those who begin to mature into their full stature.

Question: Do you know how to be still and listen?

283. Who Hears

*"For Thou didst form my inward parts; Thou
didst weave me in my mother's womb. I will give
thanks to Thee, for I am fearfully and
wonderfully made." ~ Psalm 139:13-14*

The call of God can rest on someone even before they are born. *"But when He who had set me apart, even from my mother's womb, and called me through His grace, was pleased to reveal His Son in me, that I might preach Him among the Gentiles ..."* (Galatians 1:15-16). Paul realized that God had guided him for an entire lifetime, guiding his path with an invisible hand. Jeremiah experienced a similar call. This passage relates what the Lord said to him: *"'Before I formed you in the womb I knew you, and before you were born I consecrated you; I have appointed you a prophet to the nations.' Then I said, 'Alas, Lord God! Behold, I do not know how to speak. Because I am a youth.' 'Do not say, I am a youth,' because everywhere I send you, you shall go, and all that I command you, you shall speak"* (Jeremiah 1:5-7). When God calls or designs us with Kingdom purposes in mind, He is with us. We are not called to take action on His behalf; He is with us and works through us. Learning to hear the voice of the Lord helps each person understand who they were created to be.

Question: *How long did it take you to discover what you were created for? How did you discover this?*

284. Children Respond

"Train up a child in the way he should go, even
when he is old he will not depart from it."
~ Proverbs 22:6

When Jeremiah was called, even as a young man, he cooperated. *"And the word of the Lord came to me saying, 'What do you see, Jeremiah?' And I said, 'I see a rod of an almond tree.' Then the Lord said to me, 'You have seen well, for I am watching over My word to perform it'"* (Jeremiah 1:11-12). In the Hebrew, there is a play on words here. The word for 'almond' and 'watching' are similar, moreover, the almond tree is the first to blossom in spring suggesting God's eager "wakefulness" over His word. The Lord continued to coach Jeremiah in hearing, then sent him on his mission.

Samuel heard the voice of the Lord while he was still a small child serving in the tabernacle. Prior to being conceived his mother prayed for a child and dedicated him to the Lord before he was even born (1 Samuel 1:27-28). Those were dark days in the history of Israel, the ways of the Lord were perverted. God acted on His behalf and raised up Samuel to be a priest and a prophet.

The Lord can raise up children, give them His Spirit, train them in His ways, and then release them into fruitful ministry. There is no junior Holy Spirit. How are we teaching young people to listen, to learn, and to lead?

Question: *Do you know a child who is demonstrating spiritual hunger? Pray for them.*

285. Called and Sent Ones

*"Go into all the world and preach the gospel
to all creation." ~ Mark 16:15*

Jesus called each disciple to come and follow Him, before releasing them to go in His name. He invited them to leave their former lives behind, and enter into a relationship with Him. Living with Jesus, then filled with the Holy Spirit, they were sent out as apostles to establish the Kingdom of God. We are missing this ancient pattern of discipleship today. People who come to Jesus often become church attenders, but fail to mature in Christ. An invitation to come and sit is different than a call to hear, observe, learn, and do. Though we call Christians followers of Christ, few follow the pattern Jesus set out in Matthew 28:19-20, *"Go therefore and make disciples of all the nations, baptizing them in the name of the Father and the Son and the Holy Spirit, teaching them to observe all that I commanded you."* Jesus was never content to just gain a following. He came to create an entire body that would go into the world with the message of the gospel.

Question: Where is the Lord asking you to learn to follow Him today? Where is He sending you?

286. Listen and Obey

*"Thus says the Lord, your Redeemer, the Holy
One of Israel, 'I am the Lord your God, who teaches
you to profit, who leads you in the way
you should go.'"* ~ Isaiah 48:17

The Lord called Abraham to follow Him, and *"By faith Abraham, when he was called, obeyed by going out to a place which he was to receive for an inheritance; and he went out, not knowing where he was going"* (Hebrews 11:8). When we are called to follow Christ, we begin a similar journey. Our life begins to be informed by the will and the word of the Lord—day by day listening, and day by day obeying. Isaiah describes our training like this: *"To whom would He teach knowledge? And to whom would He interpret the message? Those just weaned from milk? Those just taken from the breast? For He says, 'Order on order, order on order, line on line, line on line, a little here, a little there'"* (Isaiah 28:9-10). Our life is not prescribed, to be performed for Him. Our life is to be surrendered as an offering, allowing His life to flourish in and through our own.

Question: Which part of your spiritual journey is taking you places that you have never been before?

287. Spirit Given to All

*"Do not call to mind the former things, or ponder
things of the past. Behold, I will do something new,
now it will spring forth; will you not be aware of it?
I will even make a roadway in the wilderness, rivers
in the desert."* ~ Isaiah 43:18-19

The prophet Joel prophesied that God would *"pour out My
Spirit on all mankind; and your sons and daughters will prophesy,
your old men will dream dreams, your young men will see visions.
And even on the male and female servants I will pour out My Spirit
in those days"* (Joel 2:28-29). In the Old Testament, only a select
few prophets, priests, and kings spoke on behalf of God. The
Lord spoke through Joel of a day when He would abide in the
midst of all of His people, using each one to bear witness of
Himself. Mankind, originally designed to bear the image and
likeness of God, could not represent the One they were not
yet restored to. Following Christ's death, resurrection and
ascension, a new creation was formed. *"Therefore if any man is
in Christ, he is a new creature; the old things passed away; behold,
new things have come"* (2 Corinthians 5:17). With the formation
of a new tabernacle upon the earth, God poured out His
Spirit, allowing His glory to once more clothe mankind, filling
them with His own power and authority.

Question: *As a church body, are you experiencing the fullness of
Christ's authority and power?*

288. Does God Still Speak?

*"Make your ear attentive to wisdom, incline your
heart to understanding." ~ Proverbs 2:2*

In English we use the same word to describe many things..
For example, previously I shared how when my daughter was
two, she said, "I love Jesus, I love mommy, I love French
fries." She was using the word "love" for different things.

Another example is what experiences we describe as "hearing". Scripture indicates that some heard the audible voice of
God, while others responded to an inner voice or a mental
impression. Hearing Him today also takes a variety of forms.
As New Testament followers of Jesus, we have access to the
word of God in the scriptures. It is *"living and active and sharper
than any two-edged sword, and piercing as far as the division of soul
and spirit, of both joints and marrow, and able to judge the thoughts
and intentions of the heart"* (Hebrews 4:12). Being exposed to
His word is a dynamic experience, sometimes deeply convicting, other times personally encouraging. Our time with the
Spirit, leading us through the word, becomes a place of communion and hearing His voice. Since we are a people who
have been filled with the Holy Spirit, it is imperative that we
learn how He wants to lead us, both personally and corporately. *"I urge you therefore, brethren, by the mercies of God, to
present your bodies a living and holy sacrifice, acceptable to God,
which is your spiritual service of worship. And do not be conformed
to this world, but be transformed by the renewing of your mind, that
you may prove what the will of God is, that which is good and acceptable and perfect"* (Romans 12:1-2).

Question: *Have you experienced the voice of the Lord as He has convicted you about something? Have you heard any personal promises?*

289. Living Word

*"It is the Spirit who gives life; the flesh profits
nothing; the words that I have spoken to you are
spirit and are life." ~ John 6:63*

In order for us to understand the nature of faith, God
clothed His Son, the Living Word, in flesh, and sent Him to
dwell in our midst. *"What was from the beginning, what we have
heard, what we have seen with our eyes, what we beheld and our
hands handled, concerning the Word of Life—and the life was manifested, and we have seen and bear witness and proclaim to you the
eternal life, which was with the Father and was manifested to us—
what we have seen and heard we proclaim to you also, that you also
may have fellowship with us; and indeed our fellowship is with the
Father, and with His Son Jesus Christ"* (1 John 1:1-3). A life of
walking in the Spirit brings us into a fellowship with the
Word—the person. We are not given a creed to memorize, or
a doctrine that demands our allegiance. Instead, we are given
access to the same Word that created the world, preparing
what is seen out of things which are invisible. This is the One
who has the ability to penetrate our spirit with His truth, and
transform us into our original design.

*Question: How do you discern the difference between words taught by
the Spirit and knowledge gained from the world?*

290. Learning Communication

*"Now we have received, not the spirit of the
world, but the Spirit who is from God, that we
might know the things freely given to us by God,
which things we also speak, not in words taught by
human wisdom, but in those taught by the Spirit,
combining spiritual thoughts with spiritual words."*
~ I Corinthians 2:12-13

Children learn to understand and speak the language of
their culture in a very short amount of time. In fact, children
have a phenomenal capacity to gain a new language, when
they are placed in a new, unfamiliar culture. Some of the ways
that children learn to hear and speak help us learn the language of our Heavenly Father. Daily repetition and repeated
exposure to the scriptures and prayer effect our capacity to
hear. If we take note of the simple commands and sayings of
Jesus, we begin to comprehend His will. If learning how to
hear His voice is important to you, or you have a need, you
will be more likely to listen. When we hear others speak about
the Lord, we can imitate their ways. When we understand
how deeply we are loved by the Father, we are able to comprehend His voice, and we hear discipline as love rather than
punishment.

*Question: What does the Lord say to you repeatedly, but you still
haven't obeyed?*

291. He Makes Himself Known

"For since the creation of the world His invisible attributes, His eternal power and divine nature, have been clearly seen, being understood through what has been made ...." ~ Romans 1:20

The Lord is careful to make Himself known to a creation that has eyes, but sees not, and has ears, but hears not. He used multiple means of accessing the hearts of His people, and making Himself understood. In the Old Testament, He appeared as an unquenchable fire in a bush to get the attention of Moses. He appeared as a pillar of fire in the wilderness to lead Israel from Egypt to the Promised Land. In the New Testament, the Father made Himself visible in His Son. *"God, after He spoke long ago to the father's in the prophets in many portions and in many ways, in these last days has spoken to us in His Son, whom He appointed heir of all things, through whom also He made the world. And He is the radiance of His glory and the exact representation of His nature, and upholds all things by the word of His power"* (Hebrews 1:1-3). Now the Lord speaks to His people through the Holy Spirit. We might sense an internal voice that gives us wisdom and counsel, have an impression, see an image, recall a verse and receive insight from it, or be given instruction through a word of wisdom or a word of knowledge. As we live in submission to His word and gain our understanding through the Holy Spirit, we too, encounter the Living God.

Question: Do you consider hearing the voice of the Lord vital to daily living?

292. Holy Spirit Bears Witness

*"You search the Scriptures, because you think
that in them you have eternal life; and it is these
that bear witness of Me." ~ John 5:39*

"When the Helper comes, whom I will send to you from the Father,
that is the Spirit of truth, who proceeds from the Father, He will bear
witness of Me, and you will bear witness also, because you have been
with Me from the beginning" (John 15:26). It is the work of the
Holy Spirit to bear witness to that which is born of God. As
we are learning to coordinate and cooperate as one body of
Christ, under His leadership, there will be a variety of people
with different levels of maturity, attempting to walk in the
Spirit. As we walk in the oneness of His body, each can bear
witness to the others what they sense concerning the Spirit's
movement. These senses must be continually tested, and then
corrected, lest we operate from strength of soul and forfeit being led. If someone shares what they sense the Spirit is saying,
and it does not bear witness in your spirit—seems off some-
how—pay attention. Do not allow the body to proceed without contributing your sense as well. In this way, we walk in
submission to Him, and to one another.

Question: *How does the church discern truth when it is exposed to so
much mixture?*

293. Holy Spirit Reminds You

*"Therefore, I shall always be ready to remind you
of these things, even though you already know
them, and have been established in the truth which
is present with you. And I consider it right, as long
as I am in this earthly dwelling, to stir you up by
way of reminder ..." ~ 2 Peter 1:12-13*

When my godson was four years old, he asked me how to hear the voice of the Lord. The reply that came into my heart was, "It's like remembering something that you didn't know before." Just like memories come into our minds, thoughts from the Spirit of God arise in us, and give us an inner sense of what the Lord is saying. Jesus said, *"But the Helper, the Holy Spirit, whom the Father will send in My name, He will teach you all things, and bring to your remembrance all that I said to you"* (John 14:26). The Spirit is able to take seed that has been sown in one situation and extract a truth for another scenario. He is able to bring back a thought that was given, before we knew the reason for it. He combines lessons learned from a former trial and streamlines the application for a current situation. Unlike an earthly parent, whose reminders are often veiled opportunities to nag, the Spirit knows that apart from Him we can do nothing.

Question: Does God promise to remember anything? What does He promise to forget?

294. Guides into Truth

"But for all this, you did not trust the Lord your
God, who goes before you on your way, to seek out a
place for you to encamp, in fire by night and cloud
by day, to show you the way in which
you should go." ~ Deuteronomy 1:32-33

"But when He, the Spirit of truth, comes, He will guide you into all the truth; for He will not speak on His own initiative, but whatever He hears, He will speak; and He will disclose to you what is to come. He shall glorify Me; for He shall take of Mine, and shall disclose it to you. All things that the Father has are Mine; therefore I said, that He takes of Mine, and will disclose it to you" (John 16:13-15). Truth is a person, more than a correct theology. The Lord, by the Spirit, wants to disclose Himself, His word, and His ways, as we walk with Him. The Spirit longs to guide us in paths we have not known before. Even as the pillar of fire was sent to lead Israel on their wilderness journey, the Lord is among us to serve as the Head of the body. Because we grow accustomed to whatever culture we live in, we tend to live lives formed by that environment. To repent of one kingdom, so that we might repent to another, the Spirit of truth must convict, cleanse, guide, and reorient us to His ways.

Question: How does a guide accomplish his task or assignment?

295. Holy Spirit Grants Assurance

"... in order that He might redeem those who
were under the Law, that we might receive the
adoption as sons. And because you are sons, God
has sent forth the Spirit of His Son into our hearts,
crying, 'Abba! Father!' Therefore you are no longer
a slave, but a son; and if a son, then an
heir through God." ~ Galatians 4:5-7

The Holy Spirit grants God's people the confidence to trust in and act upon His promises and calling. *"The Spirit Himself bears witness with our spirit that we are children of God, and if children, heirs also, heirs of God and fellow heirs with Christ, if indeed we suffer with Him in order that we may also be glorified with Him"* (Romans 8:16-17). Because the accuser of the brethren is continually threatening us with fear, guilt, and shame, the Father has given us a strong defense in the form of His Spirit. The Spirit's work is to bring about a deep conviction in our identity concerning our adoption as sons. We belong to Him, and no one can take us out of His grasp. It is not our responsibility to become what we have been called for—only to believe it.

Question: Is there an area of your spiritual life where you experience insecurity?

296. Hearing the Lord in the Scriptures

*"One thing I have asked from the Lord, that I shall
seek: that I may dwell in the house of the Lord all
the days of my life, to behold the beauty of the Lord,
and to meditate in His temple." ~ Psalm 27:4*

We meditate upon the Lord in order to know Him and be familiar with His voice, character, and activity. Biblical meditation is to ponder a verse with a receptive heart, allowing the Holy Spirit to take the written word and apply it as the Living Word to our inner being. This results in the impartation of divine truth to our spirit—and our responsiveness to God.

Begin by asking the Holy Spirit to lead by teaching you the scriptures. Pray that your time and thoughts are protected as you set time aside to listen. Sometimes, if you choose a portion of scripture that you are very familiar with, it helps to meditate on that portion from a different translation. This allows the different phrasing to recapture your attention. Meditation is to read until something catches your attention, allowing words to stick out in a fresh way. You begin to notice thoughts and words you hadn't seen before, or a question from your heart is answered, or you have a sense of conviction. Meditation is about learning to linger, to digest, be inspired, or have a heart revelation—rather than information and a cognitive response.

Question: How much time can you carve out for solitude on a given day or week? What are you tempted to do with solitude?

297. Revelation, Inspiration, Illumination

"The Lord by wisdom founded the earth; by
understanding He established the heavens."
~ Proverbs 3:19

Accessing the truth of the scriptures requires the presence of the Holy Spirit. He is able to teach us, giving us wisdom and understanding. There are three words that describe this process of giving insight to the one who seeks Him.

Revelation is when God reveals truths by the Holy Spirit. It comes from the Greek word, *apokalupis*, which means to uncover. This would describe a truth that has always been present, but a lid has been lifted so that it can be seen.

The next word is **inspiration**, a divine influence directly exerted upon the mind or soul. It includes the idea of drawing in a breath. The Holy Spirit breathing upon a person can infuse them with His means of understanding.

The last word, **illumination**, is when light is shed on our understanding. When we are given insight about future happenings, it is called prophecy. When light is shed on something current, giving us understanding and helping us apply knowledge already given, it is called illumination.

Question: Have you experienced any of these personally?

298. Discovering Treasure

*"... He gives wisdom to wise men, and knowledge
to men of understanding. It is He who reveals the
profound and hidden things; He knows what is in
the darkness, and the light dwells with Him."*
~ Daniel 2:21-22

The Lord has placed His truth in plain sight, yet it remains hidden. This is how Jesus describes the nature of His Kingdom. *"To you it has been granted to know the mysteries of the kingdom of heaven, but to them it has not been granted ... therefore I speak to them in parables; because while seeing they do not see, and while hearing they do not hear, nor do they understand"* (Matthew 13:11, 13). This mystery is something hidden or not fully manifest. It is some sacred thing hidden or secret which is naturally unknown to human reason and is only known by the revelation of God. It is a spiritual truth couched under an external representation or similitude—thereby concealed or hidden unless some explanation is given. These mysteries are promised to all, but received by only a few. When Jesus teaches mysteries, it makes us convert to using our other eye—the lamp of the Spirit. Just like an infant has eyes and ears, but must learn what they are seeing, we too must learn the language of the kingdom, and its interpretation.

Question: *What do you do when you encounter a spiritual situation that you don't understand or a portion of scripture that you can't grasp?*

299. Developing Discernment

*"But solid food is for the mature, who because of
practice have their senses trained to discern good
and evil." ~ Hebrews 5:14*

Discernment is the process of learning to listen to the voice of the Lord, and developing the ability to recognize *"wisdom from above"* (James 3:17). It is not necessarily the activity of choosing good as opposed to evil, or better as opposed to best, but one who can recognize the differences and source of each. *"Things which eye has not seen and ear has not heard, and which have not entered the heart of man, all that God has prepared for those who love Him. For to us God revealed them through the Spirit; for the Spirit searches all things, even the depths of God"* (1 Corinthians 2:9-10). This is a quality of spiritual understanding that begins to develop in a believer as they mature; as they no longer lean on their own understanding. With maturity, we are able to distinguish the difference between the wisdom of the world, and the wisdom that comes from God. We are able to navigate situations by the Word of God and the counsel of the Holy Spirit. Discernment can apprehend a correct direction, while at the same time, guard us from error. With the help of the Holy Spirit, we are able to discover deception and counterfeits, put spirits to the test, and disclose the source of spiritual manifestations. As we learn to see by the Spirit, instead of the flesh, we become those who display discernment, and walk in maturity.

Question: How do you recognize the wisdom of the world? In conversations? In teachings? In what you read? In your plans and goals? How is it acquired?

300. Seated in Heavenly Places

*"Set your mind on the things above, not on the
things that are on earth. For you have died and your
life is hidden with Christ in God."*
~ Colossians 3:2-3

"For if we have become united with Him in the likeness of His death, certainly we shall be also in the likeness of His resurrection..." (Romans 6:5). Part of our maturing process in Christ is to become united with Him in all things. When we are identified with His crucifixion, we consider ourselves dead to sin; our old self is crucified with Him. When we are united in the likeness of His resurrection, death is no longer master over us, and we live in newness of life. There is a third way to become united with Him in our spiritual journey. *"But God, being rich in mercy, because of His great love with which He loved us, even when we were dead in our transgressions, made us alive together with Christ (by grace you have been saved), and raised us up with Him, and seated us with Him in the heavenly places, in Christ Jesus ..."* (Ephesians 2:4-6). Following the ascension, God seated Jesus *"at His right hand in the heavenly places, far above all rule and authority and power and dominion, and every name that is named, not only in this age, but also in the one to come"* (Ephesians 1:20-21). We have been joined to Christ in the likeness of His ascension, seated above the fray. Instead of the world overcoming us—we overcome the world.

Question: *How do you sustain a heavenly perspective while in the midst of a trial?*

301. Spiritual Blindness

"Let them alone; they are blind guides of the blind.
And if a blind man guides a blind man, both will
fall into a pit." ~ Matthew 15:14

Until we learn to navigate by the eye of our heart being enlightened, we walk in spiritual darkness. Our natural eyes and ears have the capacity to observe in the natural realm, but they are unable to serve us in accessing the spiritual realm. If we continue to operate in the oldness of the letter and law, attempting to suppress our old nature, we will not discern our means of freedom in the Spirit of God. Suppressed sin remains sin, and has the ability to interrupt our capacity to perceive. One of the strategies of the god of this world, is to *"... blind the minds of the unbelieving, that they might not see the light of the gospel of the glory of Christ, who is the image of God"* (2 *Corinthians* 4:4). If the evil one is able to prompt us to hate (1 John 2:8-11), we are blinded. When a bribe is taken, involving us in moral corruption, we are blinded (Exodus 23:8). Rebellion and idolatry are both enemy strategies to rob God's people of spiritual sight.

Question: *What outward circumstances cause blindness? What inward circumstances cause blindness?*

302. Responsive to the Spirit

*"Then the Lord came and stood and called as at
other times, 'Samuel! Samuel!' And Samuel said,
'Speak, for Thy servant is listening.'"*
~ I Samuel 3:10

"And the angel of the Lord appeared to him (Moses) in a blazing
fire from the midst of a bush; and he looked, and behold, the bush
was burning with fire, yet the bush was not consumed. So Moses
said, 'I must turn aside now, and see this marvelous sight, why the
bush is not burned up.' When the Lord saw that he turned aside to
look, God called to him from the midst of the bush, and said, 'Moses,
Moses!' And he said, 'Here I am'"* (Exodus 3:2-4). God displayed
Himself to Moses in a familiar place. When there is an inter-
ruption to our normal environment, it is time to be particularly attentive. Moses did not interpret the current situation
with previous experiences. He turned aside from his ways,
and approached the Lord. The immediate response from Moses was wonder, rather than cynicism and doubt. Have our
senses been so overstimulated by what the world continually
offers us, that we are slow to see, slow to respond, and quick
to turn away? One of the benefits of fasting is to restore our
senses to their designed sensitivity to the Holy Spirit. To deny
our body its usual satisfaction has a way of reminding our
soul to turn its attention to God.

---

*Question: Has the Lord ever captivated your attention by something in
order to speak to you there?*

303. Fluency

"How blessed are those who observe His
testimonies, who seek Him with all their heart."
~ Psalm 119:2

Responsiveness to the Spirit of God progresses through a number of stages. When we are first filled with the Spirit, there is a change of belief concerning how we learn. We are introduced to the possibility that He speaks to us, and wants to begin functioning as our indwelling guide. This challenges our independence and our reliance on knowledge alone. As we continue to abide with Him, we begin to recognize the difference between His works and our own—the strength of soul versus. the life of the Spirit. A dependency develops on His life for wisdom and understanding. Fluency is developed from intimacy of relationship with the Holy Spirit, and walking by the wisdom He imparts. Our proximity to others who understand the voice of the Lord increases our ability to know and recognize Him. As we become more familiar with His ways, and take the opportunity to listen, we mature in our understanding. Your desire for friendship with God and the fellowship of His Spirit brings you into an intimacy with Christ.

Question: How fluent are you in the language of the Holy Spirit?

304. Holy Spirit Brings Conviction

"And He, when He comes, will convict the world concerning sin and righteousness, and judgment."
~ John 16:8

One of the responsibilities of the Holy Spirit is to bring to light things that are hidden from our understanding. When we respond to His revelation concerning sin, righteousness, or judgment, that is called conviction. The Spirit examines our life, discerning where we have missed the mark and gone astray from the will of God. Even those who would claim an inability to hear the voice of the Lord are usually aware of His conviction. We learn to recognize the difference between conviction and condemnation by the content of what we are hearing. If it is specific, and is drawing you to repentance and reuniting your heart to the Lord, it is the work of the Holy Spirit. As the accuser of the brethren, the enemy attempts to separate us from the Lord. He brings vague charges against us, loading us with large portions of guilt and shame. He must be resisted verbally, as you bring your heart and mind in submission to the Father.

Question: *How can the church make room for conviction to take place corporately? See Revelation 2-3.*

328

Part 11

Faith

305. Logos and Rhema

"So faith comes from hearing, and hearing by the
word of Christ." ~ Romans 10:17

It takes two Greek words to translate "word" in the New Testament. The first, *logos*, refers to the entirety of inspired scripture, as well as to Jesus, the Word made flesh. The second word, *rhema*, refers to the spoken word. It is how the Holy Spirit takes from the scriptures and enlivens it to our heart. When the Lord calls us to faith, in Romans 10:17, it is a call to respond to His *rhema*: *"So faith comes from hearing, and hearing by the word [rhema] of Christ."* As we learn to hear and respond to the voice of the Lord, our exposure to the Holy Scriptures becomes an initial way of discerning and testing what we are perceiving. The Lord is able to take from the scriptures and plant His word as seed in our hearts. This living and powerful word of God quickens us as we believe.

Question: Do you approach the scriptures anticipating an encounter with the Living Word?

306. Little Faith

> *"And He said to them, 'Why are you timid, you*
> *men of little faith?' Then He arose, and rebuked the*
> *winds and the sea; and it became*
> *perfectly calm." ~ Matthew 8:26*

Following the transfiguration of Jesus, a man brought his demon possessed son to Jesus, because the disciples had not delivered him. When they asked Jesus why they had been unable to cast it out, He replied, *"Because of the littleness of your faith; for truly, I say to you, if you have faith as a mustard seed, you shall say to this mountain, 'Move from here to there,' and it shall move; and nothing shall be impossible to you'"* (Matthew 17:20). This is followed by an explanation that *"this kind does not go out except by prayer and fasting"* (Matthew 17:21). We tend to key in on verse 21, when there is real insight to be gained in verse 20. When faith comes to us, it comes in seed form. What we do with the seed determines what our ultimate fruit will be. In this story, if you have a seed of faith, you are to speak to the obstacle and command it to move. When we hear a *rhema* from God, our first response is to speak to whatever obstacle lies in its way.

Question: *Has the Lord entrusted you with a promise from the scriptures? What scriptures have become alive in your heart?*

307. Faith is a Seed

"But what does it say? 'The word is near you, in
your mouth and in your heart' — that is, the word of
faith which we are preaching." ~ Romans 10:8

A seed holds all the potential of full fruit, but remains within the limitation of itself until it is activated. Activation is only accomplished as we become doers of the word, and not merely hearers. *"Therefore putting aside all filthiest and all that remains of wickedness, in humility receive the word implanted, which is able to save your souls. But prove yourselves doers of the word, and not merely hearers who delude themselves"* (James 1:21-22). When you hear a gifted teacher, you are being exposed to their fruit, but you receive it as seed. When we read a book, attend a study, or listen to a sermon, we tend to eat the seed, treating it as a one-time meal. Instead, when we hear the word we can become effectual doers, being nourished, but also able to nourish others as we sow what has been given to us. It takes time, nourishment, and light to bring seed to full fruit, and how we steward this gift determines its fulfillment.

Question: *How have you exercised faith this week?*

308. Unbelieving Generation

"Then He said to Thomas, 'Reach here your finger, and see My hands; and reach here your hand, and put it into My side; and be not unbelieving, but believing.'" ~ John 20:27

When the disciples were unable to bring deliverance to a demon possessed boy, Jesus responded by saying, *"O unbelieving generation, how long shall I be with you? How long shall I put up with you...?"* (Mark 9:19). Sometimes an entire people can fail to believe. This happens when a generation is being conformed to the culture rather than bearing the image and likeness of God. Jesus knew who He was, so He did what He did. An entire generation can lose its way if they don't understand their corporate identity. *"But realize this, that in the last days difficult times will come. For men will be lovers of self, lovers of money, boastful, arrogant, revivers, disobedient to parents, ungrateful, uphold, unloving, irreconcilable, malicious gossips, without self-control, brutal, haters of good, treacherous, reckless, conceited, lovers of pleasure rather than lovers of God; holding to a form of godliness, although they have denied its power; and avoid such men as these"* (2 Timothy 3:1-5).

Question: When and where are you confronted with unbelief?

309. Faith to Faith

"For by faith, and trust and holy fervor born of
faith, the men of old had divine testimony borne to
them and obtained a good report."
~ Hebrews 11:2 (AMPC)

Perhaps movement in the Kingdom is from faith to faith, rather than from experience to experience. *"Now faith is the assurance (the confirmation, the title deed) of the things we hope for, being the proof of things we do not see and the conviction of their reality—faith perceiving as real fact what is not revealed to the senses"* (Hebrews 11:1, AMPC). From the moment we hear a *rhema* word of God, what He has activated toward us and for us, we have received the title-deed to what we are to possess. Our prayer is answered the moment we hear. When our spiritual eye and ear begin to lay hold of things that are imperceptible to our natural senses, faith is at work. Faith becomes enlarged as we lay hold of the promise, continually activating it under the direction of the Holy Spirit.

Question: *Do you know someone who seems to have a lot of faith?*

310. Father of Faith

"But as it is, they desire a better country, that is a heavenly one. Therefore God is not ashamed to be called their God; for He has prepared a city for them." ~ Hebrews 11:16

After the fall, in Genesis 3, God promises to send a Seed that would ultimately defeat Satan. Genesis 1-11 unfolds the creation story, the fall, the defiance of rebellious mankind, and then a cleansing flood. The narrative in Genesis 12 introduces us to a man who will be considered the father of faith and the chosen lineage for the promised Seed. This is where the story narrows to focus on one couple who will be God's illustration to a world that needs to relearn His ways. God speaks, and Abraham listens and believes. He is called to leave his home and follow to a land he will be shown. *"By faith Abraham, when he was called, obeyed by going out to a place which he was to receive for an inheritance; and he went out, not knowing where he was going"* (Hebrews 11:8). All that he had been is left behind for a promise to inherit what he had never seen. Walking by the Spirit takes us on a similar journey. We listen, obey, wait, and then, following a passage of time, we receive.

Question: *Do you have anyone in your earthly family who modeled the ways of God for you?*

311. Exposing Soil Conditions

"Behold, the sower went out to sow ..."
~Matthew 13:3

When the seed of God's word is sown into our hearts, it begins to expose the state of our soil. In the parable of the soils (Matthew 13, Luke 8), we find that three out of four types of soil bring no fruit to maturity. Those who hear the word without understanding it, the hard soil, are robbed of the seed as the evil one snatches it away. When God's word is sown on rocky soil, it springs up quickly, having no firm root. It dies, just as quickly, when persecution, affliction, or trials take place. The word sown among thorns—the worry of the world and the deceitfulness of riches—is choked out and it never matures. The seeds sown on good soil are those who hear the word and understand it. They persevere to the point of bringing forth fruit, some 30, some 60, and some 100-fold.

Question: When the word of the Lord is sown in your heart, what kind of soil does it find?

312. Pleasing God

"For the mind set on the flesh is death, but the mind set on the Spirit is life—and peace ... and those who are in the flesh cannot please God."
~ Romans 8:6, 8

In teaching His people the way of faith, God lets us know what is pleasing to Him. *"And without faith it is impossible to please Him for he who comes to God must believe that He is, and that He is a rewarder of those who seek Him"* (Hebrews 11:6).

A number of years ago, I sensed the Lord calling me to seek Him. I thought I knew what "seek" meant—until I lost a $900 check. When we realized it was missing, I looked in the normal, predictable locations. With every passing hour, my search became more frantic and almost absurd as I looked for it in every inch of our house, from Christmas decorations to boxes in the garage. I searched for 17 hours to no avail. The next morning, as I was out walking and praying (and weeping about the loss), the Lord remained quiet for a long time. Then, when I began to quiet myself, I heard Him speak to my heart: "Now do you know what the word seek means?"

We tend to seek the Lord within certain time constraints and in places we expect to meet Him. I broke every normal bound seeking a check. We learn the way of faith and how to walk in the Spirit by seeking Him.

Question: Where in your spiritual journey could you stand to press a bit more when it comes to seeking the Lord?

313. Leave a Known Way

"... for he was looking for the city which has
foundations, whose architect and builder is God."
~ Hebrews 11:10

When Abraham acknowledged God's call, he was a 75 year old man. He had lived his entire life in one country, one culture, one family, and set of friends. He had work that he was familiar with. He was asked to leave the known for the unknown. When he finally arrived in Shechem, the Lord appeared to him and promised land and an heir. As he encountered the Lord there, Abraham built an altar and worshipped.

God still calls people to follow Him, to leave the known way. A number of years ago, He challenged me, "If you will give up what you are satisfied with, I will give you what you are hungry for." A promise beckoned me to take up my cross and follow Him, to die to my ways in order to lay hold of Him. I didn't know where I was going, but I knew the One who bid me come. And that choice has made all the difference.

Question: *What are you hungry for?*

314. Earthly and Heavenly Inheritance

*"And just as we have borne the image of the
earthy, we shall also bear the image of the
heavenly." ~ I Corinthians 15:49*

Abraham inherited an earthly location that was a shadow of
His heavenly inheritance. His heirs were to be as the *"dust of
the earth"* (Genesis 13:15-18), and as the *"stars of the sky"*
(Genesis 15:5). One represented an earthly promise with a
natural fulfillment, while the other was a spiritual promise
with heavenly implications. Because Abraham knew and
believed God, he had his eyes fixed on the realm of the Spirit,
and not just the tangible, physical realm. He was able to wait
and watch, with hope and perseverance, because he knew the
One who fulfills all of His word. The earthly promises were
fulfilled as a down payment on His spiritual inheritance. By
observing Abraham's story, we learn to fix our own eyes
upon Jesus—who is the author and perfecter of our faith, and
has *"blessed us with every spiritual blessing in the heavenly places"*
(Ephesians 1:3).

*Question: Have you received a good gift that you know is just a shadow
of something greater?*

315. No Ability or Capacity

"By faith even Sarah herself received ability to conceive, even beyond the proper time of life, since she considered Him faithful who had promised ..."
~ Hebrews 11:11

Our faith is based in the Lord and what He promises, not our abilities or capacity. When God made His promise of an heir to Abraham and Sarah, the conception was not due to being overshadowed by the Holy Spirit as Mary was when—as a virgin—she conceived and gave birth to Jesus. It was more like Elizabeth, who was given supernatural ability to conceive, though advanced in years. All Abraham, Sarah, and Elizabeth had to bring was their faith—not their strength or fertility. When His word unites with our faith, conception is the result. *"For the word of God is living and active and sharper than any two-edged sword, and piercing as far as the division of soul and spirit, of both joints and marrow, and able to judge the thoughts and intentions of the heart ... For indeed we have had good news preached to us, just as they also; but the word they heard did not profit them, because it was not united by faith in those who heard"* (Hebrews 4:12, 2). By faith we receive the word implanted, and then we wait for the fullness of time to bear.

Question: Do you have an impossible situation that you would like to invite the Lord to respond and speak to?

316. Delay of Promise

*"Even so Abraham believed God, and it was
reckoned to him as righteousness. Therefore, be sure
that it is those who are of faith who are sons of
Abraham." ~ Galatians 3:6-7*

When God promised children to Abraham, it was good
news—something that he had longed for, but no longer
expected. From the time the promise that he would have an
heir was given to Abraham when he was 75, until it was
fulfilled when he was 99, there was a significant delay.
During this long interval, Abraham and Sarah attempted to
satisfy the promise with human effort and ingenuity. The
result was Ishmael. *"For it is written that Abraham had two sons,
one by the bond woman and one by the free woman. But the son by
the bond woman was born according to the flesh, and the son by the
free woman through the promise ... But as at that time he who was
born according to the flesh persecuted him who was born according
to the Spirit, so it is now also"* (Galatians 4:22-23, 29). Our own
Ishmaels can take place when we take the promises of God
and try to fulfill them with our own human ways, strengths,
ideas, or programs. We can often delay what God intends
through our fleshly attempts at helping Him. The deeds of the
flesh are continually at odds with the fruit of the Spirit, even
as Ishmael lived at odds with Isaac.

Question: Have you ever tried to help God? What was the result?

317. On Earth as it is in Heaven

"As Thou didst send Me into the world, I also
have sent them into the world." ~ John 17:18

Faith is not a denial of current conditions, but lays hold of what is true in the Kingdom of God and cries for that will *"to be done on earth as it is in heaven"* (Matthew 6:10). When Abraham heard the Lord's voice, and later when the Lord appear to him, he was awakened to the reality of God's Kingdom and the nature of creation prior to the fall. He set his heart on pilgrimage, even after he began to receive the promises in the natural realm (Hebrews 11:13-16). When the creation was first entrusted to Adam and Eve, they were told to be fruitful and multiply, fill the earth and subdue it, and rule over the natural realm. When the Lord gives us His Kingdom, we are entrusted with a similar stewardship. We are to exercise His authority and power to bring everything into submission to Him. We are sent into the whole world to make disciples because our assignment is to steward and possess.

Question: How can you make His Kingdom known today?

318. Welcome Promise From Afar

*"I speak the things which I have seen with
My Father ..." ~ John 8:38*

We can fail to activate the promises of God and therefore postpone their fulfillment. When God speaks a word to our hearts, we must learn how to walk by faith, and not just by sight (2 Corinthians 5:7). In Hebrews 11:13-16 it says that they saw the promises and *"welcomed them from a distance."* To welcome someone or something means we prepare a place for them. So, we can begin to make room in our heart, our mind, our plans, and our confession. We can speak what we are believing, instead of rehearsing our lack. We can give testimony to what we have heard, rehearsing God's goodness. Hebrews also states that they viewed themselves as strangers and exiles upon the earth. Jesus states something similar in John 18:36, *"My kingdom is not of this world ... is not of this realm."* When we have received a promise from God, we are invited to participate in its transfer from the unseen into the seen for the sake of the Kingdom.

Question: Is there an area of your life where the way that you speak needs to be realigned to your faith?

---

319. Manifest Your Hearts Desire

"But as it is, they desire a better country, that is a
heavenly one. Therefore God is not ashamed to be
called their God, for He has prepared
a city for them." ~ Hebrews 11:16

I am not sure that we are always aware of what our heart is set upon. The year I turned 50, I shared frequently with my husband that I wanted a Jeep for my birthday (1 am a jeep, but that is another story). One night, as the church gathered in our living room for worship, I heard the Lord ask me a question. "Jody, if I were to manifest your heart's desire right now, in the middle of this room ... would you like it to be a Jeep?" My heart was taken aback, as I replied, "No Lord. If You were to manifest my heart's desire right now, I would want it to be You." He spoke again. "If I were to manifest your heart's desire right now ... would you want it to be a fulfillment of all you have prayed for your son?" I began to weep as I considered all my heart had been set upon. Even good things must have their rightful place in our heart. May He be made manifest when we gather to worship.

Question: *If the Lord were to manifest your heart's desire in the midst of your room, right now, what would it be?*

320. *Testing Faith*

*"Blessed is a man who perseveres under trial; for
once he has been approved, he will receive the crown
of life, which the Lord has promised to those who
love Him." ~ James 1:12*

Scriptures indicate that faith is something that gets tested. Some might think that faith is too fragile for that, that if it is tested, it could be destroyed. Faith has within it all the life and power it needs to produce its end. Tests are designed to move obstacles out of the way that could impede our faith in the future. Consider James 1:2-4, *"Consider it all joy, my brethren, when you encounter various trials, knowing that the testing of your faith produces endurance. And let endurance have its perfect result, that you may be perfect and complete, lacking in nothing."* Testing produces endurance—the capacity for something to last and to withstand what obstacles it faces. In the midst of a trial we begin to develop the persistence, fortitude, stamina, and courage necessary to steward His promises.

Question: *Where has God tested your faith to the point that you developed endurance? Or patience, or perhaps longsuffering?*

321. Trust

"And those who know Thy name will put their trust in Thee; for Thou O Lord, hast not forsaken those who seek Thee." ~ Psalm 9:10

Faith lays hold of the promises of God, and trust gives stability to our faith. Trust looks past the promise and sees the Promiser; it rests in a relationship, more than a result. Ultimately, the testing of our faith exposes who or what we will turn to under pressure. The evil one hopes to gain an advantage in our trial, tempting us in our sufferings. Eve, when she was tested, trusted herself and believed a lie. While God was delaying, Abraham trusted himself in his trial, and received Ishmael—what his flesh could produce. Later Abraham, when he was tested, trusted God on the mount and received his son back as a type (Genesis 22:1-18). A key to trust is: believe that the One you trust is good—and will express that in your relationship.

Question: When do you know that you can trust someone?

322. Spiritual Heritage

"And they forgot His deeds, and His miracles that
He had shown them." ~ Psalm 78:11

Abraham is known as the father of faith, but his children were inheritors in their own right. Even as Abraham was called to follow, Isaac, Jacob and his sons also encountered the Lord, and are mentioned in Hebrews 11 for their faith. Our children need to have their own encounter with the Lord. We have the privilege of cultivating their heart. Psalm 78:2-8 instructs us on how to transfer our faith to the next generation. *"I will open my mouth in a parable; I will utter dark sayings of old, which we have heard and known, and our fathers have told us. We will not conceal them from their children, but tell to the generation to come the praises of the Lord, and His strength and His wondrous works that He has done. For He established a testimony in Jacob, and appointed a law in Israel, which He commanded our fathers, that they should teach them to their children, that the generation to come might know, even the children yet to be born, that they may arise and tell them to their children, that they should put their confidence in God, and not forget the works of God, but keep His commandments, and not be like their fathers, a stubborn and rebellious generation, a generation that did not prepare its heart, and whose spirit was not faithful to God."* We are exhorted to pass on both the statutes (God's Law) and the stories (Bible stories and our own God stories). One gives instruction concerning God's holiness and His ways, and the other fuels hearts with faith.

Question: Do you have a way of remembering and rehearsing your God stories?

---

323. Law will not Possess the Land

"But the Lord said to Moses and Aaron, 'Because you have not believed Me, to treat Me as holy in the sight of the sons of Israel, therefore you shall not bring this assembly into the land which I have given them.'" ~ Numbers 20:12

Moses, the great Old Testament leader, who led Israel from Egypt through the wilderness to the Promised Land, was forbidden to enter himself. Though he was the one chosen to receive the Law on Mount Sinai, he was considered a man of faith in Hebrews 11. *"By faith he left Egypt, not fearing the wrath of the King; for he endured, as seeing Him who is unseen"* (Hebrews 11:27). In Exodus 17, when Israel desperately needed water, Moses was instructed to strike a rock to release water for the people (a type of Christ). Later, in Numbers 20, Israel was in need of water again. The Lord instructed Moses to speak to the rock to release water (another type of Christ). Moses disobeyed and struck the rock again, thus marring the image of Christ. The consequence of this act of disobedience was that He was forbidden from entering the Promised Land. The lesson: Law can never bring us into the Kingdom (Promised Land). It is accessed by faith, a willingness to follow the Lord—walking by His Spirit.

Question: *Is there an area of your life where you think you know how to respond—but the Lord wants to speak to you?*

324. Triumph or Suffering

*"For consider Him who has endured such hostility
by sinners against Himself, so that you may not
grow weary and lose heart." ~ Hebrews 12:3*

Sometimes faith looks like triumph, and sometimes it looks like suffering. Works of faith are not based on their outcome, but in their source. Not all heroes of our faith received the promises in their lifetime. *"And all these, having gained approval through their faith, did not receive what was promised, because God had provided something better for us, so that apart from us they should not be made perfect"* (Hebrews 11:39-40). They endured with faith intact, having their eyes fixed on the unseen realm. We are called this same way. Our eyes are to be fixed on Jesus, the author and perfecter of our faith, who took the path of suffering to achieve the triumph. This same Author is writing our stories and perfecting us in the process.

Question: How do you sustain obedience—over the long-haul—when it is costly?

349

325. Living Word

"'Is not My word like fire?' declares the Lord,
'And like a hammer which shatters a rock?'"
~ Jeremiah 23:29

An encounter with God in the scriptures was always an encounter with the Living Word. When God spoke, it was always living and powerful. His commands, aimed at the heart of mankind, were sharper than a two-edged sword, piercing and dividing their soul from their spirit. When God spoke, the world was created, and by His breath it is all sustained. God still has a longing for His word to be made flesh. As we present our lives as a living sacrifice, He inhabits us as His living temple. As we carry His word, by His Spirit in our hearts, He is free to move in us and through us in the world today. When we hear Him speak to our hearts and respond in faith, this is walking in the Spirit.

Question: If the author and perfecter of faith was writing a book with your life right now, what would the title be?

326. Conceive the Word

*"... Behold, the bondslave of the Lord; be it done
to me according to your word." ~ Luke 1:38*

Faith is the pregnancy of God's Word, alive and growing in the womb of our heart. Just as it happens in the natural, conceiving takes place when there is an intimate encounter with God. As we are before Him with a prepared heart, He speaks His living word, and we are filled with His seed. In the natural, this is a time of delight for two lovers. With the Lord, such intimacy is an expression of our abiding in oneness with Him. The scriptures are filled with stories of intimate encounters of man (and woman) with their Maker. God often spoke with great blessing, making promises that would take generations to come to full term. Just as Mary heard from the Lord, and *"treasured up all these things, pondering them in her heart"* (Luke 2:19), everyone who walks by faith must do likewise. Receiving seed is not the same as bearing fruit—but it is the beginning of His will being borne in you.

Question: What kinds of settings are most conducive to your experience of intimacy with Christ?

327. Believe the Word

*"And blessed is she who believed that there would
be a fulfillment of what had been spoken to her
by the Lord." ~ Luke 1:45*

Once we have conceived the word of God in our hearts, we must continually believe the word as we wait upon God to fulfill what He has planted within us. Believing is the process God uses to enlarge our heart to bear His will through our lives. It is a season of holy trust in the One who has pierced our soul for the accomplishing of His purposes. Just as a human pregnancy requires nine months to move from a small embryo to a full term infant, it takes fulfilling the timing of God for His fullness to be released. As we wait, we nourish the gift, we rest in His love, we confess what we can't yet see, and we wait patiently for its appearing. May we learn the patience of believing from Abraham, who, *"in hope against hope he believed, in order that he might become a father of many nations, according to that which had been spoken, 'So shall your descendants be' ... with respect to the promises of God, he did not waver in unbelief, but grew strong in faith, giving glory to God ..."* (Romans 4:18, 20).

Question: What promise have you held in your heart the longest? Have you struggled to believe?

328. Receive the Word

"Let us hold fast the confession of our hope
without wavering, for He who promised is
faithful ..." ~ Hebrews 10:23

When God sent His Son into the world, *"He came to His own, and those who were His own did not receive Him. But as many as received Him, to them He gave the right to become children of God, even to those who believe in His name ..."* (John 1:11-12). Those who were willing to receive His word were filled with faith. God brought simple people to Himself, disclosed His will and purposes to them, and then worked through them as they agreed to yield their lives to Him. Mary had been quick to believe, agreeing with God's purposes and allowing her body to be the "Ark of God" —bearing His presence into the world at Bethlehem. If we misunderstand the process of faith, we can forfeit the prize that comes to those who patiently wait upon the Lord. Followers of Jesus are known as believers. We are those who have the privilege of conceiving the word, believing the word, and then, in the fullness of time, receiving the word.

Question: *How do you express your thanksgiving when God brings one of His promises to fulfillment for you?*

353

329. Believing a Lie

"You are of your father the devil, and you want to
do the desires of your father. He was a murderer
from the beginning, and does not stand in the truth,
because there is no truth in him. Whenever he
speaks a lie, he speaks from his own nature; for he is
a liar and the father of lies." ~ John 8:44

Even as the Lord sows His word into prepared hearts, the evil one, known as the father of lies, is stalking in search of unprepared hearts. Whenever he speaks, it is directly from his nature as the deceiver. He preys upon those who are disappointed in God, those who have succumbed to despair, doubting God's goodness. He waits patiently for an offense among the brethren, so he can sow thoughts of contempt, unforgiveness, and deep resentment into their wounds. Where faith has waited long, the deceiver sows doubt, anxiety, and fear. In John 8:37-38, Jesus said, *"I know that you are Abraham's offspring; yet you seek to kill Me, because My word has no place in you. I speak the things which I have seen with My Father; therefore you also do the things which you heard from your father."* The phrase "has no place in you" means "it makes no progress". The passage goes on to identify the father of lies as His opposition. We discover a key to believing in this passage. If the father of lies gets to our hearts first, and we begin to be doers of his word, we keep the deception, and it begins to grow in our heart. We may want to believe Jesus—but just can't—because the father of lies filled us with his deceptions first.

Question: *Do you struggle with doubt? Does it expose any deceptions you are believing?*

330. Currency of Faith

"For whatever is born of God overcomes the
world; and this is the victory that has overcome the
world —our faith." ~ I John 5:4

Every nation has its own form of currency, and in order to operate in each economy, an exchange of one form for another must take place. The same is true for the Kingdom of God. Money is the medium of exchange for earthly goods, while faith is the medium of exchange for heavenly things. No amount of money can purchase divine health, wisdom from above, reconciled relationships, endurance in the face of affliction, or the ability to deliver from evil. Investments depreciate, costs rise, and debt grows. Faith, on the other hand, allows the will of the Father in heaven to take place on earth. It lays hold of the unseen realm, and confesses its reality while it is still a long way off. It has the capacity to move mountains, cast out demons, heal the sick, and raise the dead. It grows as it is exercised, and multiplies as it is given away.

Question: When has distress or pressure perfected your faith?

331. Activate Your Faith

*"... that the proof of your faith, being more
precious than gold which is perishable, even though
tested by fire, may be found to result in praise and
glory and honor at the revelation
of Jesus Christ ..." ~ I Peter 1:7*

Faith hears. Faith sees. Faith acts. God's word is living and active and given to us to accomplish His will and purposes. Faith comes by hearing the word of God, or seeing (perceiving) His will through our spiritual vision. But it comes in seed form, and must be activated in order to accomplish what it was sent for. Too often, we take the seed and put it in our pocket, and take it out when we pray to remind God of what He said to us. Rather than sending us answers as we pray, in the form of fruit, we are given the means for fruit—seed. Every time we are exposed to the word of God, there is an opportunity to receive seed. We must consider how the Lord would have us become doers of the word, and not hearers only, stewarding the seed that has been entrusted to us for the furtherance of His Kingdom.

Question: Have you received a promise from God that needs to be activated? Do you know how to respond in faith?

332. Steward What You Have

*"For to everyone who has shall more be given, and
he shall have an abundance; but from the one who
does not have, even what he does have shall
be taken away." ~ Matthew 25:29*

There is a theory among some motivational speakers that encourages their listeners to envision a dream that they want to make reality. They are instructed to make a vision board, speak of the dream, and do whatever is necessary to keep their focus on that dream. We can learn a lesson from the parable of the talents that will guide us in a different way. In the parable, the master gives to each of his servants according to their ability. When they are faithful with what they receive, they are rewarded with multiplication and blessing. The servant entrusted with five talents, made five talents more. The servant entrusted with two talents, made two talents more. Neither of them had the ability to steward the double portion until they had faithfully stewarded the original grant. The servant who received only one talent, hid the talent out of fear, and gave it back to the master, preserved. He lost all. The way to see sustained growth in our stewardship is to steward what we have, not what we want. By taking the gift given, and acting upon it by faith, we lay hold of the prize.

Question: Where is the Lord asking you to steward something that is little?

333. What Do You Have in Your Hand?

> *"I urge you therefore, brethren, by the mercies of
> God, to present your bodies a living and holy
> sacrifice, acceptable to God, which is your spiritual
> service of worship." ~ Romans 12:1*

Sometimes faith is taking a little thing and allowing God to make much of it. When Moses was called to deliver Israel from cruel bondage in Egypt, he asked the Lord, *"What if they will not believe me, or listen to what I say? For they may say, 'The Lord has not appeared to you.' And the Lord said to him, 'What is that in your hand?' And he said, 'A staff'"* (Exodus 4:1-4). The staff of Moses, used to herd sheep on the back side of the desert, became the staff of God when Moses yielded to Him. A small boy, in the midst of 5,000 hungry souls gathered to listen to Jesus, carried his lunch in his hands. What he had in his hands, became much in the hands of the Savior. The widow at Zarephath was asked by Elijah for the last of her oil and flour, that he might eat (1 Kings 17:12-16). The result: *"For thus says the Lord God of Israel, 'The bowl of flour shall not be exhausted, nor shall the jar of oil be empty, until the day that the Lord sends rain on the face of the earth'"* (v. 14). Each surrendered what they had, devoted it to the Lord, and then lived with expectation.

Question: What do you have in your hand?

334. *What is Impossible*

"But He said, "The things impossible with men
are possible with God.'" ~ Luke 18:27

The word impossible means *not able to occur, exist, or be done.* In that context, each day of creation was impossible. When Sarah reached old age without bearing a child parenthood was no longer possible. When Israel found itself hemmed in, between Pharaoh and the Red Sea, escape was impossible. When Joshua led God's people silently around Jericho for seven days, then shouted with a shout to bring the great city down, it was an impossible military strategy. Daniel surviving the lion's den was an impossible outcome, as was a daily supply of bread from heaven in the Exodus wanderings. Under natural circumstances, and by human means, none of it could be done. Christ came to break the power of darkness and bring us back into the life and power of the Living God. He healed the sick, gave sight to the blind, multiplied provision, calmed the sea, and set the demon possessed free. He raised the dead, ransomed the lost, and regained the Kingdom for His Father. Nothing is impossible with God.

Question: Have you asked for anything in prayer that would be considered a miracle?

359

Part 12
Move of God

335. Initiated and Sustained

*"For I am confident of this very thing, that He
who began a good work in you will perfect it until
the day of Christ Jesus." ~ Philippians 1:6*

Dr. Joe Aldrich, when he was president of Multnomah
School of the Bible, met with a group of spiritual leaders in
Salem, Oregon. He asked them, "What would it take to see a
move of God, initiated and sustained, in a given city or re-
gion?" With that question, he invited the pastors away for
four days of seeking the Lord with no agenda. At the time in
1989, there were still significant barriers between denomina-
tions, race, and gender. When the Lord is given four days to
be Head of the church with no teaching, no preaching, no prescribed program—He shows up. Holy communion took place
among prayers of confession, repentance, and requests for
forgiveness. Man's ways were set aside, and unity was found
in the shared life of Jesus, not uniformity of doctrine. The report of those four days stirred up a hunger worldwide, and
hundreds of prayer summits followed. I was transformed forever, and picked up the mantle for this vision: believing for a
move of God to be initiated and sustained in the hearts of
God's people, an abiding habitation for the Holy One.

Question: Do you have a vision for Kingdom mission?

336. Author and Perfecter of Faith

"... fixing our eyes on Jesus, the author and
perfecter of faith, who for the joy set before Him
endured the cross, despising the shame, and has sat
down at the right hand of the throne of God."
~ Hebrews 12:2

It would appear that the Lord enjoys writing. Through prophets and priests, shepherds and kings, He has made His word known. *"My heart overflows with a good theme; I address my verses to the King; my tongue is the pen of a ready writer"* (Psalm 45:1). His preferred instruments are the stylus of His word, finding the tablets of our hearts. He is writing His story throughout history on innumerable lives and witnesses. He begins a good work in each of our lives, and writes His God story through our testimonies—that a new generation can receive more than the statutes, they can also observe the stories. An author usually begins with a story in mind. *"'For I know the plans that I have for you,' declares the Lord, 'plans for welfare and not for calamity to give you a future and a hope'"* (Jeremiah 29:11). He uses each element of our daily lives to write His redemption story with the goal of perfecting our faith. Faith is the expression of His word, heard and conceived in our heart. As He continues to write—prepare for a great conclusion!

Question: If your current circumstances were a chapter in the book of your life, what would this chapter be called?

337. Fill the Earth

*"For from Him and through Him and to Him are
all things. To Him be the glory forever. Amen."*
~ Romans 11:36

The early chapters of Genesis not only rehearse the destruction that took place in Eden, but they also unfold the intention of God for His creation as well. From the beginning as Creator, God chose to display replication of life through every aspect of His design. *"Then God said, 'Behold, I have given you every plant yielding seed that is on the surface of all the earth, and every tree which has fruit yielding seed; it shall be food for you'"* (Genesis 1:29). Life would beget life, seed would beget seed, and the earth would be filled, as God blessed mankind to be fruitful and multiply.

This is a creation pattern that was rehearsed again as the ark came to rest on solid ground. *"And God blessed Noah and his sons and said to them, 'Be fruitful and multiply, and fill the earth'"* (Genesis 9:1). At the close of the Gospel of Matthew, each of us is invited to participate in the Great Commission. *"All authority has been given to Me in heaven and on earth. Go therefore and make disciples of all the nations, baptizing them in the name of the Father and the Son and the Holy Spirit, teaching them to observe all that I commanded you; and lo, I am with you always, even to the end of the age"* (Matthew 28:18-20). The seed of the Kingdom has within it the power to bear its fruit. May we take up the command to be fruitful, and multiply.

Question: How are you purposing to obey the commandment of the Great Commission?

338. Sustained by Love

*"And we have come to know and have believed the
love which God has for us. God is love, and the one
who abides in love abides in God, and God
abides in him." ~ 1 John 4:16*

God is love, and He has chosen to form His creation after
His image and likeness. We, who were conceived in the love
of God, are designed to bear witness to all that He has lavished upon us, His beloved. *"But God demonstrates His own
love toward us, in that while we were yet sinners, Christ died for
us"* (Romans 5:8). Love remains the theme in the entire narrative of the scriptures. The Father loves the Son and shows
Him all things that He Himself is doing (John 5:20). The Son
loves the Father and obeys and submits to Him (John 14:31).
The Holy Spirit is given to display the love of the Father to us:
*"... and hope does not disappoint, because the love of God has been
poured out within our hearts through the Holy Spirit who was given
to us"* (Romans 5:5). Love is something we must receive in order to give, and we must believe in order to sustain. The new
commandment given by Christ is sourced in Him: *"A new
commandment I give to you, that you love one another, even as I
have loved you, that you also love one another. By this all men will
know that you are My disciples, if you have love for one another"*
(John 13:34-35). As we are willing to be the delivery system of
His love, His kingdom is sustained.

*Question: Do you recall when you came to know and believe the love
God has for you?*

339. Who Will Receive the Message

*"Who has believed our message? And to whom
has the arm of the Lord been revealed?"*
~ Isaiah 53:1

Jesus sent His disciples out, two by two, to every city that He intended to reach. They were given power and authority to cast out unclean spirits, and heal every kind of sickness and disease. Jesus gave them this strategy upon entering a city, *"inquire who is worthy in it; and abide there until you go away"* (Matthew 10:11). They were to look for a man of peace, greeting him with a blessing of peace: *"and if a man of peace is there, your peace will rest upon him; but if not it will return to you. And stay in that house, eating and drinking what they give you; for the laborer is worthy of his wages. Do not keep moving from house to house"* (Luke 10:5-7). In an unfamiliar city or village, God's strategy was to find someone who was willing to receive the message of the Kingdom. They would have the influence to bring entire households to faith. Whether their influence was due to their status (the jailer in Acts 16), or due to their shame (woman at the well in John 4), the Lord uses those who have influence in an area to be the open door for the gospel.

Question: Where are you being sent with the gospel? Have you discovered the person of peace in that location?

340. Nature of the Two Kingdoms

*"Thou alone art the Lord. Thou hast made the
heavens, the heaven of heavens with all their host,
the earth and all that is on it, the seas and all that is
in them. Thou dost give life to all of them and the
heavenly host bows down before Thee."*
~ Nehemiah 9:6

---

*"For He delivered us from the domain of darkness, and transferred
us to the kingdom of His beloved Son, in whom we have redemption,
the forgiveness of sins. And He is the image of the invisible God, the
first-born of all creation. For by Him all things were created, both
in the heavens and on earth, visible and invisible, whether thrones
or dominions or rulers or authorities—all things have been created
by Him and for Him"* (Colossians 1:13-16). A kingdom is a
country, state, or territory ruled by a king. There are two kingdoms at work in our world, and they are engaged in an ancient conflict with one another. One is the spiritual reign and
sovereignty of Christ, and the other is the kingdom of this
world, led by the evil one, Satan. This conflict between God
Almighty (*Pantokrator* and the ruler of this world (*Kosmokrater*) is for the rule of men's hearts. The kingdom of this
world is in rebellion to the righteous rule of the Almighty, and
has developed world systems (religion, education, governments, media, art and entertainment, business) that are independent from and opposed to the Lord. The Kingdom of God
is the fellowship of those who have accepted His offer of the
Kingdom, submitted to His rule, and entered into its blessing.

Question: How does a rival kingdom establish itself and gain territory?

367

341. Seasons

*"A time to give birth, and a time to die; a time to
plant, and a time to uproot what is planted"*
~ Ecclesiastes 3:2

With God, timing is everything. On the third day, when God created *"... the lights in the expanse of the heavens to separate the day from the night,"* He said they were for *"signs and for seasons, and for days and years ..."* (Genesis 1:14). We are better at discerning the passage of natural seasons than we are at comprehending spiritual ones. When the Father sent the Son, He was aware that Jesus would serve as a fulfillment of one season and the beginning of the next. Jesus was able to navigate each day with the sense of accomplishing His mission in the fullness of time. *"There is an appointed time for everything. And there is a time for every event under heaven"* (Ecclesiastes 3:1). The Lord often uses prophetic voices to announce a change of season, and the scriptures have preserved God's word concerning what is yet to come. Moves of God require a season change and people who will cooperate, rather than resist.

Question: *How would you describe the spiritual season in which you find yourself?*

342. The Big Story

*"Thy word is a lamp to my feet, and a light
to my path." ~ Psalm 119:105*

The Bible is made up of 66 individual books, written by a many different authors, in many different times and places. Even so, it is one, unified meta-narrative of the story of God. When we are able to view the scriptures as one story with a variety of characters, all contributing to the same plot, we begin to understand "His-story". This lens of God allows a view of mankind from the perspective of God. We see His original design and the attempt of the evil one to overcome and destroy creation. We observe the redemption plan, from the promised seed to the sacrificed Savior. Throughout each book, God weaves men's lives into His purposes, and makes His ways known. It contains both history, from God's perspective, and prophecy, His intended future. The wisdom acquired from submission to His word is our means of comprehending Him and bearing witness to the truth of His message.

Question: Do you have a life verse—a scripture that gives direction to your life mission?

343. Enough Roots for Fruit

"I am the vine, you are the branches; he who
abides in Me, and I in him, he bears much fruit; for
apart from Me you can do nothing." ~ John 15:5

If you follow the life of a seed, you watch it transform from seed to fruit: *"The kingdom of God is like a man who casts seed upon the soil; and goes to bed at night and gets up by day, and the seed sprouts up and grows—how, he himself does not know. The soil produces crops by itself; first the blade, then the head, then the mature grain in the head. But when the crop permits, he immediately puts in the sickle, because the harvest has com"* (Mark 4:26-29). But the first stage in the life of a seed, after the seed is sown in the soil, is death to its previous state: *"... unless a grain of wheat falls into the earth and dies, it remains by itself alone; but if it dies, it bears much fruit"* (John 12:24). For every word of God, sown in the soil of our heart, requires a tomb time before it resurrects in the promised fruit. When it is secured in us by the Holy Spirit, it must *"take root downward and bear fruit upward"* (Isaiah 37:31). While the seed establishes a root system, it is securing its future strength. Those roots are necessary to nourish the grown plant. To the degree that fruit is borne above ground, there is a need to be equally stabilized below ground. These are truths for our spiritual journey. Our hidden life is what sustains our visible ministry. If we would bear much fruit, the secret is in the root.

Question: How do you spend your hidden life in Christ? What have you learned from investing in the root?

344. Who Initiates

"We love, because He first loved us." ~ I John 4:19

In music, a call and response is a succession of two distinct phrases usually played by different musicians, where the second phrase is heard as a direct commentary on, or response, to the first. It is also a time-tested technique for getting attention in the classroom, with the military, in churches, or at sporting events. There is the initiator of the call, and there is the role of the responder. As the people of God, we are to display the role of the responder. Our model for this is Jesus, who said, *"I can do nothing on My own initiative. As I hear, I judge; and My judgment is just, because I do not seek My own will, but the will of Him who sent Me"* (John 5:30). When we learn to be sensitive to the impulse of the Lord, we begin to be sensitive to His presence, and responsive to His will. The Lord speaks—we listen. The Lord leads—we follow. The Lord initiates—we respond.

Question: Who has been a good example of "following" for you?

345. *When God Goes off Script*

*"For who has known the mind of the Lord, that he
should instruct Him? But we have
the mind of Christ." ~ I Corinthians 2:16*

Because we are creatures of habit, we tend to build a formula based on any way the Lord has chosen to speak or act in the past. We attempt to prescribe the movement of God by preparing for the ways He has shown Himself thus far in our journey. When scripture teaches that Jesus is the same, yesterday, today, and forever (Hebrews 13:8), it is speaking of His nature and character, not the way He demonstrates His relationship to us. Since the Lord is the Spirit (2 Corinthians 3:17), we need to learn how to follow an invisible presence giving leadership to the church. When we gather together in His name, He is among us to lead and guide. Learning to discern His word by the Spirit and to allow the Spirit's gifts to function, is the way the body matures and the Head of the church is glorified. Some churches become rigid, demanding that all must be kept within a familiar pattern, time, and place. In their desire to make sure that all is *"done properly and in an orderly manner"* (1 Corinthians 14:40), they can quench the Spirit in their midst.

Question: Is there anything that takes place in church that makes you uncomfortable? Is it biblical?

346. *Whole Body Functions*

*"For just as we have many members in one body
and all the members do not have the same function,
so we, who are many, are one body in Christ, and
individually members one of another."*
~ Romans 12:4-5

When the church gathers, there is only One who is the Head. He gathers with the body, and desires to speak and guide us into all truth. Since He is among us by His Spirit, we must learn how to discern His presence as a people, corporately. It takes the entire congregation functioning under His leadership to be an accurate reflection of His nature. The body grows as *"we all attain to the unity of the faith, and of the knowledge of the Son of God, to a mature man, to the measure of the stature which belongs to the fullness of Christ. As a result, we are no longer to be children, tossed here and there by waves, and carried about by every wind of doctrine, by the trickery of men, by craftiness in deceitful scheming; but speaking the truth in love, we are to grow up in all aspects into Him, who is the head, even Christ, from whom the whole body, being fitted and held together by that which every joint supplies, according to the proper working of each individual part, causes the growth of the body for the building up of itself in love"* (Ephesians 4:13-16). Learning to trust His active presence in our midst is the way to see the church mature.

Question: When you gather together with other believers, how do you make room for the Holy Spirit to speak?

347. Growth through Multiplication

*"Truly, truly, I say to you, unless a grain of
wheat falls into the earth and dies, it remains by
itself alone; but if it dies, it bears much fruit."*
~ John 12:24

We can see the purposes of God achieved by "doing the math". If one person were to disciple just twelve others in their lifetime and each of those twelve turned around and discipled twelve others, in just eight generations the world would be reached. Jesus began this mission with twelve and then commissioned them to go into the entire world with the gospel. He lived as an observable model of Sonship among them and then sent them out to be a living demonstration of the will of God. This is a relational message that is passed on relationally. It is entrusted to each of us, and requires the participation of all of us. We must be involved with raising up disciple makers, not just disciples who follow but never go. God has invested Himself in a body of believers, who are able to respond through their variety of gifts to a world that is needing every messenger who will proclaim His name among the nations.

Question: Who is God sending you to this week?

348. Two Ways

"There is a way which seems right to a man, but its end is the way of death." ~ Proverbs 14:12

Because we were created to bear the image and likeness of the Father, we were designed with the capacity for free will. God is sovereign and our free will is a reflection of this. In order to train us in the correct use of such a gift, He continually demonstrates the way to navigate our choices. Scripture sets in place two ways, and then offers the counsel needed to choose correctly. The two ways are often in contrast to one another. We tend to see the contrast as a way of avoiding sin, but it is often the way to lay hold to our destiny as well. There were two trees in the garden, one offering life and one that was forbidden, which brought about death. There are two kingdoms, and two Rulers we can live in submission to. We are given the choice to build our lives on the Rock, or on the sand (Matthew 7:24-27); to live from His thoughts or our own (Isaiah 55:8-11); to walk in wisdom, or live as a fool (Proverbs 8:3-5, 14-21). Therefore, *"Enter by the narrow gate; for the gate is wide, and the way is broad that leads to destruction, and many are those who enter by it. For the gate is small, and the way is narrow that leads to life, and few are those who find it"* (Matthew 7:13-14).

Question: *Do you have any choices before you that require God's wisdom and understanding?*

349. Front Follower

"If anyone wishes to come after Me, let him deny himself, and take up his cross, and follow Me."
~ Matthew 16:24

The role of a leader in the body of Christ is to be a "front follower". In order to lead in spiritual matters, we must first learn the lessons of being led. Humility in the Kingdom of God is demonstrated by the willingness to learn following in order to demonstrate leading. For a man to be a bridegroom to his bride, he must first learn to be a bride to his Bridegroom. Ever since the garden, man has had the tendency to go astray. Our souls have rivaled the leading of the Spirit, and our flesh is resistant to governing. Jesus came to live among us and demonstrate His own willingness to live a life laid down—a willingness to trust His Father to lead Him in every word He spoke, and action He took. Before the disciples became "sent ones" (apostles), they were first called to follow. The individual calling to follow Jesus involved becoming engaged in an abiding fellowship with Him, cleaving to Him in believing trust and obedience, and then modeling daily what it meant to follow.

Question: *Who, by their lifestyle, has modeled following the Spirit to you?*

350. Guide or Guard

"But when He, the Spirit of truth, comes, He will
guide you into all the truth; for He will not speak on
His own initiative, but whatever He hears, He will
speak; and He will disclose to you what is to come."
~ John 16:13

As the church learns to follow the Lord corporately, we must repent to being led. For too many years we have focused on keeping everything decent and in order without learning how to follow the Holy Spirit's lead when the body of Christ gathers.

I have had the privilege of facilitating four day prayer summits where the spiritual leadership of a given city takes time to be led by Jesus, the Head of the church. What each congregation has learned separately becomes part of the gathering. The result is a clearer view of the Lord's full picture for His people in the city. As a facilitator, I am not the director. My goal is to discern the path the Holy Spirit is moving, and then guard that from being derailed. As we steward His will, instead of our own ideas, we are privileged to host His presence.

Question: *Do you know how to practice listening together corporately in prayer?*

---

351. Removing Obstacles

"Put on the full armor of God, that you may be
able to stand firm against the schemes of the devil."
~ Ephesians 6:11

Before Israel could possess the Promised Land, she had to dispossess the inhabitants of that territory. Those who exalted themselves against the rule of God were destined for removal. While those enemies of Israel in the Old Testament were actual flesh and blood, ours are not. Our opposition is *"against the rulers, against the powers, against the world forces of this darkness, against the spiritual forces of wickedness in the heavenly places"* (Ephesians 6:12). *"For though we walk in the flesh, we do not war according to the flesh, for the weapons of our warfare are not of the flesh, but divinely powerful for the destruction of fortresses. We are destroying speculations and every lofty thing raised up against the knowledge of God, and we are taking every thought captive to the obedience of Christ ..."* (2 Corinthians 10:3-5). For the Kingdom of God to rule in this realm, a people must bow to His righteous reign. Pride, arrogance, fear, control, violence, lust, greed, and hatred must be dispossessed in the hearts of man, and the Prince of Peace enthroned.

Question: Where have you faced the greatest spiritual opposition in your walk with the Lord?

352. Holy or Human Effort

*"... holding to a form of godliness, although they
have denied its power ..." ~ 2 Timothy 3:5*

The Lord instructed His disciples to remain in Jerusalem until they had received power from on high. When the church received the gift of the Holy Spirit, they were no longer left to the limitations of the Law.

The Law only reminds us of our sin, and is without any ability to overcome the opposition of our flesh. When the Spirit was poured out, each one received His indwelling presence, demonstrated by the tongues of fire resting on each head. His desire is that we carry His presence into every daily situation, and His Spirit produces His will through us. When we fail to acknowledge the Spirit, we practice self-improvement but neglect the way of the Lord. When we walk in the strength of our own soul (mind, will, and emotions), we live a form of godliness, but deny its power. Soul strength is the power of religion, but is useless for walking in the Spirit.

Question: How does the kingdom of the world depend on human effort?

379

353. Of His Fullness

"... and to know the love of Christ which
surpasses knowledge that you may be filled up to all
the fullness of God." ~ Ephesians 3:19

Even though we, as believers, have been filled with the Holy Spirit, none of us carry within ourselves the fullness of Deity the way Jesus did: *"For in Him all the fullness of Deity dwells in bodily form ..."* (Colossians 2:9). Jesus, as Son of God, carried the fullness of His Father within His earthly body and modeled for us, operating from the infilling of the Holy Spirit. Note the Lord has entrusted His fullness to "us," plural: *"For of His fullness we have all received, and grace upon grace"* (John 1:16). It is imperative for the body of Christ to live into the oneness that Jesus prayed for His church. It is only then that we will experience all God had in mind for His people. *"And He put all things in subjection under His feet, and gave Him as head over all things to the church, which is His body, the fullness of Him who fills all in all"* (Ephesians 1:22-23). Just as Jesus put on flesh, and dwelt among us the first time, He is longing to be present, in and through our flesh, dwelling as the Head to the body. When Paul expresses what the mature church will look like, it is dependent on a people who have learned to walk in *"the unity of the faith, and of the knowledge of the Son of God, to a mature man, to the measure of the stature which belongs to the fullness of Christ"* (Ephesians 4:13).

Question: *Where are you convicted by the Holy Spirit to walk in greater oneness with the Body of Christ?*

354. Filled with His Glory

*"And the glory which Thou hast given Me I have
given to them; that they may be one, just
as We are one." ~ John 17:22*

The world was plunged into an unholy darkness at the time of the fall. When man sinned and was separated from God, he was disrobed of glory. Glory is the visible evidence of the presence of God and once it is withdrawn it leaves a sense of vulnerability and nakedness in its wake.

When God drew near to man again in the Exodus wilderness journey when the tabernacle was complete the residence was filled with glory. When man sinned, God withdrew. When he repented, glory once more found a resting place.

Learning to walk by the Spirit consistently exposes us to the glory of the Lord. *"Now the Lord is the Spirit; and where the Spirit of the Lord is, there is liberty. But we all, with unveiled face beholding as in a mirror the glory of the Lord, are being transformed into the same image from glory to glory, just as from the Lord, the Spirit"* (2 Corinthians 3:17-18). There is a promise in the scriptures: *"For the earth will be filled with the knowledge of the glory of the Lord, as the waters cover the sea"* (Habakkuk 2:14). If we submit ourselves to being an active display of His residence, glory can radiate to every corner of our planet.

Question: How would evangelism be affected through an ongoing display of His glory?

355. Revival and Restoration

"... when He comes to be glorified in His saints
on that day, and to be marveled at among all who
have believed—for our testimony to you was
believed." ~ 2 Thessalonians 1:10

A.W. Tozer once said, "The Christian is a holy rebel loose in the world with access to the throne of God." We, who have been given permission to be joined with Him in the likeness of His ascension, have a heavenly perspective, and can cooperate with His will being "done on earth, as it is in heaven." It is time for us to be about our intended design, through personal and corporate revival. Revival is a time when God restores His own people from their declining spiritual state, and brings them once more into a place where His abiding presence dwells. The word revive means to restore to life or consciousness, to resuscitate. *"Repent therefore and return, that your sins may be wiped away, in order that times of refreshing may come from the presence of the Lord; and that He may send Jesus, the Christ appointed for you, whom heaven must receive until the period of restoration of all things about which God spoke by the mouth of His holy prophets from ancient time"* (Acts 3:19-21).

Question: Is there any place in your life where you need to receive fresh breath from the Spirit of God?

356. Transfer of Faith

"This will be written for the generation to come;
that a people yet to be created may praise the Lord."
~ Psalm 102:18

During track and field events, there is an event called the "relay." It is a race that is run in stages or legs and each leg run by a different member of the team. As each member finishes their stage of the race, they pass a baton to the next runner, and both run together until the baton is securely transferred. The Kingdom Race has been set in front of each generation since Jesus handed us the baton. The gospel is transferred by one generation of believers who run the race set before them, to the next generation who pick up where they left off. We cannot transfer faith by just passing on the statutes of God without the stories of faith that each succeeding generation gets to tell to their children and grandchildren. *"I will open my mouth in a parable; I will utter dark sayings of old, which we have heard and known, and our fathers have told us. We will not conceal them from their children, but tell to the generation to come the praises of the Lord, and His strength and His wondrous works that He has done ... that they should teach them to their children, that the generation to come might know, even the children yet to be born, that they may arise and tell them to their children, that they should put their confidence in God, and not forget the works of God ..."* (Psalm 78:2-7).

Question: Do your family members know the God stories being written through your life?

357. Thanksgiving

"It is good to give thanks to the Lord, and to sing praises to Thy name, O Most High; to declare Thy loving kindness in the morning, and Thy faithfulness by night." ~ Psalm 92:1-2

God offers us continual access to His presence through thanksgiving. *"Enter His gates with thanksgiving, and His courts with praise. Give thanks to Him; bless His name"* (Psalm 100:4). Thanksgiving is an offering from our lips that the Lord prescribes for His people. *"Through Him then, let us continually offer up a sacrifice of praise to God, that is, the fruit of lips that give thanks to His name"* (Hebrews 13:15). In the Old Testament, Israel came before the Lord with blood sacrifices. Their offerings reminded them of their sin and separation from God. Now that the final payment has been made on the debt of our sin—the final Lamb has been slain—we can approach Him with gladness and an offering of thanks. When we enter His courts, we have access to His presence. Where His presence abides, there is fullness of joy (Psalm 16:11). When we experience the joy of the Lord, we walk in His strength (Nehemiah 8:10).

Question: How do you practice the giving of thanks on a daily basis?

358. God with Us

*"Behold, the virgin shall be with child, and shall
bear a Son, and they shall call His name Immanuel,
which translated means, 'God with us.'"*
~ Matthew 1:23

Apart from Him, we can do nothing. The way and work of Jesus has restored us to living a merged life. He is with us as the Head of the church. All that we say, or do, should be an active expression of submission to the Head. He is with us as a Father restored to His children. Our identity and inheritance once more reflect this love relationship. He is with us as a Teacher to His disciples. We are to come to Him, learn from Him, and then go in His name. He is with us as Master to a generation of bond-slaves. Jesus demonstrated this role and then said, *"Do you know what I have done to you? You call Me Teacher and Lord; and you are right, for so I am. If I then, the Lord and the Teacher, washed your feet, you also ought to wash one another's feet. For I gave you an example that you also should do as I did to you. Truly, truly, I say to you, a slave is not greater than his master; neither is one who is sent greater than the one who sent him. If you know these things, you are blessed if you do them"* (John 13:12-17). He is betrothed to us as a Bridegroom to His Bride. Make yourself ready. Live your life faithfully. Long for His appearing.

Question: Are you ready for His return? Is there someone who needs to hear about Him?

359. Forward Movement with Worship

*"Worthy art Thou, our Lord and our God, to
receive glory and honor and power; for Thou didst
create all things, and because of Thy will they
existed, and were created." Revelation 4:11*

Forward movement in the Kingdom of God is accomplished through worship. In the Old Testament, the musicians preceded the army, routing the enemy with the presence of the Lord and His attending glory. We enter His presence, carry His presence, and establish His throne upon our praises. The scene in heaven in Revelation 4, demonstrates that worship is one thing that will continue for all eternity: *"And from the throne proceed flashes of lightning and sounds and peals of thunder. And there were seven lamps of fire burning before the throne, which are the seven Spirits of God ... And the four living creatures, each one of them having six wings, are full of eyes around and within; and day and night they do not cease to say, 'Holy, Holy, Holy, is the Lord God, the Almighty, who was and who is and who is to come.' And when the living creatures give glory and honor and thanks to Him who sits on the throne, to Him who lives forever and ever, the twenty-four elders will fall down before Him who sits on the throne, and will worship Him who lives forever and ever, and will cast their crowns before the throne ..."* (Revelation 4:5, 8-10).

Question: Are there ways that you practice worship on a daily basis?

360. Big Vision

"Set your mind on the things above, not on the things that are on earth." ~ Colossians 3:2

People of faith have eyes to see and ears to hear what the Holy Spirit is communicating. They have learned not to lean on their own understanding, but to contend for what they have "seen" with the eye of their heart. Abraham *"obeyed by going out to a place which he was to receive for an inheritance; and he went out, not knowing where he was going"* (Hebrews 11:8). An exchange is made for those who walk by faith—their vision for the vision of God. He invites us to see things from His perspective when He seats us with Him in heavenly places. *"If then you have been raised up with Christ, keep seeking the things above, where Christ is, seated at the right hand of God. Set your mind on the things above, not on the things that are on earth. For you have died and your life is hidden with Christ in God"* (Colossians 3:1-3). From His perspective, we see the promises fulfilled while they are yet unseen, and live with hope: *"... Things which eye has not seen and ear has not heard, and which have not entered the heart of man, all that God has prepared for those who love Him. For to us God revealed them through the Spirit; for the Spirit searches all things, even the depths of God"* (1 Corinthians 2:9-10).

Question: *Do you have a promise from God that is not yet fulfilled? How are you contending in faith for it?*

361. Prepare a Place for You

*"And he carried me away in the Spirit to a great
and high mountain, and showed me the holy city,
Jerusalem, coming down out of heaven from God,
having the glory of God ..." ~ Revelation 21:10-11a*

"Let not your heart be troubled; believe in God, believe also in Me. In My Father's house are many dwelling places; if it were not so, I would have told you; for I go to prepare a place for you. And if I go and prepare a place for you, I will come again, and receive you to Myself; that where I am, there you may be also" (John 14:1-3). This familiar passage is often read as a word of comfort to mourners at a funeral. In reality, it is intended to convey wedding imagery. Jesus has betrothed His church to Himself as a bride. We have remained in the midst of the world, preparing for that appointed day, when the marriage supper of the Lamb takes place. *"And I saw a new heaven and a new earth for the first heaven and the first earth passed away, and there is no longer any sea. And I saw the holy city, new Jerusalem, coming down out of heaven from God, made ready as a bride adorned for her husband. And I heard a loud voice from the throne, saying, "Behold, the tabernacle of God is among men, and He shall dwell among them, and they shall be His people, and God Himself shall be among them ..."* (Revelation 21:1-3).

Question: *How is your walk with the Lord impacted by seeing Him as your Bridegroom?*

362. Overcoming

"He who has an ear, let him hear what the Spirit
says to the churches. To him who overcomes, I will
grant to eat of the tree of life, which is in the
paradise of God." ~ Revelation 2:7

From the day we were born, we began to experience the eternal conflict in the heavenlies as it played out on the earth. Each of us takes up our life in a world that has rebelled against the Creator, and has the opportunity to surrender and be reconciled, or resist and join the apostate. Jesus lived His life as the exact representation of the image and likeness of His Father. He submitted His will, as well as His ways, to complete obedience. From this position of authority and power, He set Himself to His mission: *"The Son of God appeared for this purpose, that He might destroy the works of the devil"* (1 John 3:8). The evil one is continually at odds with the will and purposes of God, attempting to steal, kill, and destroy (John 10:10). As we learn the way of submission, and set our hearts to please the Father, we are invited to participate in the fulfillment of His prayer: *"Thy Kingdom come, Thy will be done, on earth as it is in heaven"* (Matthew 6:10).

Question: What is the nature of your current spiritual opposition — Sin? Self? Satan?

389

363. Restoration to Oneness

"For by one Spirit we were all baptized into one
body, whether Jews or Greeks, whether slaves or
free, and we were all made to drink of one Spirit.
For the body is not one member, but many."
~ I Corinthians 12:13-14

The original design at creation was a replication of the unity experienced among the Godhead. As the Father, Son, and Spirit are One, we were invited into this same community. We were created to live a merged life with God and a merged life with one another. When sin separated us from the Father, we quickly defaulted to strife, enmity, hatred, and factions. When Christ paid our debt of sin, we were restored to oneness with Him, and He has filled us with His Spirit that we might return to a merged life with one another. *"And the glory which Thou hast given Me I have given to them; that they may be one, just as We are one; I in them, and Thou in Me, that they may be perfected in unity, that the world may know that Thou didst send Me, and didst love them, even as Thou didst love Me"* (John 17:22-23). Though oneness is available to us, most of us continue to live parallel lives—headed the same direction, at the same time, but independent and isolated from God and one another.

Question: Where does the church need to learn to operate in oneness? What is hindering this?

364. Repenting From and Repenting To

"Therefore putting aside all filthiness and all that
remains of wickedness, in humility receive the word
implanted, which is able to save your souls."
~ James 1:21

It is not a great gift to be able to point out what is wrong in a situation, without being able to point to the right path, as well. As the world continues in its destructive ways, the church cannot satisfy itself by pronouncing judgment on the darkness. We must be those who bear His light, and point to a narrow way that leads to His life. We have been set free from the kingdom of this world, in order to live in the Kingdom of our God. After being delivered from Egypt, Israel wandered for forty years in the wilderness because they were unwilling to obey the Lord and possess the Promised Land. In order for repentance to be complete, we must repent from our old, sinful practices, and *repent to* living as new creatures, in His Spirit: *"… in reference to your former manner of life, you lay aside the old self, which is being corrupted in accordance with the lusts of deceit, and that you be renewed in the spirit of your mind, and put on the new self, which in the likeness of God has been created in righteousness and holiness of the truth … for you were formerly darkness, but now you are light in the Lord; walk as children of light (for the fruit of the light consists in all goodness and righteousness and truth), trying to learn what is pleasing to the Lord"* (Ephesians 4:22-24, 5:8-10).

Question: Where are you trying to restrain old life, without putting on new life?

365. Doers of His Will

*"Therefore everyone who hears these words of
Mine, and acts upon them, may be compared to a
wise man, who built his house upon the rock."*
~ *Matthew 7:24*

The message of the gospel has been proclaimed for more than 2,000 years. It has been carried to the nations in a variety of ways, through a host of messengers. It has been sown in hostile environments as well as fertile communities. It carries with it the power to convert lost lives, heal shattered hearts, and call for a people to return to their God. The word of the Lord is living and powerful and able to accomplish all that He sent it for ... under one condition: We must become doers of His word, and not hearers only. We have to follow directions: *"But prove yourselves doers of the word, and not merely hearers who delude themselves. For if anyone is a hearer of the word and not a doer, he is like a man who looks at his natural face in a mirror; for once he has looked at himself and gone away, he has immediately forgotten what kind of person he was. But one who looks intently at the perfect law, the law of Liberty, and abides by it, not having become a forgetful hearer but an effectual doer, this man shall be blessed in what he does"* (James 1:22-25).

Question: *What have you learned from this devotional? What kind of action should you take?*

About the Author

Jody Mayhew has been a consultant and director of women's ministries for over 30 years. As a teacher, she has carried her message of intimacy with God and a passion for His presence to four continents. In her role as women's representative for International Renewal Ministries, Jody facilitates Prayer Summits worldwide and advises leadership teams in corporate prayer. She is a founding member of Abide Ministries with the purpose of calling women to deeper relationship with the Lord and into active service in ministry.

When at home in Portland, Oregon Jody ministers with her husband, Dan, teaching Bible studies, serving a traditional congregation, and coaching a community of house churches. The Mayhews have been married for 45 years and have three grown children and five grandchildren.